RED GUIDES

BUYING A PROPERTY IN
FRANCE

Reader survey 2

CW00815745

Dear Reader,

We'd really like you to fill in this questionnaire and we promise that it'll help make a difference to future Red Guides. Send us the completed survey and you could win £5000 towards the cost of your dream French home! What's more, it won't even cost you the price of a stamp as you can return the form to us via Freepost. Your answers will help us to shape this book according to your needs and interests, helping us to give you just what you want with every issue.

Good luck with the competition!

LISA DOERR
Publisher, Merricks Media

SECTION A You and Red Guides

1. Why did you buy this Red Guide?
(PLEASE TICK ALL THAT APPLY)
☐ A friend recommended it
☐ The cover appealed to me
☐ I'm interested in buying property abroad
☐ I flicked through it at the newsstand
☐ I buy all magazines on property

2. Compared with other magazines, do you think this Red Guide is good value for money?
☐ Yes   ☐ No

3. Which of the following best describe your feeling about this Red Guide?
☐ The best overseas property book I've seen
☐ A very good property book
☐ I don't feel strongly
☐ I'm not keen on the book

4. How often do you think you'll refer back to this Red Guide?
☐ Very often   ☐ Occasionally   ☐ Not very often

5. How long do you plan to keep this Red Guide for?
☐ A week   ☐ A month   ☐ 2-6 months
☐ 6-12 months   ☐ Longer than 12 months

6. How many other people have looked at your copy of this Red Guide?
☐ No one   ☐ 1 person   ☐ 2-3 people
☐ 4-5 people   ☐ More than 5 people

7. What do you like about this Red Guide?
_____
_____
_____
_____

8. What do you dislike about this Red Guide?
_____
_____
_____
_____

9. Would you buy this guide twice a year?
☐ Yes   ☐ No

10. Would the advertising in this Red Guide help you decide:
Where to buy in France?   ☐ Yes   ☐ No
What kind of property to buy?   ☐ Yes   ☐ No
Who to bank with?   ☐ Yes   ☐ No
Who to exchange currency with?   ☐ Yes   ☐ No

11. How useful have you found the following sections?
(PLEASE USE THE KEY PROVIDED AND WRITE IN YOUR ANSWERS)
1 = Very important   **2 = Quite important**
3 = Not very important   **4 = Not at all important**

Maps	_____
The Economy	_____
Buy-to-let	_____
Property Guide	_____
Case Studies	_____
Steps to buying	_____
Hotspots	_____
Regional Guides	_____
Buyers Reference	_____
Price Matrix	_____

SECTION B About you

12. Are you: ☐ Male   ☐ Female

13. Are you:
☐ Under 25   ☐ 25-34   ☐ 35-44
☐ 45-54   ☐ 55-64   ☐ 65 or older

14. Are you:
☐ Single   ☐ Living with partner
☐ Married   ☐ Divorced/widowed/separated

15. Where do you live?
☐ South east   ☐ South west   ☐ South
☐ Midlands   ☐ Wales   ☐ East Anglia
☐ North east   ☐ North west   ☐ Scotland
☐ N Ireland   ☐ Greater London

16. Do you work
☐ Full time (30+ hours per week)
☐ Part time (up to 29 hours per week))
☐ Housewife / husband ☐ Student
☐ Self-employed ☐ Unemployed
☐ Semi-retired ☐ Retired

17. What is your occupation?
_____

18. What is your approximate household annual income before tax?
☐ Under £25,000 ☐ £25-49,000
☐ £50-74,999 ☐ £75-99,000
☐ £100,000+

19. How many children do you have?
☐ None ☐ 1 ☐ 2 ☐ 3 ☐ Other:
_____

20. How many children under 18 do you have living at home?
_____

SECTION C Other media

21. Which of these newspapers do you read?
☐ Financial Times ☐ Daily Mail ☐ Daily Mirror
☐ Daily Express ☐ Guardian ☐ Independent
☐ Daily Telegraph ☐ Times ☐ Sun
☐ Other:
_____

22. Have you used the internet to research overseas property? ☐ Yes ☐ No

23. Which online sites have you referred to?
_____
_____
_____
_____

24. Which of these overseas property magazines do you read?
☐ A Place in the Sun ☐ Homes Worldwide
☐ Homes Overseas ☐ Buying Abroad
☐ Other (please state)
_____

25. Which other brand of French property Magazines do you/would you buy
☐ Living France ☐ French Magazine
☐ Destination France ☐ France
☐ Other (please state)
_____

26. Have you read any Red Guides before? If yes, which one(s)?
☐ None ☐ France ☐ Italy
☐ Spain ☐ Eastern Europe ☐ Greece
☐ Florida ☐ Portugal ☐ Gap Travel
☐ Living & Working Abroad

SECTION D Your overseas property

27. How long have you been looking for a property in France?
☐ Just started looking ☐ 1-6 months
☐ 6-12 months ☐ 1-2 years
☐ Other (please state)
_____

28. How many viewing trips do you plan to make before you buy?
☐ 1 ☐ 2 ☐ 3 ☐ 4
☐ Other (please state)
_____

29. How much are you planning to spend on your overseas property?
☐ Less than £49,999
☐ £50,000 – £99,000
☐ £100,000 – £199,000
☐ £200,000 – £299,000
☐ £300,000 – £399,000
☐ £400,000 – £499,000
☐ £500,000 – £999,000
☐ More than £1,000,000

30. What are your main reasons for buying / thinking about buying abroad?
☐ UK market too expensive
☐ To own a holiday / second home
☐ For permanent / first home
☐ For retirement
☐ As an investment - from rental income
☐ As an investment - to resell
☐ As a renovation project
☐ Job relocation

31. How important were the following factors in influencing your decision to buy abroad?
(PLEASE USE THE KEY PROVIDED AND WRITE IN YOUR ANSWERS)
1 = Very important   2 = Quite important
3 = Not very important   4 = Not at all important

Better lifestyle	_____
Different culture	_____
Weather / climate	_____
Cost of properties	_____
Cost of living	_____
Work opportunities	_____
Increased budget flights	_____
To be nearer family	_____
Expanding economy	_____
Number of UK citizens living there	_____

32. Where in France are you interested in buying?
(YOU MAY TICK MORE THAN ONE)
☐ Brittany ☐ Normandy ☐ Loire
☐ Nord-Calais ☐ Ill-de France ☐ Burgundy
☐ Champagne ☐ Alsace, Lorraine ☐ Poitou
☐ Limousin ☐ Rhone ☐ Aquitaine
☐ Cote d'azur ☐ Languedoc ☐ Pyrenees

33. What is your biggest concern when considering your property purchase abroad?
☐ Language barrier
☐ Being ripped off i.e. paying too much
☐ Tax implications
☐ Security of property when empty
☐ Other (please state)
_____

34. How do you plan to finance your overseas property purchase?
☐ Cash purchase
☐ Remortgage your UK property
☐ Euro Mortgage
☐ Other (please state)
_____

35. Do you feel confident you understand the all finance options available to you?
☐ Yes very confident
☐ Only a little confident
☐ No not confident at all

36. What first gave you the idea to buy a property abroad?
☐ TV programme
☐ Holiday in the area
☐ Press article
☐ Security of property when empty
☐ Other (please state)
_____

Thank you for taking the time to fill out this questionnaire. Please send it freepost to the address below to be in with a chance of winning £5000 courtesy of Barclays Bank PLC

BARCLAYS

SECTION E Your details

NAME
_____

ADDRESS
_____
_____
_____
_____

HOME TEL
_____
WORK TEL
_____
MOBILE
_____
EMAIL
_____

Post your entry in an envelope to:
Red Guide Reader Survey, FREEPOST SWB 10668, Bath, BA1 2ZZ

BUYING A PROPERTY IN

France

THE ULTIMATE GUIDE TO BUYING AND LETTING IN FRANCE

Compiled, edited and designed by
Merricks Media Ltd
3 & 4 Riverside Court
Lower Bristol Road
Bath, BA2 3DZ
Tel: 01225 786800
redguides@merricksmedia.co.uk
www.redguides.co.uk

Senior Editor Michael Shakespeare
Consultant editor Leaonne Hall
Researcher Kelly-Marie Dudley
Art editor Angela Ashton
Managing director Lisa Doerr
Production manager Cee Pike
Advertising manager Karen Wragg
Senior sales executive Matt Hobbs
Advertisement design Becky Hamblin

RED GUIDES is a trademark of Merricks Media Ltd

Regional maps by Jamie Symmonds
© **Merricks Media Ltd** 2004
France touring map © **Michelin**
Illustrations by Felix Packer
© **Merricks Media Ltd** 2004

Fifth edition 2007

Copyright © **Merricks Media Ltd** 2007
Printed and bound by Cayfo Quebecor S. A. in Spain.
ISBN 1-905049-28-5
British Library Cataloguing in Publication Data.
A catalogue record for this bookazine is available from the British Library.

Michael Shakespeare

A staunch advocate of the overseas lifestyle, Michael has lived in countries as diverse as Hong Kong, Dubai and Poland. He is the editor of Spanish Homes Magazine but has a wealth of knowledge about overeseas property purchase across the whole of Europe an many other parts of the world.

"Buying abroad is a wonderfully exciting adventure, and we hope you find this book helpful"

Welcome

I t seems incredible but we are already on the fifth edition of Buying In France, and the UK property market is still strong enough to support the overseas property dreams of thousands of people every year. But here we are, five editions in, and France is proving as popular a destination as it always has been, and for very good reason; it's close, accessible, beautiful, full of great food, even better wine, and has some of Europe's most amazing countryside. And that's before we even get to the property! No one will try to convince you that the market is as ripe for quick profits as it once was, but there are still great bargains to be had; in fact there are fantastic properties at all prices, as you'll soon discover.

It is an enormous undertaking, buying abroad, and one that you should consider fully before you make any plans. But it's a also a wonderfully exciting adventure to do, and we hope you find this book helpful in your quest. All the information has been updated while our band of property and finance experts have given us their lowdown on France for the coming year, while there are some great properties for you to get an idea of what you can afford in each region, while our ever popular price matrices make a welcome return near the back.

Michael

Michael Shakespeare
Editor

INTRODUCTION

Contents

PROPERTY GUIDES

15 in-depth regional guides to the property market, hotspots and typical property prices throughout France

REAL LIFE

029 Landes of the living!

Quintin and Merrilyn Hetherington (and baby Jaydon!) on how they found a home and made a life in the lovely resort of Landes

BUYER'S REFERENCE

How to use this guide

The guide's three sections – the Buyer's Guide, Property Guide and Buyer's Reference – cover every aspect of finding and buying a home in France.

1 Buyer's guide

THE LATEST INFORMATION ABOUT THE financial and legal processes of buying property in France, including articles on the lettings market written by our experts (see p8), plus an in-depth Steps to Buying section covering everything from obtaining a survey to completing the sale

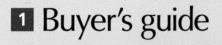

The property market
The latest facts and up-to-the-minute information about buying and letting property in France. Informative articles on the economy and property market by our panel of experts

Steps to buying
A comprehensive section taking you through every stage of the financial process and the conveyancing system, from currency conversion to signing the contract.

Real life
We did it! Be inspired by our case study on moving to Burgundy, showing how to turn a dream into reality. Invaluable hints and tips based on firsthand experience. Q & A format for easy reference

Living and working
A guide to the French healthcare and education systems, obtaining a driving licence, connecting utilities, insurance and pet travel. Checklist of essentials

2 Property guide

UP-TO-THE-MINUTE INFORMATION ABOUT
each region's property market, with detailed
profiles of its top hotspots. The guide is divided
into 15 regional chapters, from Normandy and
the Loire to Languedoc-Roussillon and Provence

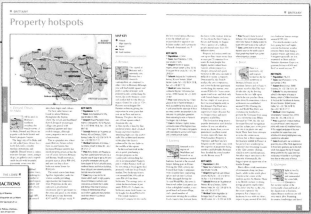

Regional profiles

General information on the
featured region, its geography,
history, economy, key
attractions and cultural
treasures, plus the top tourist
draws for each area. You'll also
find a Travel factfile to help you
get there and feature boxes
highlighting locally produced
food and wine.

Hotspots

The top places in which to buy
a property in France, with
information on the lettings
market, current price trends
and the nearest hospitals and
schools. Detailed hotspot
profiles provide cultural
information and highlight
typical average rental and
purchase prices.

3 Buyer's reference

INCLUDES THREE PRICE MATRICES, a glossary of
French house-buying and legal terms; a directory
of useful contacts for professionals and
organisations, from architects to lawyers; plus an
index to estate agents specialising in France and
French property purchase.

Price guides

A guide to typical properties in
each area with sample
properties showing you what
you can get for your budget.
Property price charts give sale
prices for two, three, four and
five-bedroom properties,
Agents' three-letter codes are
listed in our Index to Agents on
page 193.

Price matrices

Includes three matrices – for
houses, apartments and
lettings – to enable you to
calculate potential outlay and
rental return on a wide range
of prospective properties.
Prices are based on current
market prices and the average
house sale prices are in the top
hotspots.

Panel of experts

All our contributors are professionally qualified experts in their own field

NICHOLAS STALLWOOD

Unique Homes France Director and Midi-Pyrenees specialist Nicholas Stallwood has a deep knowledge of the French property market, gleaned from his years as executive director of the French Property Shop and his deep involvement in property acquisition and development throughout 12 years in his home region, the Midi-Pyrenees. Nicholas wrote our lettings feature.

TRISHA MASON

Trisha Mason is founder and Managing Director of VEF French property which, over the last 18 years, has helped 1000s of people buy property in France. A regular commentator on the French property market in the national press – as well as on television and radio – there is little that Trisha doesn't know about buying in France. Trisha wrote our Property Market article.

STEFANO LUCATELLO

Stefano Lucatello is a senior partner at the International Property law centre. Stefano has provided legal advice and support to people and businesses alike for over 20 years. Stefano wrote our Steps to Buying article.

PENNY ZOLDAN

Penny Zoldan is the MD of Latitudes French Property Agents, who specialise in the sale of property in France. Penny is the author of 'Buying Property in France', a common sense guide that covers the questions you need to know before making a purchase. Penny holds seminars on buying and investing in France, and writes frequently about French property. Tel 020 8951 5155, sales@latitudes.co.uk, www.latitudes.co.uk

MILES DOBSON

Miles worked in the insurance industry for 20 years in the City of London finishing his career as a senior manager in an international insurance company. Miles is now one of four Directors at affordablefrenchhomes.com, a small company which was a new venture for 2004. Miles wrote our Living and Working article.

ALL PHOTOS MAISON DE LA FRANCE

Regional map of France

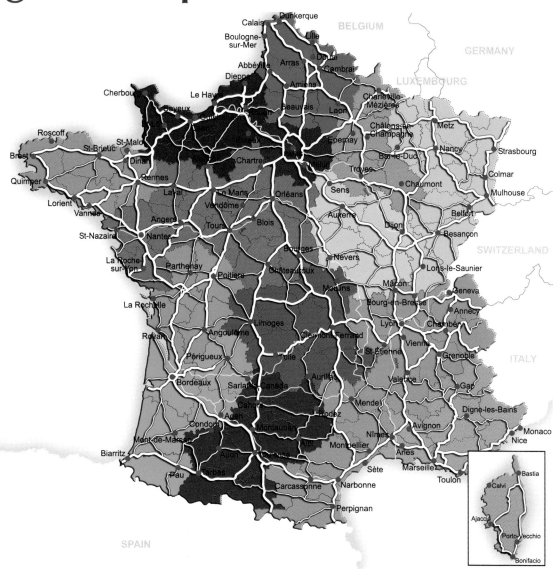

1 BRITTANY

2 NORMANDY

3 NORD-PAS-DE-CALAIS & PICARDY

4 ÎLE-DE-FRANCE

5 CHAMPAGNE-ARDENNE

6 ALSACE, LORRAINE & FRANCHE-COMTÉ

7 THE LOIRE

8 BURGUNDY

9 POITOU-CHARENTES

10 LIMOUSIN & AUVERGNE

11 RHÔNE-ALPES

12 AQUITAINE

13 MIDI-PYRÉNÉES

14 LANGUEDOC-ROUSSILLON

15 CÔTE D'AZUR, PROVENCE & CORSICA

Touring map and facts

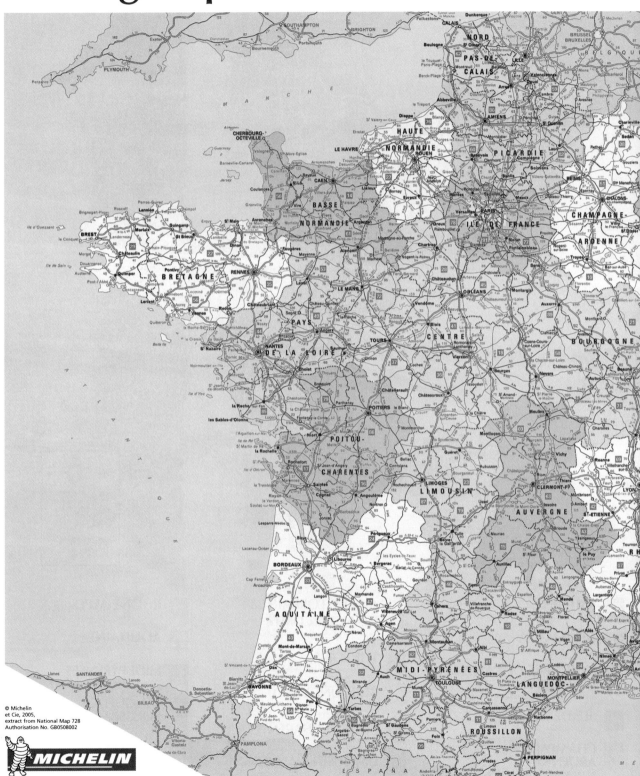

© Michelin
et Cie, 2005,
extract from National Map 728
Authorisation No. GB0508002

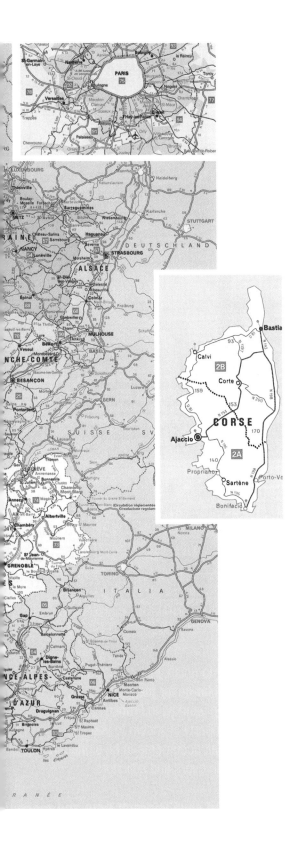

POPULATION

■ The total population of France currently stands at 60.5 million
■ The population is growing at a rate of 0.37% per year, and has increased by 2.9 million in the last 10 years
■ The median age in France is 38.8 years
■ The most populous metropolitan area is around Paris, with a population of 2.2 million
■ Population growth in rural areas is outpacing that of urban areas

GEOGRAPHY

■ France covers 547,030km2 in total
■ The total length of France's borders is 6,316km, of which 3,427km is coastline
■ France is bordered by Spain, Andorra, Italy, Monaco, Switzerland, Germany, Luxembourg and Belgium
■ The terrain of France mostly consists of rolling hills in the North and West, with mountain ranges in the South and East
■ The highest point in France is Mont Blanc at 4,807m
■ The lowest point in France is the Rhône river delta at -2m

CLIMATE

■ Northwest and Midwest France have an oceanic climate, with mild winters, cool summers and frequent rain
■ Inland France has a continental climate with cold winters, hot summers and medium rainfall
■ The mountain ranges have very cold, snowy winters and hot but often wet summers
■ The South coast has a Mediterranean climate, with mild winters and hot dry summers
■ The French climate is one of the most temperate in Europe

ECONOMY

■ The 2004 deficit was 3.6% of the GDP, an improvement from 4% in 2003 but still above the EU's 3% debt limit
■ Unemployment currently stands at 10.2% and has risen every year since 2001
■ There has been recent movement towards privatisation of many large companies
■ A dynamic service sector accounts for an increasingly large share of economic activity (72%) and is responsible for nearly all recent job creation

Buyer's guide

Buying property abroad is a big step, so before you rush
headlong into the decision, read our expert advice on finding
and buying your dream home in France

The economy

France has the fifth largest economy in the world, with predicted growth of 1.8 per cent in the near future

"In the real estate sector, much activity has been buoyed by continuing low interest rates"

FRANCE'S RIGHT-OF-CENTRE GOVERNMENT WILL struggle to set any sort of agenda in 2007, as attention turns to the presidential and legislative elections in the spring.

The second round of the presidential election is likely to pit Nicolas Sarkozy, the current minister of the interior, against Segolene Royal of the Parti socialiste (PS), but general and widespread dissatisfaction with the mainstream alternatives, plus another swathe protest candidates, could see France endure another contest similar to 2002, when the contest was dogged by controversy, not least surrounding the limited but still significant success of far right nationalist Jean-Marie Le Pen.

Last year the government was forced to backtrack on its attempts to push through a series of pretty modest labour market reforms after much opposition from students; there'll be no more attempts until after the elections, but the economy is showing signs of growth, helped by a cyclical fall in unemployment. That said, real GDP growth is forecast to slow from 2% in 2006 to 1.8% in 2007 and to pick up only modestly in 2008. Inflation has fallen sharply since the middle of 2006.

State of the French economy

France has the second largest economy in the euro area and the fifth largest economy in the world. Excluding Luxembourg, it has, with Germany, the joint fifth highest per capita GDP in the euro area.

In recent years, France has tended to perform better than other euro area countries, most notably Germany and Italy. Economic activity has been more vigorous, partly owing to public support for sustainable consumption, and partly owing to a lower sensitivity to the euro/dollar exchange rate (which stems from the fact that France is exporting less to fast-growing countries than Germany is). Looking forward, growth ought to be slower in 2006, but is expected to remain brisk and higher

Recent French economic activity has been vigorous

than the euro area average (1.6 per cent in 2005 for France against a projected 1.3 per cent for the euro area, and 2.2 per cent for 2006 against 1.8 per cent for the euro area). There are two major risks to the short-term economic outlook: housing prices and consumer confidence.

In the real estate sector, a great deal of activity has been buoyed by continuing low interest rates and easier lending conditions (a typical mortgage period is lengthening significantly) as well as a lot of interest from overseas, including Britain.

Property prices continue to rise throughout France (15.3 per cent overall in 2004 against 7.2 per cent for the whole euro area). However, most

France has the second largest economy in the euro area and the fifth largest economy in the world

analysts are not overly concerned about the direction France is heading in as housing demand is supported by much more buoyant demographics than in the rest of the euro area, not least of which is other European citizens buying holiday property in France (prices have risen faster outside Paris in this cycle than within Paris). Nevertheless, the general sentiment is that prices have reached a peak and that there will be a deceleration in housing inflation (10.1 per cent housing price growth in 2005 in France, 5.8 per cent for the euro area). This outcome could become bleaker if interest rates were to rise faster than expected, thus ending the upward trend in house prices quite abruptly.

Another risk is consumer confidence, which has been quite depressed since early 2005, owing to the persistently high unemployment rate. Unemployment has fallen, but consumer confidence has not risen in accordance with it, and the labour market looks to have peaked in 2006 and is ready to deflate again. The government in 2005 decided to boost support for publicly subsidised jobs, and while this hasn't solved long term labour market issues, in the short term it has helped reduced the unemployment rate which, in turn, has boosted business confidence.

Economic reform

France is in the midst of transition from a well-to-do modern economy that has featured extensive government ownership and intervention to one that relies more on market mechanisms. Looking forward, France has initiated some important structural reforms, but much remains to be done, especially in the labour market, pension systems and health care service.

Some impressive (though little publicised) steps have been taken. Most notably, a new law reforming the budgetary procedure should allow more flexibility to cut public spending. Pension reform was initiated in 2003, with the aim of solving about 40 per cent of the problem in the next 20 years. A major health-care reform was also launched in 2004. Rated as one of the best healthcare systems in OECD (Organisation for Economic Co-operation and Development) countries, the French system is very expensive and social security funds are running high deficits. The reform focuses primarily on enhancing the use of generic drugs, reviewing the reimbursement of drugs and controlling doctors' visits through a centralised management system. Although the latter is taking longer than foreseen to be implemented (and it is unclear how much impact

Low interest rates have enhanced the French market

"France has initiated some important structural reforms, but much remains to be done"

it will have), lower drug spending does seem to have been implemented. And lastly, public services such as transport are slowly opening up to competition.

Government attempts to boost employment through increased labor market flexibility garnered much opposition, which hampered the government's ability to revitalize the economy. Labour costs remain high, the labour code remains rigid, and the public employment services fail to help reduce unemployment. Small actions taken over the years have accumulated so that the labour code is hugely complex, and employers are sceptical about any new labour market policy measures. However, in the present political context, it seems difficult to see any significant reform before this year's elections.

Rigidity in the labour market, alongside high labour costs, is dampening French competitiveness and French entrepreneurial appetites, so that France has a larger proportion of very small enterprises than other OECD countries, all afraid to grow for fear of increasing red tape. It is well known, however, that exporting businesses are generally of a large size. France's exports are negligible when compared to Germany's, for example, and could weigh increasingly on GDP growth as the global competition intensifies.

Positive demographics

The national statistical office is currently running a thorough analysis of French demographics. Early results show that French growth could well be supported by a relatively favourable demographic outlook (by European standards) with a working age population projected to increase 1.6 per cent per year over the next five years, and a fecundity rate of close to two children against a European average closer to one child. ●

The French Property Market

2006 has been a year when we have seen very different property price trends in France according to the type and location of properties sold.

"The price increase of 8-10% for resale character properties in 2006 has not been experienced with new build properties"

AT THE START OF THE YEAR THE MARKET WAS still fairly slow following a general slow down which we witnessed from the fourth quarter of 2005. By the end of the first quarter 0f 2006 the speed of the market had accelerated but some areas and some types of properties were selling at considerably less than the asking price (around 10% or even higher is some cases). The types of property where prices fell were those traditionally bought by the French purchaser, apartments, recently constructed villas and pavilions and everything within 20 – 30 minutes of centres of employment. The type of property sought by overseas buyers continued to show price increases, although not generally to the same level as that experienced in 2004 and most of 2005.

The average overseas buyer of resale property is looking for a traditionally built house in a fairly rural setting. There is a finite supply of such properties and as ever, with anything in finite supply, prices are determined by the market and the market for such properties continues to increase. In most areas of France character properties continued to show increases of around 8-10% throughout 2007. Some areas which were subject to particular conditions saw higher increases and some slightly lower. An intimate knowledge of France, its economy and its property market is essential for anyone hoping to maximise capital growth with their purchase of a French property.

The factors affecting property prices continue to be the same. The supply and demand factor will obviously always affect prices, hence character properties in idyllic situations saw price increases continue. What affects demand hardly varies either. The development of a local airport offering international flights, the development of a tram

BECKY HAMBLIN

More families are moving to and buying in France

system in a city with the accompanying pedestrianisation of the centre, other improved transport links such as the arrival of the TGV making nearby cities more accessible and other economic factors in the local area, such as closing down or opening up of new factories. Ironically, to illustrate the power of the press, media attention can also cause prices to rise or fall. Since 2003 the Limousin has attracted a lot of attention from the UK press and throughout 2003, 2004 and 2005 we saw prices increase above what I believed to be a sustainable level. In 2006 we have seen them stabilise and I believe that this will continue throughout 2007 until they are once again in line with national prices and the press turn their attention to another area.

The price increase of 8-10% for resale character properties in 2006 has not been experienced with new build properties. 2006 has been a year when off-plan properties have remained similarly priced to 2005.

So, why have off-plan properties, recently constructed properties and town apartments failed to see the same increases in 2006 as resale property? I believe the reason to be that the criteria for borrowing money for property purchase in France is much less liberal than in the UK. All borrowing is still subject to a 3 times net income rule and having witnessed average price increases of more than 25% over 3 years, some French purchasers have found the market closing to them. Lending institutions in France are now looking at their financial products and I believe that we will see a more liberal approach to lending amongst French institutions in 2007. I

REGIONAL PRICE INCREASES AND AVERAGE PRICES

Poitou-Charentes	28%	€214,536
Centre	24%	€216,547
Aquitaine	21%	€309,995
Burgundy	22%	€141,621
Limousin	22%	€140,029
Nord-Pas-de-Calais	18%	€259,120
Auvergne	18%	€161,813
Midi-Pyrénées	17%	€239,693
Provence	15%	€406,623
Brittany	12%	€225,453

believe that this will result in an increase in prices for off-plan and newly constructed properties and for town apartments. However, this will not happen immediately and the first few months of 2007 should be a very good time to buy for anyone intending to purchase such property.

The leaseback scheme continues to attract overseas buyers and although prices are not rising as much as we were seeing in 2003 and 2004, we are now noticing that developers are reducing some of the attractive rental returns on offer in 2004 and 2005, suggesting that the market is still buoyant. Leaseback purchase is an ideal way to split the use of a property in France between occasional holiday use and investment and will continue to attract purchasers both with France and from overseas. In 2006 we have also witnessed a growing interest amongst the overseas investor in buy-to-let property in France, whether this be off plan or exisiting apartments to let on the local market, to professional workers or students. Interestingly, the apart-hotel type developments are also creating a lot of interest in the market and in 2006 have shown the highest increase in capital growth amongst all off-plan purchases.

There are still bargains to be had with off-plan and all investment-type property and with the benefit of a stable economy, a well regulated property market and proven exit strategy, I believe that France is still a sensible option for investors looking for medium to long term, medium level risk.

So, who has been buying property in France in 2006? More than ever it has been people intending to move to France full time in the very short term. We have seen a growth in the number of people who intend to move themselves and their families to France and to commute back to the UK regularly for work and we have also seen a growth in young families who are releasing sufficient equity in the current home to buy a family home in France and maintain themselves financially for 3 years or so while they look into employment possibilities. We have also seen many of our buyers from several years ago who are now living in France turn to leaseback and buy to let property to invest funds which they have released from pensions. And a final, small but significantly growing group of people are young people under the age of 25 who are buying in France to get onto the property ladder, something which they cannot afford to do in the UK. However, the majority of buyers are still early retirees who want to maximise on the quality of life which France offers and which they believe to be no longer available in the UK.

Predictions for 2007? I anticipate a steady growth in the number of British people buying in France coupled with a steady growth in resale property prices of those styles of properties favoured by the overseas buyer. I also anticipate a faster-than-steady growth in purchases of off-plan properties as investors turn to France for a 'safer' investment after much bad press being received by many relatively new property buying destinations as well as the old favourite of Spain. Investors are becoming more and more aware that a balance of high and medium risk investment is what is needed to create a sensible portfolio and France certainly has proved itself long term as the home for medium risk investors.

So, whatever you are buying for, France will remain one of the most popular destinations in 2007 for property purchase and may well exceed Spain and fix itself firmly at the top of the list. ●

> *"Predictions for 2007? I anticipate a steady growth in the number of British people buying in France coupled with a steady growth in resale property prices"*

The laidback French lifestyle attracts a lot of British people to buy in the country

JUSTIN POSTLETHWAITE

The lettings market

Although the number of seasonal lettings has been going down, landlords with a small and loyal customer base are continuing to be successful

"Many tenants want higher quality furniture and outdoor facilities. Those owners who continue to offer basic furnishings are increasingly missing out"

IF YOU ARE QUESTIONING WHETHER OR NOT TO purchase a holiday home in France, primarily because you are uncertain as to how much use you will get out of it, it may be worth considering letting out your home. There are a number of rental options open to a potential landlord. These are dependent upon the property type and location, which will determine whether residential properties can be rented in the short- or long-term. The length of the holiday letting season also differs greatly from region to region, in particular because of the fact that there is a differing climate across France which affects the number of months a landlord can secure rentals for.For example, in the Rhône-Alpes the peak season is predominantly winter because of the ski season, while in the Côte d'Azur it is obviously summer, due to the proximity of the beach. It also differs depending on whether you buy in the town or country. If you buy in a city, you may be able to let to businessmen and holidaymakers for short periods and, in addition, find French tenants looking for long-term lets. As a general rule, cities yield the best rents and number of prospective tenants for long-term lets, while the country is better for the short-term and holiday lets.

A beautiful property can attract higher rental income

The market

Agents report that seasonal letting in France was slightly up in 2006, after a downturn in 2005 and a poor year in 2004. In fact 2002 was the last exceptionally good letting year. Tenants are increasingly booking late and seeking "deals". Larger properties have suffered most as tenants are not leaving enough time to get a large party together. Many people benefit from a loyal customer base,especially if they are a small and personal business who get to know both the owners and their properties as well as the tenants. Despite this trend, many agents are doing better than average and are able to increase their turnover. Many tenants want, and pay for, higher quality furniture and outdoor facilities. Those owners who continue to offer basic furnishings and properties are increasingly missing out. Demand is still primarily from the UK,though the Irish, Dutch and Belgians are increasing in numbers. The French and Germans tend to be attracted to the expensive seaside resorts and there are some Americans, but not as many as pre-2001.

Earning an income

The general rule of thumb is that a letting property will produce no more than four to five per cent gross income based on today's property values. This has halved (from nearly 10 per cent) over the past five years as property values have increased but, at the same time, the lettings market has become more competitive. Consequently, lettings prices have been pretty static in recent years. There are always exceptions, but on the whole how well the property photographs is the most important consideration. Prospective tenants are increasingly concerned with aesthetics. After this, it is the quality of the property and its management that will bring the same tenants (or their friends) back year after year.

Check the regulations on pools before you make the plunge

Finding tenants

Owners of French property have a range of options when it comes to finding tenants and managing their holiday home. If you choose to let privately you can place an advertisement in a specialist publication with lettings advertisements in France,as well as in the home country of your target audience and on specialist websites.In France,local papers also have listings sections of properties for rent. If you would prefer someone else to market your property you can,for a certain percentage of the rent,do it through a local estate agency or holiday- lettings specialist,or,in the case of new-builds,a management company that services the entire building or complex.Tourist offices also market holiday properties.Contact Maison de la Francefor more details.

Managing lets

Overseeing the cleaning and changeover days of properties let for short periods can be difficult to manage from a distance, though not impossible. Some holiday home owners find they can rely on their clients to leave the property in a good state and simply send a key to them, though help can usually be hired in most of France's towns and villages. A local job centre,or Agence Nationale Pour L'Emploi, can be good source of help. Any owner who lets their property for commercial or residential use must,by law, be licensed to do so. Anyone hiring a lettings agent, or agent locataire, should ensure that they draw up a contract to protect their rights and interests. A lettings agent will probably have standard tenancy agreements, but these can contain clauses that are disadvantageous to the landlord. If you are presented with such an agreement, consider asking an independent legal advisor to review it, even if it has been translated into your own language. If you are

Get a professional photgraph taken of your property

FRENCH PROPERTY SHOP

VEF

There are maintenance companies in most French cities who will look after your property

letting directly to tenants, you should have an agreement drawn up by an experienced lawyer which contains the necessary clauses to protect you as the landlord, and a schedule of the condition of the property (état de lieux).

Tax

As the property owner,you are also obliged to inform the authorities that you are generating income from your property and pay the relevant tax bill. Non-residents must file an annual return for income tax - impôt sur le revenu - if they receive income from letting property or from providing bed-and-breakfast accommodation. If you become involved in the management of any lettings, it may be possible to offset a proportion of your expenses against any income tax paid in another country.

Swimming pool regulations

The French have clamped down on the safety laws surrounding swimming pools.The final details are still after many years hazy but for more details visit ehst wimming pool section on www.frenchentree. com (the actual link is www.frenchentree.com/fe-lavie/DisplayArticle.asp?ID=271). It's worth bearing in mind, though, that while a pool does add substantially to your property's appeal and it's rental and resale value, it will also need constant attention and maintenance. ●

"Owners of French property have a range of options when it comes to finding tenants and managing their holiday home"

Sterling $€ Exchange

Steps to buying

Beautiful France offers something for everyone, and more and more people from the UK are buying homes in Europe's third largest country.

Buying a property abroad is not a decision to be taken lightly, nor is it a decision that should be made on impulse, even when the turnover of properties in your area of choice is swift. Buying a house you fall in love with at the end of a holiday, for example, can be a recipe for disaster. In a foreign country in particular, there are legal, cost and other practical issues to be considered before embarking on a house purchase.

One of the first questions to ask is how much you can afford to spend. When you know how much finance you can raise, consider the purchasing costs, then set yourself a realistic house price limit. Once you've set your budget and decided roughly on the area in which you want to search, you will have more of an idea whether you should be looking for a stone fermette (small farmhouse), a townhouse or a much grander manoir (manor house). Bear in mind, though, that some regions of France are more expensive than others. By casting your net wider, you can open up your options, particularly as budget flight routes and high-speed train links have made areas once inconceivable to visit for a long weekend, for example, easily accessible from the UK.

STEP 1 Finding the right property

Be practical when choosing a property. An isolated farmhouse can be perfect for escaping the bustle of city life, but if you need medical assistance close at hand, or would like neighbours to look after your property when you are away, you should think of buying somewhere within easy reach of other households and village amenities. Try to spend time getting to know your preferred locality – if you find your dream location during the winter, it may be spoilt by hordes of tourists in the summer; and what might appear idyllic in summer could be ruined by howling gales in winter. There are several different ways to track down that ideal French home. You can simply trail around the region of your choice, hunting out à vendre (for sale) signs and looking in the windows of agents immobiliers (estate agents) and notaires (public notaries), but this is

MAISON DE LA FRANCE

You might fall in love with an isolated farmhouse, but do consider the practical implications

time-consuming – fine if you are combining it with a holiday, not so good if you are trying to fit in such trips around a busy life.

A good way to start is by searching through specialist magazines and websites, as well as attending the growing number of overseas property fairs held outside France. You should also consider using a property search agent, or 'homefinder'. Based in France or the UK, they can cut out the legwork by presenting a range of properties for you to view. These might be on the books of local estate agents, selected from forthcoming auctions, or even private sales.

Whether or not you choose an intermediary, at some point you will have to organise a trip to France to arrange viewings of your shortlist of properties. Find out as much as you can about these properties before you go. Particulars provided for French properties are rarely as thorough as those produced for British houses, with details such as room measurements often left out. By asking for extensive details and photographs of the properties, you might save yourself a wasted trip.

New-builds & leasebacks

Foreigners moving to France or looking for a holiday home there are often keen to find a charming period house, but building a home in the right location can prove to be a practical alternative. Building land in France is cheaper and more readily available than in other countries, particularly in the

countryside, and many French families choose to buy a plot of land and have a new home built for them. New homes can provide more comfort from day one, and be sited closer to schools and workplaces.

A newly built home is often easier to maintain than an old home (an important consideration if it is to be let out) and is usually much cheaper to buy. New-builds can therefore represent a good holiday-rental investment. There is, however, a significant disadvantage to buying a property under five years old that is being sold for the first time: TVA, taxe sur la valeur ajoutée – the French term for VAT – is usually charged on the sale. There is, however, a way of avoiding this.

A new property leased back immediately to the developers, who then rent the property to holiday-makers over a period of about nine years, is exempt from TVA if the property is held for at least 20 years (if it is sold before the twentieth year, a proportion of the saved TVA must be repaid). Owners can expect to earn a net return on their investment of around six per cent per annum, as well as save on the initial cost of their purchase. So-called 'leaseback schemes' are restricted to areas popular with tourists, and are only available if the property is accepted as being up to tourism standard by the local authorities. Tax breaks are given to developers building tourist accommodation, and the VAT refund is passed on to buyers. In effect, you will pay only 80 per cent of the purchase price at the outset. This is a government initiative, and shouldn't be confused with timeshare schemes – from day one you are the owner of the property.

If you are interested in new-builds, plots of land, or parcelles, can be found through estate agents or specialist publications and websites such as www.terrain-a-batir.com and www. frenchland.com. Should you choose this option, it is best to go to the local mairie, or town hall, to scrutinise the plan local d'urbanisme, which should indicate whether or not the land can be built on, and the related coefficient d'occupation des sols, which identifies the amount of habitable space allowable on the land. In any case, you need to have in the preliminary contract a clause allowing you to pull out if planning permission is not granted. Note also that the granting of planning permission will depend on access to roads and utilities. (See also Building a new home on p.31.)

STEP 2 **The survey**

Foreign buyers are not always aware of the local market prices of property, and can run the risk of paying inflated prices. A valuation by a local valuer, or by an agent immobilier, estate agent, can help avoid this. The valuer can also help to estimate the cost of any renovation work to make the property habitable or to improve the living space.

Even an agent immobilier will not, however, provide a full structural survey. The survey, or expertise, that they carry out is, in

effect, more like a valuation. The closest equivalent to a British structural survey is an évaluation structurale. The French do not have a professional equivalent to the British chartered building surveyor. They usually either turn to an architecte (architect), who will normally provide only a brief report on the condition of a building, or rely on testimonies from local tradesmen, or artisans, to gauge a property's state of repair. One of the best ways to obtain a structural survey can be to instruct one of the growing number of properly qualified British building surveyors or architects who now live in France, or who will travel across the Channel, to carry out such surveys.

Be careful when buying an older property, as age often brings problems. The house may have been left for years without proper maintenance, perhaps because it was part of an inheritance and not subsequently lived in, and there might be neither mains electricity nor proper sewerage. The cost of renovating and connecting utilities can be onerous. British buyers should also note the need to check certain details that would not necessarily require checking when buying a property in the UK. For instance, if a property is made up of a collection of buildings, it should be determined whether or not all the buildings are actually included in the sale. Boundaries can often be blurred too, especially if land has been split up into several parcelles, or if a wood obscures part of one of these. They can be checked against a

plan cadastral, the official record of site boundaries, although this can sometimes be out of date. A géomètre, or land surveyor, can help verify such details.

Note that there is no legal protection in France allowing purchasers to pull out from the preliminary contract if the survey is unsatisfactory; it is necessary to ask for such a clause up front, as soon as the offer is made.

STEP 3 **Managing your euros**

In order to work out the total cost of buying a French property, as a rule of thumb you should add 10 per cent to the purchase price. In reality, though, the total can be much higher than this. One of the main costs is the sales commission, which is usually five to six per cent but can reach up to 20 per cent, particularly in the case of less expensive properties. Check carefully whether or not the fee is included in the advertised price, and also whether TVA has been added. Phrases like 'toutes taxes comprises' or 'TVA comprise' should indicate that this fee has been included.

Although it is sometimes the vendor who pays the agent's commission, the buyer is always responsible for paying the conveyancing fees to the notaire. The notaire's fees are fixed by law on a sliding scale based on the purchase price of the property, ranging from three per cent for a property under five years old to about 10 per cent for an older property. If two notaires are appointed, one by the buyer and one by the vendor, the fee is divided between them.

On top of their own fee, the notaire will collect other duties and fees, such as stamp and transfer duties, land registry fees, taxes and disbursements. When a mortgage is taken out, there will also be a charge payable to the notaire, usually one to three per cent of the mortgage value. This is for registering the charge of the lender with the relevant land registry, or conservation des hypothèques.

Exchange rate fluctuations can potentially increase the cost of financing if a borrower is converting sterling to make payments on a euro mortgage. However, fixing the exchange rate through a specialist currency broker over a long period of time can give the borrower peace of mind. If the property is being bought for cash, it can also be a good idea to fix the exchange rate at the beginning of the purchase process, so that the actual price of the property remains the same.

One of the biggest costs of buying an older

WHO TO BUY A FRENCH HOME FROM

Every town in France should have at least one estate agent and there is an increasing number of UK-based agents specialising in French properties who have a network of French agents providing them with local knowledge and property details. These agents understand the needs of foreign buyers, and, of course, they offer an English-speaking service, which makes buying considerably easier. All French estate agents should have a carte professionelle, proving that they have the correct professional qualifications and are backed by a financial guarantee and professional liability insurance, and also that they are members of a regulatory body such as the Fédération Nationale des Agents Immobiliers et Mandataires, or FNAIM.

Estate agents' fees are normally included in the sale price, so buyers do not usually have to worry about raising extra money to pay them. Mortgage providers usually lend only a percentage of the actual sale price and do not take additional costs into consideration. However, if an estate agent's fee is included in the price, the buyer may end up paying purchase duties on this fee as well as on the property.

To avoid paying more duties than necessary, ensure the contract includes the statement 'commission de l'agence immobilière à la charge de l'acquéreur' ('agent's commission paid for by the buyer').

For a list of estate agents in France, contact the FNAIM (see Directory of useful contacts on p.187 for further details).

property is renovation work. A would-be buyer may spot a derelict building in a field and think it's a bargain, but the cost of restoration can be at least as much as the price of the building itself. To prevent a dream home turning into a renovation project that was never completed, buyers should calculate all the outlays before proceeding with the sale, obtaining estimates (devis) from local builders.

Financing

In recent years, it has become much easier for non-residents to raise a mortgage, or prêt immobilier, on a home in France. There are two basic ways to do this: by remortgaging a property in the UK in sterling with a UK lender or by taking out a euro mortgage with a French bank against the French property – banks cannot take first legal charge on a property outside their own countries, so will only offer mortgages on properties in their own country.

Although there can be a substantial initial exchange rate fee to pay when money is raised in a currency other than the euro, remortgaging in sterling can protect the British buyer against the effect of future exchange rate fluctuations on their repayments. Taking out a mortgage in euros on a French property will always, on the other hand, reflect the true euro value of the property, and the bank will have the first legal charge on the actual property being financed. The cost of the mortgage can also potentially be offset against any income received from letting the property.

There are many French lenders for overseas buyers to choose from if a mortgage is to be raised on a property in France, but one option these days is to use the French branches of UK banks. All the paperwork can be supplied in English, and although the mortgage will be in euros, the monthly payments can be made in sterling, straight from a British bank

account. Note that a French bank usually asks for a life policy to be taken out on the life of the borrower, requiring both a medical and a blood test.

Repayment mortgages, or prêts amortissables, are most commonly offered by French banks to foreign buyers in preference to interest-only mortgages and endowment policies. British buyers are usually lent money by a French lender for between five and 20 years. Rates can be fixed (à taux fixe), or variable (à taux variable). There are likely to be early redemption charges payable on the former, but not on the latter. French variable rates are linked to the EURIBOR (Euro Interbank Offered Rate), and for foreign buyers this is usually fixed for 12 months. One main difference between UK and French variable interest rates is that, whereas in the UK the monthly payments are likely to fluctuate, in France the rates tend to stay stable, and it is only the term of the loan that changes according to the EURIBOR rate change.

A deposit of at least 20 per cent of the price of the property is usually required, and it is generally true that the higher the deposit, the better the interest rate. French lenders are usually obliged to prove that the borrower can afford the repayments, so they often insist that the monthly payments for all the borrower's mortgages and other fixed outgoings should not exceed 30 to 35 per cent of their income. A French lender will deduct your expenditure from your monthly net salary and then tell you how much it can lend based on the remaining monthly figure.

Even if properties financed by a residential mortgage are to be let out for part of the year, lenders do not usually take into consideration potential rental income when assessing the loan. Neither will they lend money to cover costs such as notary fees, though subject to the approval of relevant estimates from builders or developers, mortgages can cover the cost of renovation or construction work. As a rule, allow two months between the completed mortgage application and the mortgage offer.

Once a mortgage offer is received, French legislation requires that the borrower wait at least 10 days, but no longer than 30, before signing and accepting it. On acceptance, an arrangement fee of one to two per cent of the loan value will be payable. Borrowers are also obliged to take out a life insurance policy so that, in the event of death or disability, the outstanding loan value will be repaid.

French banks pay the money being lent to the notaire. The portion covering renovation or construction costs is paid directly to the contractor on presentation of invoices (duly authorised for payment by the customer) after the customer's personal contribution has been paid.

STEP 4 The legal process

The French legal system can be a minefield for foreign buyers. Never does the expression 'take independent advice' ring more true than in the case of buying a property abroad. There are numerous pitfalls that the unsuspecting buyer can encounter when buying a home in France, and there are also ways that a legal advisor can help the buyer best structure their purchase.

A French property can either be purchased by individuals – in single, joint or multiple names – or through a French property-holding company, a société civile immobilière (SCI), whose shares are held by the buyers. Although an SCI can cost between €1,500 and €6,000 to set up, and annual accounts must be prepared for the company, this purchase structure should be considered in many cases, as it can have tax advantages and make it easier for owners to dispose of their share of the property. It can also in some cases overcome a great deal of the restrictions put in place by France's succession law.

French law dictates that upon the death of a homeowner, the property is divided equally between the surviving spouse and any children. Shares in a company, however, are easier to distribute, especially during one's lifetime, than immovable property, thus enabling better management of inheritance and property transferring. The transfer of shares can be done under English law if you are domiciled in the UK on your death but it is still submitted to French tax law.

STEP 5 Protecting your interests

The notaire who oversees the sale of a property is primarily concerned with registering the sale, ensuring that the conveyancing is carried out according to the law, and collecting the relevant taxes on behalf of the government. Although they are qualified to provide legal advice, notaires are not acting on behalf of either side so, to make sure that you are bound by favourable terms, it would be best either to employ a separate notaire in France or to employ a British lawyer familiar with French conveyancing law from the very start of the legal process. There are quite a few UK-based solicitors who specialise in the buying and selling of French property and it's worth seeking them out.

Not only can solicitors working on behalf of the buyer draw up any necessary get-out clauses in the contract, they can also advise on the best way to structure the purchase according to personal circumstances and recommend ways of minimising the effect of French inheritance law. The latter should be considered a long time before the conveyance is signed.

Special assur'titre insurance policies can be taken out to insure the title of a property against unknown title defects, such as unforeseen claims by third parties and the violation of planning regulations by former owners, as well as mistakes on behalf of the notaire. This policy gives the buyer protection against any costs or damages that may follow as a result of any claims from third parties or subsequent owners. Such policies are being offered increasingly by estate agents as part of their service, and are a good complement to the advice of an independent solicitor.

STEP 6 **Contracts**

In France, when you buy a property you will be very quickly asked to sign a preliminary contract. A contract, known as a 'compromis de vente', a 'promesse de vente' or a 'sous-seing privé', is entered into early on in the process, and this commits the vendor and

HEADLANDS INTERNATIONAL

The conveyancing on the sale of a property is usually carried out by a notaire, or notary

buyer to a deal they will conclude with a deed of sale, or conveyance. The agreement is normally drawn up either by an estate agent or a notaire and then handed to the notaire overseeing the completion of the sale together with the deposit.

Unless special arrangements have been made, the conveyancing on the sale will be conducted by the notaire appointed by the seller of the property. The buyer may, if he wishes, appoint his own notary to protect his interests. The contract gives the details of the parties and the property, and the price and the completion date when the signing of the final deed of sale takes place. It will also

include details of the notary or notaries overseeing the transaction and of where the deed that completes the conveyancing, the 'acte de vente' – sometimes referred to as the 'acte authentique' or even the 'acte authentique de vente'– will be signed. At this stage, a deposit of 10 per cent of the purchase price is paid by the buyer to the notaire or the estate agent, backed by a financial guarantee and a professional liability insurance. Under no circumstances should money be paid directly to the vendor at this or any other point in the process, nor should the buyer agree to any side payments, or dessous la table.

There is a seven-day 'cooling-off' period from the day after the buyer receives a copy of the contract, countersigned by the vendor. During this period, the buyer can withdraw from the sale and not be liable for any penalties. If the buyer withdraws from the purchase after this cooling-off period, they will probably lose their deposit and may be liable for penalties. If a penalty clause is included in the contract, it will stipulate the amount payable in case of withdrawal. Should the vendor withdraw, the deposit will normally be refunded and the vendor must pay any damages stipulated in the contract. These damage payments will have to be settled in a court action.

If the contract contains clauses suspensives, or get-out clauses, laying out conditions to be met during the sale process, the buyer may, in some circumstances, be able to withdraw from the purchase without the risk of losing the deposit and having to pay penalties. The sale can be made conditional upon a number of factors, such as: the offer of a mortgage; the absence of rights of way across the property; the absence of a droit de préemption, or right of preemption, that gives a local authority, land commission or another third party the right to buy the property or its land; the absence of asbestos in the property, termites, dry rot and wet rot and lead piping. The vendor must declare in the contract whether the land falls within an area highlighted by the local authorities as being susceptible to lead, asbestos and termites and, if so, must annex a report to the contract saying that an inspection has taken place and that the property is free or not from termites etc.

In the case of properties whose construction has not yet been completed, a contrat de reservation precedes the conveyance. The contract should preferably provide a full description of the property to

TAXES ON RENTALS

1 If you declare the income you receive from letting a property in France to the tax authorities in the country where you are resident, France still retains principle taxation rights on French-sourced income. This is the case no matter where both landlord and tenant reside, or where and in which currency the rent is paid

2 French tax authorities may tax up to three years in arrears, and usually add interest and penalty charges on late tax returns

3 When lettings qualify as a business for the purposes of French taxation, the method used to determine the taxable income depends on the level of annual turnover from the preceding year

4 Some rentals may be subject to TVA; local taxes can also be levied on leases

5 Although the supply of food, telephone and other services to self-catering accommodation is subject to TVA at the standard rate, when an establishment provides full-board or half-board accommodation, TVA can be reduced. In some French départements, owners can obtain grants from local authorities for converting homes into rental accommodation. Contact the relevant administrative offices for further information.

NOTAIRES

Much of the property sold in France is still offered through notaires, who were the principal source of French property before estate agents set up in business. Notaries are highly trained lawyers who oversee the purchase, and their sales commission will not normally be included in the price. Properties sold through notaires can often be more reasonably priced than those sold through estate agents, as the latter are usually more aware of market trends. For details of regional notaires, contact Notaires de France (see Directory of useful contacts on p. 187 for further details).

be built, an approximate surface area, or surface habitable, a floor plan, and a proposed date for the completion of the construction. When this contract is signed, the buyer will need to pay the developer a non-interest-bearing deposit, or réservation, of up to five per cent.

If construction is due to be completed within a year of signing the contract, the deposit cannot exceed five per cent; or two per cent if within two years. No deposit is payable if the construction is not due for completion within two years.

STEP 7 **Completing the sale**

When all the procedural formalities have been concluded, the notary will summon the parties to his office for the signing of the final deed. The formalities leading to completion usually take between two and three months. The completion date in the contract will be postponed automatically by the notary if any part of the administrative process remains outstanding. This should be borne in mind by the buyers, who should not make any travel arrangements until the notary has given them a date. The notary will ask for the balance of the purchase money and the costs to be sent direct to his bank account. This process can often take up to two weeks, so buyers are advised to pursue this as soon as they are given instructions by the notaire to do so.

Many buyers complete the purchase by proxy using a power of attorney drawn up by the notary. Indeed, it is common practice for a member of the notary's staff to be appointed to sign the final deed on the buyer's behalf.

After completion, the notary will stamp and register the title deed which can take about six months. A certified copy of the purchase deed, or expédition de vente, is then sent to the notary by the land registry who usually keeps it on behalf of the buyer. This is the only evidence of ownership available. There are no title deeds. If a buyer requires evidence of his ownership, he can ask the notary for a declaration –attestation de vente– to this effect.

On completion of the purchase of an unfinished property, ownership of the land and incomplete construction (if building work has begun) passes to the buyer, though proprietorship of the rest of the building is only transferred as works proceed. In contrast to completed buildings, the balance of the purchase price is payable in instalments as construction progresses; a 30 per cent payment is usually requested on the signing of the conveyance as foundations have to be laid down for legal completion to take place. Further staged instalments are then payable on completion of the foundations, on the building being made watertight, and on completion of the building work. A final payment is made when the property has been inspected by the buyer, and it has been agreed that there are no faults with the construction.

STEP 8 **Moving in**

The new owners of a French property are allowed to take possession of it officially only after the sale has been completed by the notaire. If the property is vacant, it may be possible to arrange an earlier removal date but solely for the purpose of installing furniture. After completion, the buyer will need to start paying for utilities that are connected, as well as for local services like rubbish collection. A notaire or estate agent will often help with this. Water is supplied by a range of private companies in France. When a property is not connected, an application should be made to the local supplier. New owners also have to contact Electricité de France (EDF) and Gaz de France (GDF) to read the meters and to change the name on the accounts. A connection charge is usually payable, as is a deposit if the owner is a non- resident. In rural areas, inhabitants usually rely on cylinder gas.

Homeowners are also legally obliged to take out a third-party liability insurance policy on their property. A notaire will ask to see some proof that the buyer has adequate

insurance cover from the day they take ownership of the property. The vendor's insurance can simply be transferred into the new owner's name. This can be part of a multi-risk household insurance policy, or assurance multirisques habitation, which includes contents and buildings insurance.

Although it is possible to pay utility bills and insurance premiums from the UK, if the French home is not going to be used as a main residence it can be easier to pay by direct debit, or prélèvement automatique, from a French bank account. Not only does it simplify the process, but it also avoids supplies being cut off simply because letters and cheques never reached their destination. Opening a French bank account is easier now than it has ever been. Help is usually available from estate agents, homefinders and solicitors involved in the purchase, and today banks in France even have English-speaking branches, and non-resident as well as resident bank accounts (non-resident bank accounts do not offer overdraft facilities).

There are no restrictions on the importing of most furniture and household effects into France by an EU citizen, provided they are for personal use. However, the movement of antiques in and out of the UK can cause complications; proof of their origin should be kept ready to be produced when they are moved between countries.

Thanks to a new 'pet passport' scheme, pets are much freer to move between the UK

See as much of France as possible before buying and get to know your chosen locality

HEADLANDS INTERNATIONAL

STEPS TO BUYING

and other EU countries, without the need for quarantine periods. To enter France, they must have a current anti-rabies vaccination certificate; to return to the UK they will need a pet passport and a microchip.

STEP 9 Taxation

A foreign homeowner only usually becomes a resident of France when they spend more than 183 days in the country, or if their permanent home is there. Even if they are not a tax resident, apart from the taxes paid to the notaire at the time of the property purchase, owners of French homes may also be liable at some time or another to pay a range of other taxes.

The tax offices of France and the country in which a foreign national resides will be interested in their annual income from activities in France, which could range from bank interest to rental income. If this is above a certain figure, an annual declaration of income in France must be made.

Although a tax resident of France could, in theory, be liable for French and UK taxes, there is a double tax treaty between France and the UK that protects most British nationals with property in France from paying tax twice. Anyone planning to move permanently from the UK to France would be advised to notify the British tax authorities before leaving, and provide them with new employment and property details.

Note that direct taxes are not deducted by means of a PAYE system in France. Instead, they are paid in the year following the tax year in question, which runs from 1 January to 31 December. This is done either in three or 10 instalments, and taxation is always on a self-assessment basis. Residents' taxes are collected by the Direction Générale des Impôts, while non-residents deal with the Centre des Impôts des Non-Résidents in Paris. A tax return form, or déclaration des revenus, can be obtained from the local tax office, or centre des impôts, who can help the uninitiated to fill out their forms.

Property taxes

Based on the average rental value of a property, there are two types of local tax payable by individuals. The taxe foncière is a property ownership tax paid on unbuilt or built-up land by the owner, whether a resident in France or not. The taxe d'habitation is a residential tax paid by the occupiers, who may or may not be the

HEADLANDS INTERNATIONAL

Secure a binding estimate from your builder to cover the price and completion date

number of allowances from which you can get tax relief. A tax on investment or 'unearned' income tax, impôt sur les revenus de capitaux, is payable on property and investment income, as well as interest paid on bank accounts. There is also a separate rental income tax, or contribution sur les revenus locatifs, which is levied on gross rental income.

Wealth tax

Wealth tax, or impôt de solidarité sur la fortune, is levied on net assets held in France valued above a certain threshold, currently €750,000, if resident or with assets in France on 1 January of any year. Assets can include property, a car and bank balances; certain items or assets are excluded, such as antiques. Wealth tax cannot exceed 85 per cent of your net taxable income. The tax can be minimised if you buy a property through an SCI, or property-holding company, and the net worth of the property can be reduced by way of a mortgage or borrowing on the property or a debt. Wealth tax is levied on married couples, single persons, persons residing together under a marriage pact or under 'common law'.

Capital gains tax and social charges

There is no tax on any gain made from the sale of a principal home, but capital gains tax, or impôt sur les plus-values, is levied on profits of the sale of other property, subject to certain allowances. Non-residents do not, however, pay CSG (generalised social contributions) or CRDS (repayment of the social debt). With capital gains tax a

distinction is made between short-term gains (i.e. within two years of acquiring the asset) and long-term gains. The gross gain is worked out by taking away from the sale price the purchase price; the costs incurred when buying the property (the default cost is 7.5 per cent); and the cost of any works if you have had the property for more than five years – if you do the work, a valuer will value this or multiply material costs by three, or you may opt for the default cost of 15 per cent if the work is done by workmen if you have not kept the invoices and receipts. The gross gain can then be reduced by 10 per cent for every full year after five years since the purchase. There is also a fixed allowance of €1,000 if you are the sole owner of the property; €2,000 if you are sharing the ownership with your partner. The final figure becomes your net taxable gain. Tax for French tax residents and non-residents is currently paid at 16 per cent of the net gain; French tax residents pay a further 11 per cent in national insurance on top of that. Since 2004, long-term gains are taxed immediately on the signing of the final purchase deed.

Inheritance tax

French inheritance law – which governs inheritance tax, death and estate duties, and decides who inherits a person's assets – is quite unlike anything that a British buyer will have encountered before. In theory, inheritance tax is paid on the global assets of a French tax resident. The beneficiaries pay inheritance taxes, depending on how closely they are related to the deceased. Inheritance tax is payable on any French property owned by a non-resident.

French inheritance tax is due on the registration of the "déclaration de succession". But delays or payment by instalments can be obtained from the French Revenue, if necessary, although interest will be charged. French inheritance tax varies from 5% to 60%.

The French Finance Act 2005 changed the law to favour children of the deceased. Estates up to €100,000 are free from inheritance tax. Children have an abatement of €50,000 and the spouse a tax-free amount of €76,000.

One child is entitled to one-half of a deceased parent's estate, and two children to two-thirds shared equally between them. If three or more children exist, their reserve share is 75% of the estate divided between them.

As from July 1, 2002, the surviving spouse

is now treated as a true heir. If the deceased leaves children from the marriage with the surviving spouse, the latter may choose to receive usufruct of the deceased's assets (i.e. the right to use or collect the income from them) or assume ownership of one quarter of the estate.

There are several ways in which you can minimise an inheritance tax bill, and careful planning at the time of the house purchase is crucial. In certain circumstances, for example, changes to a marriage contract can help, as can buying through an SCI, of which the owners are the shareholders.

Be careful, though, with an SCI as the shareholder's heirs will have to pay French inheritance taxes. Usually the law of the country in which the property is located is applicable. If the property is owned by an SCI, the applicable law will be that of the deceased's last country of residence, as it is not immovable property, which is always subject to French inheritance civil law. Again, this needs to be borne in mind.

Clause tontine

To benefit the surviving spouse, provisions can also be made in the French will, or in the purchase document, of an owner to ensure that their husband or wife receives the whole of the property on the death of the first or a lifetime interest. One of the most popular methods that couples opt for is to put a 'clause tontine' in the conveyance, which, in effect, suspends the ownership of the entire property until one or other of them dies. However, this does not make the property exempt from taxation.

Change of matrimonial regime

The 1978 Hague Convention on matrimonial property regimes allows couples to change the law applicable to their matrimonial regime. Under article 6 of the Convention, couples may choose to adopt the law of a country of which at least one of them is a national or of a country in which one of them is resident. In addition, in respect of real estate only, they can choose to apply the law of the country in which that real estate is situated.

If your main concern is to ensure that the surviving spouse inherits the deceased spouse's share in the French property absolutely (thereby achieving 100% ownership and gaining full control over the property), you may adopt the French matrimonial regime of "Régime de la Communauté Universelle des Biens" in respect of your French property and any other immovable property that you may acquire in the future in France. This will have the effect of placing your property in joint ownership ("communauté").

New French Succession Rules

A new law reforming French successions will apply from 1 January 2007. It modifies over 200 articles of the French Civil Code. The reform will bring flexibility to an old system to be more adapted to the changing family groups of our society.

Please find below some of the new reforms:
■ Simplification for changing the matrimonial regime
■ Possibility for the heirs to renounce all of part of their inheritance
■ The deadline during which a heir may accept or renounce to a succession is reduced from 30 to 10 years.
■ Ascendants will no longer be treated as reserved heirs when the deceased has no children. So childless couple will be able to transfer the entire estate by will.
■ Better protection of heirs in respect of an estate's liabilities.

STEP 10 Renovations & building works

If you buy a property with a view to making alterations, you should check for any planning restrictions that may affect any building plans you have. A certificate showing planning permission, a certificat d'urbanisme, will provide precise details of the rules regarding the potential development of an individual property. Each area has an official maximum planning density, the coefficient d'occupation des sols, and some areas have no-build zones. Contact your local town hall for these. Buyers should also be aware that not all buildings can be improved and turned into gîtes. Some buildings may be too small in the first place to do so – check the planning regulations. Some minor works require no formalities, but even before building a swimming pool, you may need to fill in a form called a déclaration des travaux at your local mairie. In the case of more extensive alterations to a French property, both planning permission and a building permit, or permis de construire, must be applied for through the local mairie. Once the application has been considered by the mairie, it is forwarded to the local planning office, and following approval it is then passed back to the mairie

for final signing off. The whole process usually takes about two months. Applications can be made by the owners themselves or a surveyor, unless the net surface area to be built upon exceeds 170 square metres, in which case it should be made by an architect who is a member of the ordre des architectes. A listed historical building, or a building that is situated near one, will also require review by an architecte des bâtiments de France. The majority of planning applications in France also require an environmental declaration providing an assessment of the impact of the proposals on the local area. An architect will usually organise this for you. It may be tempting to try to carry out renovation work without recourse to builders or architects, but anyone renovating or adding to a historic building must be competent in the use of local wood and stone, and understand the regulations governing the use of building material in the area. French builders are not renowned for their punctuality, but they are known to do a good job. The local chambre

TEN TIPS FOR BUYERS

1 Cast your net wider than the areas you already know
2 Cut down on wasted trips by asking for detailed descriptions of properties
3 Don't buy simply on impulse – this is a major purchase that could have any number of hidden costs
4 Visit the area in all seasons, if possible
5 Rent in the locality if you can, to get to know the area before you buy
6 Introduce yourself to the neighbours to get to know them and the neighbourhood before you commit yourself to a property
7 Be prepared to negotiate the asking price, engaging a local géometre or a valuer to offer an independent opinion
8 Seek independent legal advice before signing any contract and handing over any money, and consider instructing your own notaire who can oversee the sale alongside the vendor's notaire – there is no extra cost for this service
9 Instruct a qualified buildings surveyor to carry out a full survey and estimate the cost of necessary repairs or building work
10 Plan the move to the property as carefully as you plan the purchase itself.

des métiers, or chamber of trade, can supply details of builders registered in the area. Some British homeowners are more comfortable employing British builders, even though they may not be as knowledgeable about local materials and planning regulations. There are plenty of British builders living in France or willing to travel to France to work. It is essential, though, to check that the work of builders, electricians, plumbers and other tradesmen complies with French standards. If you cannot be on site to supervise the project, employing an architect or surveyor, French or British, to see the project through can end up saving you money as well as time. When work has been completed, you will need to obtain a certificate, or certificat de conformité, proving that it complies with the planning permission. All new building works come with a 10-year guarantee from the contractor who has carried out that work, provided that they are properly registered with the French authorities. The guarantee will be backed by the contractor's professional insurance. What is rarely guaranteed is the actual cost of the work. Estimates form the basis of a fixed-price deal if the builder carrying out the works signs an estimate endorsed with the words 'prix global au forfait'. This binds them to completing the job for the price shown. Completion dates can also be hard to guarantee, but again there is a way to help fix the date. By inserting a few more words on the paperwork, such as 'le délai d'achèvement des travaux sera le 31 juillet 2007' ('building work will be completed on 31 July 2007), the builder will feel obliged to stick to that date. A penalty clause can also be included, such as 'avec une pénalité de 20 euros par jour de retard', in which case if completion is delayed, the bill will be reduced by 20 euros for each day the work is delayed.

A nationwide organisation called the Conseil d'Architecture, d'Urbanisme et de l'Environnement (CAUE), which has local branches in all of France's regions, can offer advice on renovating or extending traditional buildings. It is also well worth checking with a mairie to discover if the local council provides grants for restoring buildings in the area. Some offer particular help to anyone converting buildings into holiday accommodation, as part of a drive to attract tourism into the regions. The larger gîte rental companies also offer money for this purpose, with the proviso that they have the right to let out the property afterwards.

Building a new home

If you buy a home to be constructed by a developer, they will oversee the construction of your new home, and your choice of architectural style may be limited by the designs drawn up for that particular development. If you are not buying from a developer, you can choose between hiring an architect to draw up plans or buying a ready-made plan from the builder you engage to construct it. If you choose the former option – which will give you the greatest scope for influencing the style of the building according to your personal tastes but will also probably be more expensive – you can either oversee the building of the property yourself, or engage a maître d'œuvre to do so. In any case, you will usually be expected to pay the cost in stages over the course of the construction.

In France, if you buy a new apartment or villa under construction which forms part of a development, you should be protected by the code de la construction (construction law) from the developer being made bankrupt during its construction, and from other possible pitfalls. By law, when the keys to your newly built home are handed over, there will be a one-month guarantee against obvious structural defects and a 10-year warranty against latent defects affecting the structure of the building. There will also be a two-year warranty against defects in equipment, such as central heating. ●

HOW TO BUY....

Through a developer

It's quite common in France to buy a property before it is completed – la vente en l'état futur d'achevement – from a developer, or promoteur constructeur. This can be an apartment in a building, a villa, a townhouse on an estate, or a lotissement. French developers buy land, obtain planning permission and then try to attract buyers. You can obtain details of developers through the Fédération Nationale des Promoteurs Constructeurs (see Directory of useful contacts on p. 187 for further details)

Through a user group

You can purchase a share in a new multipropriété or an existing one – re-sales do become available – set up by a group of individuals or a specialist company. Check out publications or newspaper sections advertising French property for announcements of the sale of shares in multipropriétés, or contact specialists like Owner Groups Company (www.ownergroups.com)

At auction

Auctions can be a source of real bargains, as here properties are often sold as a result of inheritance disputes or mortgage defaults, and consequently are priced keenly for a swift sale. At an auction, or vente aux enchères, a notary must usually bid on behalf of the buyer. Written authorisation, in the form of a mandate to bid up to a certain value, must be given to the notary before they attend the sale. Be prepared also to pay 20 per cent of the highest price you are prepared to bid to them in advance. The balance of a successful bid must be paid between one and three months after the sale date.

Note that there is no prospect of including get-out clauses in the sale agreement, so it is essential to examine carefully the property and details such as third-party rights of way over it. Any loans should be in place before the sale. Auction details will appear in local newspapers, in national publications such as the bi-monthly Le Journal des Enchères and Les Ventes aux Encheres des Notaires, and on websites like www.encheres-paris.com and www.ventes-judiciaires.com. Both estate agents and notaries should also have details of properties up for auction in their area

Direct from the owner

Homes in France can also be bought direct from the owner. Private sales are advertised in specialist magazines and on websites based in France itself and in many other countries. If you buy from an owner, do not be pressurised into handing over a deposit to the owner themselves. There may be no guarantee that they will return it if either party withdraws from the sale for valid reasons. Deposits should be handled by the notaire in charge of overseeing the sale. It is also preferable not to hand over any deposit without seeking independent advice, as it may prove to be non-refundable.

LANDES OF THE LIVING

Not content with running a ski chalet business in the Alps, outdoor lovers Quintin and Merrilyn Hetherington decided to set up a second business in Soustons, Landes.

BOTH ACTIVE TYPES, QUINTIN AND Merrilyn met whilst on a ski season in Courchevel in 1997. They subsequently settled in Merrilyn's home country of Australia, but dreamed of returning to France to set up their own chalet business there.

Three years later, the intrepid couple arrived in Courcheval to make their dreams a reality, despite having never run a business before and with a grasp of only the most basic French. Their gamble paid off and soon they were looking around for a new venture to occupy their time during the summer months.

With a criteria of sun, sea and plenty of sporting activities on offer, their search lead them to the department of Landes in south-west France, and to the magnificent 19th-century stately home, Domaine de Bellegarde in Soustons. Quintin and Merrilyn now run the beautifully restored property as a luxury catered villa for guests between April and November, and feel that in Landes, they have finally found a place to call home.

Busy all year round, they couldn't be happier and are delighted with the family focus and hospitality found in Landes, having recently had a little boy called Jaydon.

Q What attracted you to life in France?

A We were living in Avalon Beach, Sydney. Merrilyn was working at Sydney Hospital in the city, travelling up to three hours a day, while I was working at Flightcentre in addition to other work. We found it difficult to save enough money to get our foot on the property ladder and were not

In Landes, the Hetherington's have found a home

really finding much time to enjoy a quality outdoor lifestyle. We had always talked about setting up a business in Courchevel as this is where we met one another doing a ski season in 1997, so we decided to take the plunge and give it a go! In addition, we loved the varied lifestyle and landscapes offered in France – our winters are spent in the Alps with its blue sky, sunshine and clean air; during the long summers we're in southwest France. Both places suit our outdoor lifestyle; we can ski, snowboard, surf, cycle and swim when time permits!

Q What preparations did you make before you went out?

A We believed that there was a niche in the highly competitive ski market for a luxury catered chalet company with real personal service, qualified chefs, and a high ratio of staff to guests. We contacted the ski company we had worked for in the past, explained our intentions and they offered us the opportunity to operate one of their luxury chalets in Courchevel 1850. This was an ideal way to see if it really was what we wanted to do, if it was possible to make it work, and it gave us some time to find a suitable chalet to rent for the following ski season.

Q How did you get started with your ski business?

A We arrived in France in November 2000 to have a short break before starting the winter season. I took this opportunity to surprise Merrilyn with a marriage proposal at the top of the Eiffel Tower – and she said yes! During the season, we found a ski chalet in the centre of Courchevel 1850 for the following year and began preparations for the launch of our business – designing a website, renovations, attending the London ski show, plus marketing and PR. We opened our first chalet in December 2001, with Merrilyn as the chef and me as the host along with one employee. The season was a great success and we signed on a second chalet for the next year. We also managed to plan and prepare for our wedding, which took place the following Spring.

Q When did you decide to start your summer venture?

A In September 2004 I travelled to Hossegor for a week's surfing holiday and spent time contacting agents and looking at potential areas. The main objective was to find something within easy reach (less than 10 kilometres) of the coast, in a village with plenty of things to interest our guests. It was a tough criteria to fulfil, but we think Domaine

LOCATION

■ Situated along the south-west coastline of the Aquitaine region, this department is home to the longest stretch of beach in Europe, the Côte d'Argent. Ideal for surfers, its flat, forested landscape inland also attracts cyclists and campers.

■ A typical landaise farmhouse is characterised by its large size, low roofs and wooden beams. Prices start from €160,000 for unrenovated properties away from the coast.

"In the Alps our favourite time of the year is Christmas; there's a real buzz in the resort. Autumn and Spring in Landes are special times as they lack the crowds, and the weather is truly superb"

de Bellegarde did this and more! We found the property in March 2005 and finally moved in after a difficult purchase process in August, although the house was not officially ours until late October. The purchase was one of the most difficult and challenging experiences we have ever encountered and we feel our perseverance plus a bit of luck got us there in the end.

Q Describe your property.

A We consider our real home to be the Domaine de Bellegarde in Soustons, as this is where we spend most of the year. Our property is a 19th-century stately home surrounded by six acres of private gardens with a large heated swimming pool, outdoor summer barbeque kitchen, shaded poolside terrace, tennis court and a croquet lawn. The house has been beautifully restored and thoughtfully decorated with contemporary décor and furniture throughout. It has nine individually designed en-suite bedrooms, which have four-poster beds, a Jacuzzi, sauna, marble fireplaces and balconies. There is a grand reception lounge and hall, spacious dining room, billiards room and TV lounge, all with high ornate ceilings, original oak parquet floors and an impressive staircase. The house truly is exceptional and is one of the grandest of all the houses in the region – all within six kilometres of the Atlantic coast with endless sandy blue flag beaches! We live in a converted bungalow next door, so we're on site without invading our guests' privacy.

Q Did you have to do much work on your property?

A A significant amount of work had already been done prior to the purchase: the ceiling coving, wood panelling, plasterwork details and plumbing had all been restored. We now have an on-demand hot water and heating system. We renovated the pool area and installed a summer barbeque kitchen, so that our chef can cook poolside and guests can enjoy their cuisine alfresco. The gardens have also been improved and we've also installed an outside shower and toilet alongside the pool house. The property and gardens are now as they were originally designed.

Q Could you speak the language?

A On our arrival in France we both had a basic knowledge of French, but since then we have developed a good command of the language from our immersion in everyday French life. We have found that since we moved to Landes, our vocabulary has improved even more, as the locals have more time due to a slower pace of life. There's a great attitude to outsiders here, which is not always found in the French Alps.

Q Having recently had a baby in France, how would you describe the healthcare?

A The French system puts a very high value on the family unit and the emphasis is very much on the provision of the best healthcare from the start of pregnancy through to the birth. Compared to the

The Landes department incorporates the sandy blue-flag beaches of the Atlantic coast

UK and Australia, there are additional ultrasound scans and appointments with a consultant rather than a GP or midwife. The hospital ensures you are really prepared for life as a family by providing a stay of five nights in a private room with midwives available to allay any fears and provide help with many aspects of early parenting. We would not hesitate to recommend the system to anyone planning to give birth here.

Q What have been the main challenges about the move?

A The bureaucracy and endless paperwork created by operating two business in France, along with the fact that everything is done at a slower pace. August comes to a standstill and as our peak occupancy is at this time, this provides its trials and tribulations! As we operate all year round, we don't have much time to prepare for the following season's business, so life can be quite hectic especially with a new baby. We don't regret any of our decisions, but we would welcome a few more hours in each day, to work and relax!

Q How have you benefited from the move?

A We now control our own destiny and have a place we call home. We make our own decisions which is the good side of being your own boss. Despite the hard work and long hours we both get to see our baby boy Jaydon whenever we like as work is on site. The downside is that it's hard to put work to one side at times.

Q Have you found it easy to integrate into French life?

A Due to the nature of our businesses, we are often dealing with local companies. This has enabled us to meet and mix with local people relatively quickly. We have found the people in Landes to be very friendly and welcoming. It feels more of a community in Soustons as opposed to Courchevel where people are generally there to work the winter season, making it a transient population. The lifestyle in Landes is very similar to Australia, so it suits us perfectly!

Q What do you miss most?

A First and foremost we both miss our family and friends, but we also miss the people of Australia, as they live a very outdoor and 'can-do' lifestyle with a happy and fun nature that is not really part of the French culture. We are sure that not being a native plays a part in this. Cheddar cheese and a good café culture are also missed.

Q When is your favourite time of year?

A In the Alps our favourite time of the year is Christmas, as it is cosy in the chalets, there is a real buzz in the resort as most people are on holiday. The snowfall combined with the excitement is hard to beat... if we weren't working! Autumn and spring in Landes are special times as they lack the crowds of July and August, the weather is truly superb with long sunny days, and the ocean holds a temperature that is good for swimming for eight months of the year.

Q Can you describe a typical day?

A Each day can be very different, but a general day in the summer is as follows: we buy the bread, croissants and pain au chocolat from the boulangerie, visit the Soustons market on Mondays for fresh local produce, set out the pool loungers and prepare and serve breakfast for the guests, which is served poolside or in the grand dining room. We service the bedrooms and communal areas, check emails and organise any events for guests such as surfing lessons, golf, tennis or vineyard tours. On alternate days we serve a luxury four-course lunch or dinner. We tend the office and I also manage the house and garden maintenance.

Q Is your move permanent?

A We are quite happy at the moment but would like to one day own something in Australia and France so that we have the choice, but we feel that our children will probably dictate where we live as they grow up and have their own views ●

"Our winters are spent in the Alps with its blue sky, sunshine and clean air; summers are spent in the southwest. Both places suit our outdoor lifestyle; we can ski, snowboard, surf, cycle and swim"

Living and working

All the information you need for living and working in France, from work permits and visas, to healthcare and collecting your pension

I F YOU ARE AN EU NATIONAL YOU NO LONGER have to apply for a residence permit (carte/titre de séjour) after living or working in France for more than three months. You must, however, hold some other form of ID from your country of origin, which includes proof of your home address. If you are a UK resident, your passport and a recent utilities bill which includes your address are acceptable. However, many French officials are not yet familiar with how to apply the new law and in some instances, for the time being at least; it may be easier to obtain a carte de séjour. If, for example, you apply for a job or set up a business, you may still be asked for a carte de séjour because traditionally this permit has served as an ID card and as proof of the right to work. If you are planning to stay in France for more than three months, you must register your presence in the country; this would normally be done at your local mairie (town hall) or gendarmerie (police station) for larger towns. Failure to do so could result in a fine. The mairie is also a good place to start getting your new life in France up and running. Most larger mairies, such as heads of administrative cantons, have offices reserved for representatives from the various French benefit agencies. They will normally be available for a specified time once or twice a week and this is an excellent place to start getting yourself registered in the French system. You could also ask for a pamphlet produced by La Sécurité Sociable called Vous ET vos Droits (You and your Rights), which covers all social security matters and has a foreigners' section for most topics. Anyone working in France, either as an employee or self-employed, must be registered with the social security organisations (caisses) which cover their particular occupation and pay contributions to the relevant caisses.

Tax

A foreign home-owner usually becomes a resident of France after spending more than 183 days in the country. If they spend fewer than 183 days, they could still be classed as 'resident' if they practise their profession or have a permanent home in France. Non- residents must pay tax if they have income from a rental property or a French employer. See Taxation, on p.26, for further details.

Healthcare

In 2000, the World Health Organisation voted the French healthcare system the best in the world. If you are an EU national, and only visit your French home for short periods, you will qualify for free emergency

Finding a job in France is the same as in the UK, but many find work before they arrive

medical treatment in France; you used to get an E111 form from any UK post office, now you will receive a European Health Insurance Card (EHIC) which will entitle you to free medical treatment in France for three months when you present it, but be aware, it will only reimburse you between 65% and 70% of the total cost, dependent on treatment. If you live in France for over three months but you don't work there, you may be entitled to the same treatment and benefits as French nationals. In order to fully benefit from the state benefits system you should be able to supply your last two years' pay slips or submitted accounts; either way, they will want proof of how much tax you have paid during this period. This

---

CARTE DE SÉJOURCHECKLIST (RESIDENCE PERMIT)

EU nationals will typically be asked to produce the following documents to obtain a carte de séjour:
■ Valid passport
■ Birth and/or marriage certificate
■ Proof of accommodation
■ Proof that you pay contributions to the French state health insurance scheme, or have medical insurance that will cover you until you join it
■ Three passport-sized photographs
■ Proof of employment or receipt of a state pension, or proof of enrolment with a French university

LIVING AND WORKING

The French love buying their food fresh from local markets

entitlement will only cover you for so long, after which time you would be wise to make voluntary contributions to the state health insurance scheme. Should you need future medical treatment, most of the cost will hopefully be paid by the state scheme, between 65% and 70%. Otherwise you will have to take out private medical insurance, to cover the shortfall. Once you are employed in France, your employers should register you with the social security and pay state health insurance scheme contributions for you. While these payments are being made, the scheme will cover most of your healthcare costs. The same applies if you are self-employed and paying contributions to the caisse. If you are planning to retire in France and receive a state pension from another EU country, that country will usually pay your healthcare. Register for free healthcare in France with form E121. If you also receive a French state pension you will be treated as a French pensioner and France's health insurance scheme will cover your healthcare costs. If you are not yet eligible for a state pension and you won't be working in France you can obtain medical cover for up to two years by completing form E106. After this, as mentioned above, you should pay voluntary contributions or take out private medical insurance. To accommodate the ever increasing numbers of families living in France but with the main bread winner commuting back to work in the UK and paying National Insurance contributions there or another Member State; the E109 has been introduced to cover the family living in France, with the commuter utilising the EHIC. British nationals can contact the Department of Work and Pensions (DWP) for further information. In France you can get forms and advice from your local health insurance or social security office. Even when someone is living in France and has joined the state health insurance scheme, unless they fall into the 'low income' bracket or are suffering from a serious illness, the full cost of any treatment is not usually met by the state health service. You will usually need to pay for consultations, treatments and prescriptions up front before being reimbursed, in full or in part, by the relevant health insurance caisse. This applies unless treatment is carried out in an approved hospital, in which case the state will pay 80 per cent of the cost of the treatment directly to the hospital. You must then pay the balance and any fixed daily hospital charge. As of 1 July 2005, French residents now have to register with a particular Payout can visit any dentist that you choose to, but be advised that fees vary greatly. Details of local hospitals and practitioners can be obtained from a gendarmerie or by dialling 15 on any French telephone. Your local social security office can provide a list of the doctors who charge the official social security rate.

Education

Any child of non-French origin who is living in France has the right to join the French education system. He or she can attend a local state school, a private school, or one of the many bilingual schools – both state-run or private – depending on which school best suits their needs. Between the ages of three and five, children can join an école maternelle(a nursery). All six to 16-year- olds must first attend an école primaire(a primary school),then a collège(a secondary school). The last two years are spent at a lycée, where students can choose to study either for a baccalauréat (a diploma covering more subjects than the A-level system does in the UK, entitling students to go on to university) or for vocational qualifications. The French state education system has an excellent reputation but if children have a poor command of the French language when they arrive in the country they may be better off at a bilingual school. Each region has one or sometimes two académies (education districts), managed by a rectorat (local education authority) where details of the schools and universities based in their locality are held. These should be available on request.

Insurance

Home-owners are legally obliged to take out third-party liability insurance on their property. The vendor's insurance can be transferred into the new owner's name. This can be part of a multi-risk household insurance policy which includes contents and buildings insurance. Contents and insurance policies specific to holiday homes may be preferable for those who intend to visit the property only from time to time. All cars in France must have at least third-party insurance cover. Proof of insurance must be kept with the car at all times. If you purchase car insurance in France and want to benefit from your no claims discount accrued in the UK you must provide proof of this; your current insurance papers will not suffice. Try to get a letter from your current insurer stating how many years' no claims bonus you have.

Securing a driving licence

Citizens of EU countries are permitted to drive within France on the driving licence issued by their country of origin.UK licence holders moving to France should note that the DVLA does not permit foreign addresses on UK licences, so when you notify them of your foreign address, they'll send you an application form for a French licence. If you commit a driving offence in France that results in penalty points, you'll have to get a French licence. Apply for a French driving licence by contacting your local prefecture. You'll need a valid current licence, proof of address, two passport-sized photographs, and the fee. You will also have to pay to have your current UK licence translated by a recognised translator; the local prefecture will provide a list. The standard UK licence allows you to drive a vehicle of 7.5 tonnes, whereas the standard French licence allows you to drive only 2.5 tonnes. You could be asked to pass a

Fresh French bread is just one reason for living here

JUSTIN POSTLETHWAITE

medical to keep what is considered a heavy goods licence in France, together with retaining the right to tow a trailer. By law, you must carry your licence whenever you drive, and you should also be able to produce the carte grise, or registration document, and a valid insurance document for the car.

Finding a job

Looking for a job in France is much the same as in the UK. You can send speculative letters to companies of interest or apply for vacancies published in the French press or online. There are also numerous temporary employment agencies, recruitment centres and vocational guidance centres, as well as employment services to help you in your search for work. A French CV is traditionally only one page long and should be handwritten; it does no harm attaching a current passport picture of yourself. In France,www.parisfranceguide.com or the Agence Nationale Pour l'Emploi (ANPE) at www.anpe.fr are two websites worth checking out. If job-hunting from Britain, try the Recruitment and Employment Confederation's website,www.rec.uk.com, or www.ukworksearch.com. Alternatively, try an agency such as European Employment Services (EURES).

Making a will

British wills are recognised in France, but are much more costly to implement, so it's always advisable to draw up a French will. This should be done with a lawyer. Leaving no will can cause untold complications and considerable costs for your heirs.

Pet travel checklist

When exporting cats and dogs from Britain under the Pet Travel Scheme (PETS),you must ensure that they are micro chipped and vaccinated against rabies. The rabies vaccine must be given at least 30 days before departure to allow time for immunity to develop. Once a blood test confirms a sufficient level of rabies antibodies, the micro chipped pet qualifies for a British pet passport. After your pet has lived in France for three months, it's regarded as a resident and must comply with French laws. For more exotic pets, check with the French authorities as special import certificates may be required. For re-entry to the UK, a few days before travelling have your pet checked for ticks and tapeworms by a vet who can then issue you with the relevant certificate. You must sign a declaration stating that your pet hasn't been outside any PETS qualifying countries within the previous six months. Pets not meeting these requirements must spend six months in quarantine.

PET CHECKLIST

- Your pet must be vaccinated against rabies
- You are required to secure a PETS certificate, essentially a 'pet passport'
- Your pet must be micro chipped by your vet
- Your pet is required to undergo a blood test to confirm that it does not carry any rabies antibodies

"Any child of non-French origin who is living in France has the right to join the French education system"

COMMUNICATIONS

Mobile phones

Most foreigners in France use their British phone, but substitute their UK sim card for a French one. It is then possible to operate on a 'Pay as you go' tariff, purchasing a mobicarte(top-up card) from any tabac or supermarket, thus avoiding a contract and billing system for which you need a permanent address.

Internet

France's main internet service provider is www.wanadoo.fr. They provide free software for internet connection but you do have to pay through your phone bill for time online. This is only a few euros per minute but these can accumulate. There are various deals on offer through telecom providers (France Télécom) which can be faster and cheaper.

Postal services

La poste (the French post office; www.laposte.net) is easily recognisable due to its yellow and blue colouring. Not only does it function as a traditional post office, you can also pay your bills, receive welfare payments, and open a bank account of sorts.

The French postal system is quick and efficient

Retirement and pensions

Anyone moving to France to retire should inform their DWP office a few weeks before their departure date so that the necessary administrative arrangements can be set in motion. You can still receive a state pension from one country if you retire to another, but you must make sure you that you pass on details of any new bank account. If you work in France before you retire and have made contributions to the French state pension scheme, you will probably be entitled to receive a French state pension in addition to one from any other country you have lived and worked in. The level of state pension will depend on how long you contributed to the pension scheme of that particular country. In France, on reaching retirement age you should contact the Caisse Nationale d'Assurance Vieillesse (CNAV). The overseas branch of the UK's Department for Work and Pensions can provide information about pensions for British citizens moving abroad.

Utilities

Most French home utilities are state run, which makes getting connected a fairly simple process. Most of France's power (supplied by Electricité de France, or EDF) comes from nuclear reactors and hydro-electric plants, and is among the cheapest in Europe. Hence, most home heating and appliances run on electricity. Contact your local EDF office to arrange connection – you'll need proof of home-ownership and one other form of identity. Mains gas is supplied by Gaz de France (GDF) and is part of EDF. Both utilities are usually billed together. Water is privatised and supplied by Générale des Eaux. It's expensive wherever you live, although there's a wide spread of charges depending on which region you live in. Mains drainage in particular is expensive in remote areas, explaining why many rural homes rely on a

simpler, cheaper system of having a septic tank. Contact your local water company to set up a new account and be sure to avoid paying anyone else's charges by having the meter read before you move in. For telephone connection, visit your local France Télécom office with ID and proof of your address. You will be charged a call-out and connection fee.

Voting

All EU citizens resident in France are legally entitled to vote in certain French elections, specifically the local (municipal) elections and European elections. You will need a voter registration card and an identity document.

Marriage

France is different to the UK in that only civil weddings are legally recognised. Religious ceremonies have no legal standing, so if you want to marry in a French church, you will also have to have a civil ceremony elsewhere. Alternatively, you could have a civil marriage in Britain followed by a religious wedding in France. At least one of the partners must reside in the place where the wedding is to be held for at least 40 days before the wedding. After 30 days, you must display the marriage banns at the mairie for ten days. British nationals don't lose their nationality when they marry. Equally, marriage to a French citizen does not automatically grant you French citizenship. To acquire French nationality upon marrying a French citizen, you must sign a declaration before a French consul or magistrate. This will grant you dual nationality. Should you marry in France, you will be given a Liver de Familiar book in which family events (births, deaths, divorces) are recorded – invaluable when dealing with French bureaucracy. Without one, passports, birth certificates and a utilities bill will suffice. ●

We make it easier to swap your UK life for the good life.

If you're thinking of buying in France, it's nice to have a familiar face around who can help you with the difficult parts. At Barclays we'll simplify everything for you. Whether it's organising the best mortgage, navigating through local regulations or finding trustworthy tradesmen, our staff in Europe can offer advice on it all, in plain English. And with over 80 years on the continent, Barclays has more experience than any other UK bank helping people from the UK, buy a home in Europe. So here's to an easier life in the sun.

To find out how Barclays can help you buy property in France, visit www.barclays.co.uk/europe or call 0845 675 0555*

BARCLAYS
Now there's a thought

Property guide

We've travelled the length and breadth of France to reveal the up-and-coming areas and hottest property prospects

Brittany

Windswept coasts, historic villages and ancient sites

BRITTANY TOURIST BOARD

FACT BOX

- ■ **POPULATION** 2,906,197
- ■ **UNEMPLOYMENT RATE** 8.3%
- ■ **AVERAGE 4-BED HOUSE PRICE** €264, 837
- ■ **REGIONAL CAPITAL** Rennes
- ■ **REGION SIZE** 27,184km²

Contents

Area profile

Blessed with a fair climate, Brittany offers wild coves, pretty villages, stunning scenery and a wealth of history

GETTING THERE

AIR Flybe (0871 700 0535; www. flybe.co.uk) flies to Brest from Belfast, Birmingham, Edinburgh, Exeter and Southampton. **Ryanair** (0871 246 0000; www.ryanair.com) flies to Dinard, Brest and Nantes from London and the East Midlands. **Aurigny Air** (01481 822886; www.aurignyair.com) flies to Dinard from Guernsey and Jersey, and via Guernsey from Manchester, East Midlands, Bristol, Stansted, Gatwick and Southampton. **Air France** (0845 084 5111; www.airfrance. co.uk) flies to Nantes or Paris with connecting flights to Quimper and Brest.

SEA Brittany Ferries (0870 366 5333; www.brittany-ferries.com) sails to St-Malo from Portsmouth, and to Roscoff from Plymouth. **Condor Ferries** (0845 345 2000; www.condorferries.com) sails to St-Malo from Poole and Weymouth.

ROAD The N12/N165 offers easy access into Brittany, running along the coast and on to Rennes. Travelling across Brittany's more isolated areas can prove to be much slower. From Paris, the A11 runs direct to Brittany.

RAIL Brittany's rail network mainly follows the coast with limited stations inland. The high-speed **TGV** (www.tvg. co.uk) runs direct from Paris and Lille into Rennes, and across to Brest and Quimper, and there is a good local train service. For information, contact **Rail Europe** (0870 584 8848; www.raileurope.co.uk).

CLIMATE

	BRITTANY		LONDON		BRITTANY		LONDON
	8.5	Dec	7	84	Dec	81
	11.5	Nov	10	86	Nov	78
	15.5	Oct	14	79	Oct	70
	19.5	Sep	19	64	Sep	65
	23	Aug	21	46	Aug	62
	23	Jul	22	46	Jul	59
	21	Jun	20	46	Jun	58
	15	May	17	64	May	57
	15	Apr	13	51	Apr	56
	8.5	Mar	10	69	Mar	64
	7.5	Feb	7	71	Feb	72
	8.5	Jan	6	86	Jan	77

AVERAGE **TEMPERATURE** (Celsius)

AVERAGE **RAINFALL** (millimetres)

KNOWN AS THE "LAND OF THE SEA" AND accounting for a quarter of France's coastline, Brittany offers rocky coves and sheltered harbours in the north and dramatic rocky cliffs in the west, while its southern coast boasts long sandy beaches set in beautiful bays where the climate is almost Mediterranean.

Land of contrasts

Brittany sits on the western outcrop of France, a region isolated both geographically and, in many respects, culturally from the rest of the country; the ancient local Breton language is still practised and taught in certain areas. The rocky coastline stretches for over a thousand kilometres; the northern half faces the English Channel and the southern section is swept by the Atlantic in the Bay of Biscay. Gulf Stream currents brush the coast ensuring the region enjoys a very clement climate.

This region has a rich history dating back thousands of years. The first standing stones were built in 4500 BC at Carnac and numerous other megalithic sites were established – dolmens and menhirs proliferate in the southern part of Brittany.

The region's capital is Rennes, a handsome university city with a picturesque old quarter and a wealth of good restaurants and museums. Even more outstanding is the small medieval city of Dinan, home to some stunning half-timbered buildings

which date back to the 15th century. Travel 25km north of Dinan and you reach Brittany's seaside towns of St-Malo and Dinard. While the latter is a rather brash resort, St-Malo is lively yet austere, and it has a busy ferry port.

At Brittany's western point lies Brest, a city which had to be rebuilt virtually after heavy German bombing in the Second World War. It has a rich maritime history, and it is home to France's largest naval facility as well as Océanopolis, the biggest open-air aquarium in Europe. Inland, Brittany is much quieter although there is much to explore, including a number of Neolithic sites, ancient castles, regional parks and great forests.

Cultural legacy

During the Middle Ages the Duchy of Brittany was an almost constant battleground as French and English invaders fought to claim the region as their own – the granite fortresses along the border with Normandy and maritime castles along the coast are testimony of this. Châteaugiron and Fougères – one of Europe's finest castles – are particularly fine examples. During the Renaissance when Brittany lost its independence and joined the Kingdom of France, the region reached the height of its wealth and over 4,000 luxury châteaux and manor houses were built during this time by rich locals. Château de Kerjean is one of the most attractive.

FOOD AND DRINK

Breton cuisine features simple recipes cooked with first-class ingredients. Fish and shellfish dominate the menu, with mussels and oysters being particularly prevalent. The Atlantic spawns a vast array of fish including sardines, mackerel, coalfish, monkfish, tuna, red gurnard, sole, eel, John Dory, and shellfish such as coquilles Saint-Jacques (sea scallops), spiny lobster, shrimps, crab, langoustines, and lobster. Brittany is also known for its agricultural and dairy produce, not to mention its first-rate charcuterie. Salted butter and pork are two of the region's famous exports.

However, perhaps what Brittany does best is its divine crêpes, the top seller being the classic crêpe beurre-sucre made with butter and sugar, although you can choose from all manner of sweet and savoury fillings. Other regional specialities are wafer biscuits and butter cookies.

Brittany produces a good range of beers and ciders – the cider of Cornouaille has AOC status. Other beverages include pommeau (a sweet cider and apple brandy aperitif liqueur) and chouchen (fermented honey and water).

JUSTIN POSTLETHWAITE

Culturally, the Bretons are essentially Celtic – this is a land of legend and folklore – and as in northern Spain, Scotland and Ireland, the local instrument is the bagpipes. Traditional Celtic dances and songs are part and parcel of the regional culture and there are several notable Breton Celtic groups. This fiercely independent region has its own language, Breton, spoken mostly in the west but enjoying a revival throughout the region especially in schools.

The economy

Brittany is France's main agricultural producer and it has a strong livestock industry. At a local level, the government encourages new industries, and Rennes has now developed its motor trade, while Brest has a thriving engineering and electronics industry. Tourism is still a vital business in Brittany, and the fishing industry remains active in various ports.

Social groups

Traditionally, Brittany is the home of the British family holiday and it has an abundance of small villages within easy reach of the coast. The region has been dubbed "Little Britain" by the French because of its popularity with Britons looking for a holiday home or permanent residence ●

ATTRACTIONS

■ The many islands in the Golfe du Morbihan – Île d'Hoëdic and Île aux Moines are particularly attractive

■ The magical forest of Brocéliande – home to a wealth of myth and legends including Merlin's tomb

■ The town of Vannes with its medieval port, 14th- century walls and half-timbered houses

■ Quimper, the region's oldest city, and its fine Gothic cathedral

■ The world's largest megalithic site at Carnac with nearly 3,000 standing stones built between 4500 and 200 BC

■ The Sept Îles nature reserve, home to France's largest seabird colony

■ Religious processions known as pardons held on saints' days in towns and villages

■ A sunset seen from the Crozon Peninsula in Finistère where the cliffs tower 100 metres above the sea

PROFILE

Property hotspots

MAP KEY

5 Hotspot
○ Major town/city
✈ Airport
⛴ Ferry

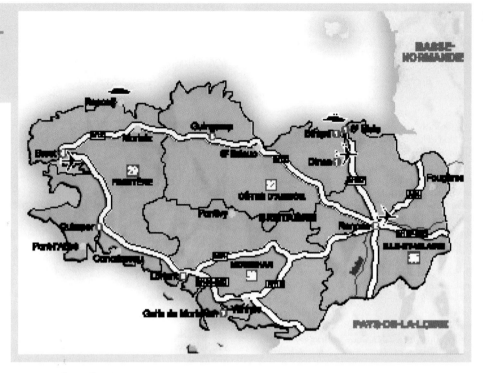

DINARD, DINAN, ST-MALO

1 All located on Brittany's northern coastline, the seaside towns of St-Malo, Dinard and Dinan are popular with both British and French property buyers.

The large city of St-Malo and its old walled Intra Muros has a lively feel, with a citadel, marinas, restaurants and nightlife. Dinard boasts a casino, seawater therapy centre, antique shops, art galleries and a superb sandy beach with beautiful panoramic views over the Rance estuary.

Dinan has been dubbed Brittany's most evocative town, its timbered houses making it a striking example of medieval architecture. The central region celebrates its local culture and traditions, with several schools still teaching the Breton language. Sea views are breathtaking, with high cliffs, islands and rock pools named after their shapes and colours.

The best value homes are found in inland Brittany, throughout the Argoat, where the woods and heathland dotted alongside picturesque villages are graced with traditional granite and slate-roofed cottages, although many properties are in need of renovation.

This is a popular area where many Britons choose to buy their second homes, but increased Parisian interest has raised property prices, as has the ease of access between Brittany and Britain. Small renovation projects start at about €100,000,

and you can buy a four-bedroom stone house from €350,000.

The rental season lasts from April to September, with the winter months providing opportunities for long-term rents. Properties in the area represent a good rental investment, due to proximity to the coast and good access routes. Rental prices vary from between €400 per week for one bedroom and €1,250 per week for five bedrooms.

Key facts

■ **POPULATION** 74,191
■ **TAXES** Taxe d'habitation 9.28%, taxe foncière 10.79%
■ **AIRPORT** Dinard/Pleurtuit/St-Malo Airport, L'Aérodrome, 35730 Pleurtuit, Tel: +33 2 99 46 18 46, Fax: +33 2 99 8817 85
■ **SCHOOLS** Rectorat de l'Académie de Rennes, 96 rue d'Antrain, 35044 Rennes Cedex, Tel: +33 2 99 28 78 78, Fax: +33 2 99 28 77 72
■ **MEDICAL** Hospitalier de St-Malo, 1 rue Marne, 35400 St-Malo, Tel: +33 2 99 21 21 21

■ **PROS** Many Britons are choosing to buy their second home here and it is a popular area ■ Easy to get to, the area is good for commuters and second-home buyers ■ Full of colourful streets, medieval houses and historic buildings, these old ports are extremely attractive, but not overun by tourists
■ **CONS** Easy access for the UK market which results in high property prices ■ Brittany's northern coast experiences a climate that is colder and damper than that of southern Brittany ■ International schools are in short supply and many families send their children to a French-speaking school.

RENNES

2 The capital of Brittany and a university city, Rennes has a distinctly cosmopolitan air compared to other cities in Brittany. Although you will find stylish squares and perfect medieval houses with pointed façades overlooking the streets, this is the business centre and market hub for the Breton region. Gutted by a fire in 1720,

Rennes was redesigned by Parisian architects, giving the impression in some parts that you are in Paris and not in Brittany. The place des Lices, one of four squares which dominate the city architecturally, is lined by fine medieval houses, their crooked beams and oriel windows stretching high over the market stalls. The architectural interest of the place des Lices is enhanced by the two halles in the middle of the square.

As the road network in the area is good, purchasing a cheaper property in the countryside surrounding the city is recommended. Property prices within Rennes itself can be very steep, as local agents deal primarily with the local French market. Two-bedroom homes cost around €195,000; add an extra €80,000 for three bedrooms. The average price of a four-bedroom home is just under €300,000. A classic six-bedroom, stone-built house can be bought for upwards of €400,000.

The rentals market is restricted. Long-term lets can be the best rental option. Rennes is too far inland and too industrialised to appeal to the holiday market, and is primarily a French-dominated city. On average you can expect to generate €343 per week for a one-bedroom property, reaching up to €1,664 for five bedrooms.

Key facts

■ **POPULATION** 212,494
■ **TAXES** Taxe d'habitation 7.19%, taxe foncière 7.54%
■ **AIRPORT** Rennes St-Jacques Airport, avenue Joseph Le Brix, 35136 St-Jacques-de-la-Lande, Tel: +33 2 99 29 60 00
■ **SCHOOLS** Rectorat de l'Académie de Rennes, 96 rue d'Antrain, 35044 Rennes Cedex, Tel: +33 2 99 28 78 78, Fax: +33 2 99 28 77 72
■ **MEDICAL** Centre Hospitalier Guillaume Régnier, 108 avenue Gén Leclerc, 35000 Rennes, Tel: +33 29 93 33 900
■ **PROS** Voted among the top 12 best places to live in France ■ Rennes is easily accessible by ferry and by air, and is well served by the autoroute ■ There are many services and amenities in the area and it is particularly geared for those relocating to work in France n The biggest city in Brittany
■ **CONS** As Brittany's capital, Rennes commands some of the highest prices in the region ■ This area is not popular with international second home buyers, and is mainly a local market.

LORIENT

3 Situated in the region of Morbihan and located on an immense natural harbour, Lorient is the second largest fishing port in France. During the 18th century, the French East India Companies were founded here, importing spices and salt into Lorient. Badly damaged during the Second World War, the town is functional rather than pretty, yet it has a delightful market, a very good beach at Larmor Plage, and a good

number of restaurants serving the excellent local country fare. Lorient hosts the Inter-Celtic festival, held for 10 days from the first Friday to the second Sunday in August. Over a quarter of a million people attend more than 150 different shows.

Property in Lorient itself can cost up to three times more than in areas just 20 minutes from town. As most people buy slightly further inland from Lorient, where property is cheaper, demand and quick turnover in this area can make it difficult to secure a property. Dominated by the French market, the area is expensive, and a two-bedroom apartment overlooking the marina costs around €300,000. For a four-bedroom house the average price sits at around €300,000, while for €100,000 less you can buy a two-bedroom property.

Some estate agents tend to try and deal only with French buyers, and over the last couple of years prices have increased significantly, as has demand. The Baud area, behind the southern coast, experiences more demand due to cheaper prices and more property availability.

The Lorient has long been a popular destination with holiday makers. If you can afford to invest in a home here, you are guaranteed excellent rental income, especially from the French market – you can expect to generate an average of around €536 for a two-bedroom house. Property is expensive and there are few bargains on the south coast, with the majority of properties being modern and habitable. Parisians have flooded the rental market on the Breton coast.

Key facts

■ **POPULATION** 61,844
■ **TAXES** Taxe d'habitation 7.22%, taxe foncière 10.82%
■ **AIRPORT** Aéroport de Lann Bihoué, Lorient, 56270, Tel: + 33 3 14 90 44 44,

Fax: + 33 3 14 90 63 28
■ **SCHOOLS** Rectorat de l'Académie de Rennes, 96 rue d'Antrain, 35044 Rennes Cedex, Tel: +33 2 99 28 78 78, Fax: +33 2 99 28 77 72
■ **MEDICAL** Centre Hospitalier de Bretagne Sud, 27 rue Doct Lettry, 56100 Lorient, Tel: +33 2 97 64 90 00
■ **PROS** The port is home to one of Brittany's most renowned festivals, the Inter-Celtic festival ■ Ideally located for those who want to be on the seafront
■ **CONS** Lorient itself is not the most dynamic town on the south coast ■ Most people buy inland from Lorient where property is cheaper.

BREST

4 Brest is a university city and seaport, located in the far northwest of Brittany. It boasts a rich maritime history and is France's premier naval facility. The river divides the city by flowing between the two hills upon which the city perches. Brest dates from Roman times when a settlement was established around 50 BC. During the Second World War, Brest was continuously bombed to prevent the Germans from using it as a submarine base. When liberated in 1944, the city was devastated beyond recognition and the architecture of the post-war city is in places raw and bleak. There have been attempts to make the centre more verdant, but as Brest experiences the heaviest rainfall in France, it has proved too windswept to respond. One remaining treasure is the 12th-century château, which is now a naval museum. Another major attraction is the futuristic Océanopolis, the biggest open-air aquarium of its kind in Europe.

Brest offers a wide assortment of restaurants along rue Jean-Jaurès, while to the north, place Guérin is the centre of the student quartier, St-Martin. There is no British enclave or strong foreign property market

here. The closer you buy to the city, the more expensive the property. For a luxury six-bedroom house with sea views, expect to pay around €350,000; two-bedroom homes average around €205,000 and for €261,000 you can have a spacious three-bedroom home.

The rentals market can be slow going here and highly seasonal. Inclement weather prevents Brest from being a popular tourist and rental area. Foreigners generally are not interested in Brest and the Finistère département. Expect to generate between €437 and €700 in rental income for a one-to-three-bedroom property.

Key facts

■ **POPULATION** 156,210
■ **TAXES** Taxe d'habitation 7.31%, taxe foncière 7.95%
■ **AIRPORT** Brest Airport, 29490 Guipavas, Tel: +33 2 98 32 01 00
■ **SCHOOLS** The only international school in the region is located in Rennes, which is 249km from Brest
■ **RECTORAT** de l'Académie de Rennes, 96 rue d'Antrain, 35044 Rennes Cedex, Tel: +33 2 99 28 78 78, Fax: +33 2 99 28 77 72
■ **MEDICAL** Centre Hospitalier Universitaire, 5 avenue Foch, 29200 Brest, Tel: +33 2 98 22 33 33
■ **PROS** Located on a natural harbour, it is one of France's most important ports, with a very rich maritime history ■ The rugged landscape of the area is excellent for nature lovers and activities ■ A strong employment area, excellent for relocation ■ **CONS** Brest's post-war architecture gives the city a rather bleak appearance n Brest lacks greenery, due to the high winds that plague the city ■ Despite being located on the coast, Brest has no beaches ■ Rainfall is much higher here than in other parts of France.

QUIMPER

5 Split in two by the Odet river and surrounded by seven hills, Quimper is the ancient capital of the Cornouaille coast and head of the

département of Finistère, where Breton traditions are still very much alive. Featuring decorative footbridges and lined by rows of trees, lights and colourful hanging flower baskets, Quimper is well placed for exploring inland towns and villages, and offers quick access to the area's spectacular beaches.

A must-see is the Gothic Cathédrale St-Corentin, named after Quimper's first bishop. Dominating the skyline, the cathedral was constructed between the 13th and 16th centuries. Walk directly to the old town from the cathedral's front to see cobbled squares, the Musée Départemental Breton and the charming narrow streets, lined with half-timbered houses and the celebrated crêperies. In the Middle Ages, each street of the vieux quartier was devoted to a single trade and each still bears the name of its original trade.

Property is very expensive around Quimper and the surrounding coastline, and this is primarily a French market, with foreign buyers reluctant to meet the prices. In the countryside within 20 minutes of Quimper, you could buy a two-bedroom stone-built property for €141,000 while the average price of a three-bedroom property is €230,000.

Quimper is popular with French holiday-makers, and rental prices are higher than elsewhere in Brittany – an average of €525 for a two-bedroom property. Up-and-coming Pays Bigouden and Pont l'Abbé generate good rental income.

Key facts
■ **POPULATION** 63,238
■ **TAXES** Taxe d'habitation 7.31%, taxe foncière 7.95%
■ **AIRPORT** Quimper Cornouaille Airport, Kermaduit, 29700 Pluguffan, Tel: +33 2 98 94 30 30
■ **SCHOOLS** Rectorat de l'Académie de Rennes, 96 rue d'Antrain, 35044 Rennes Cedex, Tel: +33 2 99 28 78 78

■ **MEDICAL** Cornouaille Centre Hospitalier, 14 avenue Yves Thépot, 29000 Quimper, Tel: +33 2 98 52 60 60
■ **PROS** Quimper is easily accessible, with its own airport, and is located on the motorway and rail network ■ The town is within easy reach of the sea
■ **CONS** More of a holiday and rentals market than a permanent home-buyers' market.

GUINGAMP

6 On Brittany's rugged north coast, Guingamp is an attractive historic town of alleyways and cobbled streets. The town's university ensures a youthful atmosphere with plenty of nightlife and bars, while the place du Centre is traffic-free. La Plomée is surrounded by fine old houses and hotels with wood and slate façades. The three-turreted Basilica of Notre-Dame-de-Bon-Secours dates back to the 13th century, and each year on the first Saturday in July it is encircled by the annual Celtic festival, or pardon, including a candlelit night procession and bonfires, and a traditional dance festival performed by children. In August, the Fête de la St-Loup continues for a week, during which there is folk-dancing in the streets. On the outskirts of town, the Warenghem Breton whisky distillery is interesting to visit: try one of the apple-based specialities, such as pomig (an apple liqueur).

Central Brittany offers some of the best bargains in the region, and is also the ideal place to look for properties suitable for renovation. Although there is demand for properties in this area, they remain cheaper than they would be on the coast, or in a slightly more upmarket area such as the Golfe du Morbihan. Two-bedroom stone properties cost around €130,000; add another €100,000 for a four-bedroom property, while you can pick up five bedrooms or more from around €265,000.

The St-Brieuc area, Côte de Granit Rose and Île de Bréhat

are popular for rentals and generate a fair amount of interest from tourists. There is a guaranteed rental season from April to September – weekly rental for a two-bedroom property averages from €400 in low to €570 in peak season.

Key facts
■ **POPULATION** 8,830
■ **TAXES** Taxe d'habitation 9.28%, taxe foncière 10.79%
■ **AIRPORT** Dinard/Pleurtuit/St-Malo Airport, L'Aérodrome, 35730 Pleurtuit, Tel: +33 2 99 46 18 46, Fax: +33 2 99 88 17 85
■ **SCHOOLS** Rectorat de l'Académie de Rennes, 96 rue d'Antrain, 35044 Rennes Cedex, Tel: +33 2 99 28 78 78, Fax: +33 2 99 28 77 72
■ **MEDICAL** Hôpital de Guingamp, 17 rue Armor, 22200 Pabu, Tel: +33 2 96 44 56 56
■ **PROS** Guingamp is near the stunningly attractive Côtes d'Armor coast ■ Property is slightly cheaper here than in coastal areas
■ **CONS** Guingamp is not an easily accessible area ■ This is not a coastal area, making it less attractive for those seeking to rent property.

GOLFE DU MORBIHAN

7 The Gulf of Morbihan in southern Brittany enjoys its own balmy microclimate and is an ideal place for nautical activities, beachcombing or walking along the many miles of coastal paths. It is dotted with hundreds of small islands, the largest being Île aux Moines, which has sub-tropical vegetation and a pretty fishing village. Although many islands are privately owned retreats, you can visit most of the bay by boat. Surrounded by the Gulf's inlets and islands, the historic town of Vannes enjoys a superb location, and has a wealth of exquisitely preserved buildings, particularly its classic half-timbered houses and medieval market square. Carnac, an elegant summer resort on the bay of Quiberon, offers low-rise villas and

apartments, not unlike the Côte d'Azur. Famed for its megalithic monuments, the town also has a prehistoric museum and delightful pine-fringed beaches.

The whole of the Gulf of Morbihan is extremely expensive, especially if you are intending to let your property. Again, this area is dominated by the French market. A four-bedroom house in the centre of Vannes can be found for €450,000. If you prefer the seclusion of a Gulf of Morbihan village, a one-bedroom country cottage close to the sea can be bought for under €250,000 and three-bedrooms for an average of €356,000. Luxury top-of-the-range homes will set you back by more than €500,000.

This is the most exclusive area in Brittany and the most popular area with British buyers and also renters. The warm climate of the Gulf guarantees the buyer the longest rental season in Brittany, and the region's stunning coastline ensures a strong interest from holiday-makers. A two-bedroom property can secure you an average of €614 a week, while for five bedrooms you are looking at more than €2,200.

Key facts
■ **POPULATION** 1999: 32,988
■ **TAXES** Taxe d'habitation 7.22%, taxe foncière 10.82%
■ **AIRPORT** Rennes St-Jacques Airport, avenue Joseph Le Brix, 35136 St-Jacques-de-la-Lande, Tel: +33 2 99 29 60 00
■ **SCHOOLS** Rectorat de l'Académie de Rennes, rue d'Antrain, 35044 Rennes Cedex, Tel: +33 2 99 28 78 78
■ **MEDICAL** Centre Hospitalier Bretagne Atlantique, 20 boulevard Gén Maurice Guillaudot, 56000 Vannes, Tel: +33 2 97 01 41 41
■ **PROS** Areas such as Vannes and Carnac are extremely popular
■ **THIS** stretch of coastline offers a Mediterranean-style climate together with a healthy standard of living
■ **CONS** The whole of the Gulf of Morbihan is extremely expensive, with prices creeping up almost to Mediterranean levels. ●

Property guide

One of France's most popular destinations for British and French purchasers, Brittany has been dubbed "Little Britain" because of the number of UK retirees and second home-owners flocking to the area

A traditional Breton house, built of granite and with a slate roof and shutters

Average house prices in Brittany range from €70,000 for inland accommodation to €425,000 for luxury coastal villas. The market is booming, with prices having doubled since 2000, but the region still remains one of the most affordable within France.

Many Britons are lured by the prospect of finding a cheap rural renovation project but increased demand is leading to a shortage of such properties. This, combined with an increase in the average budget of British buyers, is pushing up prices in popular locations. Although it's possible to purchase a property for under €50,000, you will need to spend a considerable amount to make it habitable.

Property is most exclusive and expensive along the Gulf of Morbihan, where top-end properties sell for upwards of €500,000. However, for around €200,000 you can buy a decent renovated and refurbished home, while under €100,000 will buy you a one-bedroom cottage. Closer to fast-expanding capital city, Rennes, property prices rise sharply, with a four-bedroom home now costing around €300,000. For those with bigger budgets, €800,000 plus will buy you a fully restored manor house complete with land and outbuildings.

Some new developments are being constructed, but quaint cottages and traditional farmhouses are the most frequently recurring property type, and most come with large plots of land.

The rental market is strong and there is year-round tourism, but the summer season is shorter than in the south of France. A two-person gîte has a rental yield of €250 (low season) to €400 (peak season) per week, and €150 to €200 for weekend rental. A five-bedroom house sleeping up to 12 people with pool close to Morbihan costs between €985 and €2,290 per week. Properties closer to the beach or with notable character often achieve premium rates of €800 to €1,200 per week.

With low interest rates, the rise in the investment market, frequent, year-round ferry services and low budget flights, Brittany's property prices are set to soar as its popularity and perhaps more importantly, it's accessibililty grows. ●

BRETON COTTAGES

■ The Breton farm cottage is based on the traditional French long house, which is the oldest type of communal house (maison bloc)
■ Breton cottages are traditionally long and low , typically one-storey high, with walls constructed from local granite. Roofs are usually made from smooth, grey slate but can sometimes be thatched. Windows are few in number and very small
■ At one time, members of the household would have lived together with their livestock under one roof, but at different ends of the building, with two entrances – a stable door for the livestock and a doorway to the family living quarters
■ A partition wall separating the household members from their animals became a common feature of Breton cottages only during the 19th century

WHAT CAN YOU GET FOR YOUR EUROS?

TRADITIONAL HOUSE

Traditional house built of stone with hangar set in over quarter of an acre (1025m2) garden, just 10 minutes to the beach by car. The property with a garage is in good condition & comprises: Ground floor: living room with fireplace, fitted equipped kitchen, sitting room, bathroom, wc. 1st floor: 2 bedrooms, dressing room. 2nd floor: Bedroom & convertible attic. Situated near La Haye du Puits.

€193,976 CODE LAT

MODERN PROPERTY

Spacious fermette style property with colombage, set in quarter of an acre (1059m2) pretty wooded garden. Comprising: Ground Floor: fitted kitchen, lounge with marble floor, fireplace, beamed dining room with tiled floor, fireplace & stairs, 2 bedrooms, bathroom/wc, shower room, separate wc, 5.71m2 utility room with water heater, 3 bedrooms. Situated in the Domfront area.

€267,500 CODE LAT

COUNTRY COTTAGE

In a quiet country setting in the Ploermel region, this characterful cottage offers two bedrooms, a kitchen / sitting room a second lounge area and a bathroom. With a small conservatory overlooking the back garden – which extends to one-third of an acre – its the older features that fire the imagination. Think stone walls, floors and stairs, exposed wood work, and a large fireplace. Requiring some renovation.

€145,858 CODE VEF

STONE-BUILT RENOVATION

Only a 45 minutes drive from Rennes airport, this rurally located property sits in 3/4 acre of land and is ideal for those desiring rural living. Requiring complete renovation the house has three rooms which can be converted as you choose. Situated in the Ile-et-Vilaine department, you will find yourself only a quick drive from the ferry ports, the coastline around St Malo and the capital of Rennes.

€35,000 CODE FPS

SECLUDED PROPERTY

Requiring some TLC this secluded five-bedroom property comes with one hectare of land and is only 6 kilometres from the beach and the large town of Muzillac. With a total habitable space of 180m² on the ground floor, this house does require work – mainly redecoration – and has no mains electricity connected. Nevertheless, surrounded by stunning countryside this house has huge potential.

€505,393 CODE VEF

MAISON DE MAITRE

With four bedrooms and eight bathrooms this charming maison de maitre is located in the heart of a market town, in the bay of St. Brieuc, with all shops and facilities nearby. Just 10 mins from the sea, this lovely and spacious 14th century property offers 420m2 of habitable space over three floors. Set in grounds of 3500 square metres there are a number of charming outbuildings to convert.

€918,000 CODE SIF

AVERAGE HOUSE PRICES BRITTANY

	2-bed		3-bed		4-bed		5/6-bed	
Dinard, Dinan, St-M	€220,243	(£148,813)	€288,120	(£195,000)	€377,238	(£254,891)	€425,466	(£287,500)
Rennes	€194,253	(£131,252)	€272,262	(£184,000)	€292,200	(£197,433)	€413,383	(£279,313)
Lorient	€192,000	(£129,430)	€242,427	(£163,802)	€295,118	(£199,404)	€313,443	(£212,000)
Brest	€205,000	(£138,365	€261,000	(£176,100)	€292,200	(£197,410)	€308,000	(£208,000)
Quimper	€141,140	(£95,400)	€230,000	(£155,271)	€265,000	(£179,000)	€307,000	(£207,366)
Guingamp	€129,400	(£87,412)	€169,000	(£114,000)	€240,000	(£162,000)	€265,000	(£179,000)
Golfe du Morbidan	€289,000	(195,130)	€355,500	(£240,200)	€447,000	(£302,000)	€512,000	(£346,000)

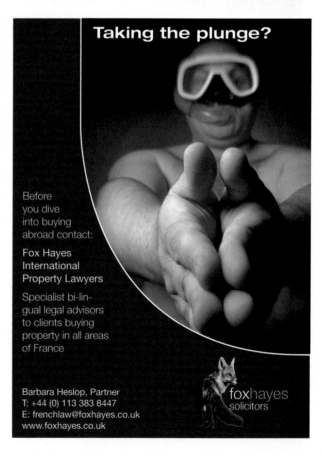

Normandy

Pretty ports, Mont St-Michel and English-style castles

MAISON DE LA FRANCE

FACT BOX

- ■ **POPULATION** 3,202,385 (+2.4% from 1990)
Basse-Normandie: 1,422,193; Haute-Normandie: 1,780,192
- ■ **UNEMPLOYMENT RATE** Basse-Normandie: 9.6%;
Haute-Normandie: 11%
- ■ **AVERAGE 4-BED HOUSE PRICE** €361,919
- ■ **REGIONAL CAPITAL** Basse-Normandie: Caen;
Haute-Normandie: Rouen
- ■ **REGION SIZE** 29,841km²

Contents

Area profile

Just a hop across the Channel, Normandy is home to creamy cheeses, rustic cider and the famed tapestry of Bayeux

GETTING THERE

AIR Ryanair (08712 460 000; www. ryanair.com) flies to Deauville and nearby Dinard from Stansted, and **Aurigny** (01481 822 886; www.aurigny.com) flies to Dinard from Bristol, Gatwick, Stansted and Manchester.

SEA Brittany Ferries (0870 366 5333; www.brittany-ferries.com) sails to Caen from Portsmouth and to Cherbourg from Poole and Portsmouth.
Transmanche Ferries (0800 917 1201; www.transmanche ferries.com) sails to Dieppe from Newhaven. **P&O** (0870 520 2020; www.poferries.com) sails to Le Havre from Portsmouth.

ROAD The A28/29 offers quick and direct access from Calais to the whole of Normandy, joining the A13 motorway, which runs west through Caen and ends in Paris. The A16 runs from Calais to Rouen, while the D100 runs down the Manche peninsula to Avranches. Main roads link the ports of Dieppe, Le Havre, Caen and Cherbourg.

RAIL The **TGV** rail network runs throughout Normandy linking Cherbourg, Caen, Le Havre and Rouen. The **Eurostar** (0870 518 6186; www.eurostar.com) arrives at Lille Europe train station, and from there TGV services operate to Rouen. From Paris there are regular services to Le Havre, Dieppe, Caen, Rouen, Cherbourg. Contact **Rail Europe** (0870 584 8848; www.raileurope.co.uk)

CLIMATE

NORMANDY		LONDON		NORMANDY		LONDON	
8	Dec	7		69	Dec	81
11	Nov	10		85	Nov	78
15	Oct	14		68	Oct	70
18	Sep	19		61	Sep	65
22	Aug	21		47	Aug	62
22	Jul	22		48	Jul	59
20	Jun	20		52	Jun	58
14	May	17		58	May	57
13	Apr	13		47	Apr	56
8	Mar	10		56	Mar	64
6	Feb	7		58	Feb	72
8	Jan	6		64	Jan	77

AVERAGE TEMPERATURE
(Celsius)

AVERAGE RAINFALL
(millimetres)

ORMANDY TAKES ITS NAME FROM THE Norsemen who arrived here (albeit uninvited) from Scandinavia in the ninth century, and it was from here that William the Conqueror crossed the English Channel to crush the English forces in the Battle of Hastings in 1066.

Home to fashionable resort towns on the coast, Normandy is characterised inland by pastoral farmland, with apple orchards, grazing for dairy cattle and, unusually for France, miles of hedgerows separating the fields. Indeed, the landscape is often likened to that of England.

The picturesque landscape of Normandy can be divided into three main areas: the eastern flatlands, home to the verdant Seine valley which divides Haute-Normandie (upper Normandy) and Basse-Normandie (lower Normandy); the lush west; and the central plains interrupted by "Swiss Normandy" south of Caen with its deep ravines and rocky outcrops. The north coast has long sandy beaches, but the best beaches are found on the Manche peninsula. The region's mild climate lends itself to ideal gardening conditions and there are several fine botanic gardens in the area.

The capital is Caen, a university city that suffered terrible bombing in the Second World War. A couple of outstanding Romanesque abbeys survived and the modern, pedestrianised centre is pleasant enough. Rouen was also heavily damaged in the war but it has been superbly restored; the Gothic cathedral and plethora of half-timbered houses are particularly impressive.

Normandy's most fashionable resort is Deauville, an expensive weekend playground for wealthy Parisians. Its seafront is lined with Victorian beach huts and the wide, sandy beaches are very popular in the summer months. Deauville's twin town, Trouville, on the eastern bank of the river Touques, is less exclusive but has some fine fish restaurants along the waterfront. Other popular resorts include Honfleur, Fécamp and Dieppe, the latter being particularly popular with English visitors because of its ferry port.

Normandy is also home to Mont-St-Michel, a small island that houses one of the most impressive and spectacular abbeys in Europe.

Conquests and invasions

Normandy has a chequered history. William the Conqueror set sail from here on his conquest of England and one of the region's major tourist attractions is the 900-year-old tapestry housed in a building next to Bayeux cathedral, depicting an 11th-century embroidered view of the Battle of Hastings. The region joined the Kingdom of France in 1204, was occupied by the English during the 15th century and saw some of the fiercest fighting during

FOOD AND DRINK

Normandy's lush pastures enable the region to produce about half of France's dairy products. Rich cream – used in many local sauces – and cheeses are particular specialities, notably Camembert, which originated in Normandy, and Brie. Normandy is also renowned for its abundance of apples and fresh seafood. Moules à la crème Normande is a satisfyingly rich traditional dish of mussels and cream, while apples form the basis of Normandy's most famous pastry dish, tarte Normande. Located in the heart of the region is Rouen, dubbed the gastronomic capital of Normandy, whose most famous recipes are those based on duck, such as canard à la Rouennaise (duck stuffed with its liver and cooked in red wine). Gournay, on Normandy's eastern border, claims ownership of the brioche. Normandy's apples are used to make the much-loved Calvados, the apple brandy named after one of the region's départements, and local ciders.

MAISON DE LA FRANCE

Normandy is renowned for its soft cheeses

ALL PHOTOS MAISON DE LA FRANCE

ATTRACTIONS

- ■ Rouen, home to the tallest spire in France and where Joan of Arc was burned
- ■ Monet's house and garden at Giverny
- ■ The city of Caen with its ancient and modern monuments
- ■ The Bayeux tapestries
- ■ The botanical gardens at the Château de Vauville
- ■ Mont-St-Michel with its fastest tides in Europe
- ■ The fine castles at Caen, Falaise and Harcourt
- ■ The lovely village of St-Cénery-le-Gérei
- ■ The Cider Route (Route du Cidre) taking in villages such as Beuvron-en-Auge

the First and Second World Wars. In 1944 Normandy beaches provided the key to the Allied victory in Europe, as can be seen in the D-Day museum built on the site of the landings at Arromanches les Bains. The city of Caen is home to the Memorial for Peace and the International Peace Museum.

Artistic heritage

The area is rich in religious treasures and has one of Europe's finest collections of stained glass. Norman artists were pioneers in this art during the Middle Ages and particularly fine examples can be seen at Evreux's Notre-Dame cathedral and St-Ouen in Rouen. There were once 120 abbeys, most of which are now in ruins such as those at Hambye and Jumièges, although several are still used – both Caen and Rouen's town halls are housed in old abbeys.

Writers such as Flaubert and Proust found ample inspiration in Normandy's pastoral landscape and two of the country's best-known artists, Monet and Poussin, painted here. Monet's residence at Giverny (open to the public) is home to the colourful water gardens and lilies depicted in some of his most famous paintings.

The economy

Normandy prospers from its production of meat, milk, butter, cheese and cider apples, with 45 per cent of upper Normandy and 30 per cent of lower Normandy given over to arable land. The coastline boasts more than 50 ports, and the region is renowned for its cuisine, producing many speciality seafood dishes. The dairy industry has suffered of late at the hands of EU regulations, with many small dairy farms being forced to close, impacting on much of inland Normandy. Recent years have seen diversification into light industry and agri-

foodstuffs, while upper Normandy specialises in petrochemicals and car manufacturing, though the region retains its agricultural character.

Social groups

Buyers target Normandy because of its easy access and abundance of cheap property. Two-thirds of foreign buyers here are British, with concentrations around the port resorts, though higher prices have driven many property seekers inland. The closer you get to Paris, the steeper the prices, and cheaper areas such as Orne have seen an explosion of interest and prices. The Seine-Maritime is in high demand from London buyers seeking easy commuting access to the UK. Prices rose almost 14 per cent in the first three quarters of 2004 and are expected to rise a further 20 to 25 per cent in the next few years, making cheap properties increasingly rare. ●

Property hotspots

MAP KEY

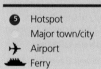

5 Hotspot
○ Major town/city
✈ Airport
⛴ Ferry

DEAUVILLE

1 Fashionable Deauville attracts the affluent weekend crowd and, indeed, strong Parisian purchasing power has caused prices to soar in this '21st arrondissement'. Frequented by film stars, millionaires and royals alike, this seaside resort is full of glamour and glitz. With a picturesque port, sandy beaches and historic wooden walkways, such as the Promenade des Planches, Deauville is an authentically preserved Norman town with half-timbered architecture.

Each year Deauville plays host to the International Festival of American Cinema, and the seafront is lined with Victorian-style beach huts named after Hollywood movie stars.

There is also a busy casino and a decent golf course, and the race track is one of the town's social hubs. Visit the Wednesday to Saturday market, which sells a wide range of regional specialities including seafood, cheeses, cider and Calvados.

A 10-minute drive takes you inland to the Calvados region, which boasts beautiful Normandy countryside.

Deauville's coastal location pushes property prices up, due to the sea views. If you are looking for a sea view, expect to pay an average of €284,000 for a two-bedroom house, and €368,400 for a three-bedroom property. A central four-bedroom house will cost around €422,000.

In such an expensive area it's hard to make money through rentals, and the British are reluctant to pay for costly

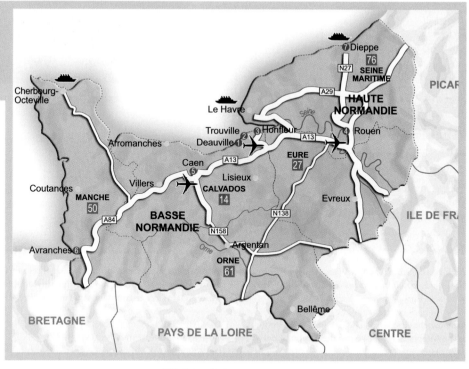

apartments and villas; the French, however, will accept this premium. A two-bedroom property will earn you an average of €629 a week, while four-bedrooms will secure you over €1,000.

Key facts
■ **POPULATION** 4,300
■ **TAXES** Taxe d'habitation 5.37%, taxe foncière 11.88%
■ **AIRPORT** Aéroport de Deauville St Gatien, 14130 St-Gatien-des-Bois, Tel: +33 2 31 65 65 65
■ **SCHOOLS** Contact the Rectorat de l'Académie de Caen, 168 rue Caponière, BP 6184, 14061 Caen Cedex, Tel: +33 2 31 30 15 00 for advice on education in the region
■ **MEDICAL** Hôpital de Trouville, 20 rue Soeurs Hôpital, 14360 Trouville-sur-Mer, +33 2 31 81 8 4 84
■ **PROS** Located on the Côte Fleurie, Deauville is known as the 'Cannes of the North' ■ Deauville has its own airport and the port of Caen is nearby
■ **CONS** A slightly pretentious resort priced the same as the Côte d'Azur ■ Mainly a French-saturated market.

TROUVILLE

2 Separated from its 'twin' resort Deauville by the estuary of the river Touques, the fishing port of Trouville can be reached in five minutes by ferry. Smart, but more modest in terms of its social calendar, Trouville is arguably more authentic and family-friendly. It's quieter yet not depressingly so, and has a native population that makes it livelier out of season.

It has an excellent beach, sports facilities, fish market and Planche promenade. Other interesting places to visit include its extravagant Napoléon III casino, Aquarium Vivarium de Trouville and Villa Montebello, Napoléon's old summer home.

British and Norman history has long been interwoven and it was the British in the 19th century, along with painters such as Turner, who made the Normandy coast fashionable. French painters too, from Delacroix to the Impressionists,

were inspired by the clear light of the coast and created many wonderful and now hugely expensive seascapes.

The love affair continues, but these days the British are reluctant to pay the average price tag of €375,000 to buy in Trouville. As property here is sold essentially to the French market – the area is popular with people who commute to Caen, Paris and Rennes – it carries a premium, but you can still find a three-bedroom home for €250,000, while the average price of a four-bedroom home is €448,000 – add an extra €200,000 for an extra bedroom.

Trouville, as with Deauville, primarily services the French rental market. Rental demand comes from Parisians and the cities of Caen and Rennes, as the British are unwilling to pay the area's high rental prices. A two-bedroom property will earn the landlord an average of €837 per week and this rises to €1,026 for four-bedrooms.

Key facts
■ **POPULATION** 6,500
■ **TAXES** Taxe d'habitation 5.37%, taxe foncière 11.88%
■ **AIRPORT** Aéroport de Deauville St Gatien, 14130 St-Gatien-des-Bois, Tel: +33 2 31 65 65 65
■ **SCHOOLS** Contact the Rectorat de l'Académie de Caen, 168 rue Caponière, BP 6184, 14061 Caen Cedex, Tel: +33 2 31 30 15 00 for advice on education in the region
■ **MEDICAL** Hôpital de Trouville, 20 rue Soeurs Hôpital, 14360 Trouville-sur-Mer, +33 2 31 81 84 84
■ **PROS** Trouville has a lovely beach and down-to-earth diversions
■ **CONS** The area is frequented by people commuting to Caen, Paris and Rennes ■ Despite the exclusive nature of the area, some people have described the town as unmemorable and pretentious.

HONFLEUR

3 Honfleur's charms are hard to resist, as it remains picturesque with an unspoilt ambiance while continuing to be a busy, working port. The Vieux Bassin or inner harbour is the hub, frequented by fishermen, yacht owners, painters and tourists rather than the explorers and corsairs of yesteryear. The tall, irregular houses that flank the harbour contain bars, antique shops and galleries, which all become crowded in season.

Miraculously still standing in the market square is the Église Ste-Catherine, the 'temporary' Gothic church built of oak by shipwrights to celebrate the departure of the English at the end of the Hundred Years' War. The original farm (Ferme St-Siméon), where local artist Boudin and friends met to drink cider and later formed the Impressionist movement, is now an exclusive hotel, while the Boudin museum displays some of the period's paintings and pastels.

Many consider Honfleur the most attractive port in Normandy and, as such, one of

the most popular spots in northern France. Along with other old ports like Étretat and Fécamp, Honfleur has long been a favourite with Parisians seeking weekend retreats on the coast away from the big city hustle. Commuters from Caen and Rennes have also driven prices up. Consequently, a two-bedroom property in the area starts at €210,000; three bedrooms costs an average of €242,400.

One of the most popular resorts on the Calvados coastline, Honfleur and the surrounding area are excellent for property lets. Popular with Parisian daytrippers, Honfleur has huge local rental potential, and the annual rental yield is good, particularly from April to September. The average rental for a three-bedroom property is €694 per week, while five bedrooms will generate a healthy average income of €1,080 per week.

Key facts
■ **POPULATION** 12,738
■ **TAXES** Taxe d'habitation 5.37%, taxe foncière 11.88%
■ **AIRPORT** Aéroport de Caen, Carpiquet, 14000 Caen, Tel: +33 2 31 71 20 10
■ **SCHOOLS** Contact the Rectorat de l'Académie de Caen, 168 rue Caponière, BP 6184, 14061 Caen Cedex, Tel: +33 2 31 30 15 00, Fax: +33 2 31 30 15 92, for advice on education in the region
■ **MEDICAL** Centre Hospitalier de La Plane-Equemauville, 14600 Honfleur, Tel: +33 2 31 89 89 89, Fax: +33 2 31 89 88 81
■ **PROS** Honfleur has become increasingly upmarket in recent years
■ **LOCATED** close to Le Havre, the area is easily accessible ■ Although popular with tourists, Honfleur retains its quaint and tranquil air
■ **CONS** Honfleur is an attractive coastal resort but lacks a beach ■ There is relatively little economic prosperity ■ Commuters from Paris, Caen and Rennes have flooded the market and raised prices.

ROUEN & SURROUNDS

4 Capital of the Seine-Maritime département and France's fifth largest port, Rouen has a vivid cultural and architectural heritage. The city is expensive and densely populated, serving as a catchment area for Parisians who commute 30 to 40 kilometres to work. The old city on the Right Bank has been called the 'museum town' due to 700 beamed, timber-framed medieval houses that make up its narrow pedestrian streets. Other attractions include the Gothic cathedral, Archbishop's Palace and the tower where Joan of Arc was kept prisoner. Arts lovers can savour the Flaubert Museum and the Museum of Fine Arts and Ceramics, which holds a collection of 17th to 19th-century paintings by Caravaggio and Monet along with 16th-century porcelain.

Central Rouen is very expensive but once you move into the countryside, property prices drop. The area is dominated by the French market and local estate agents are reluctant to deal with foreign buyers. Property styles include the traditional Norman beamed buildings, manor houses and the maison de maître built in the classical colonial style. A standard four-bedroom home can cost from €277,000 – two-bedrooms costs, little less at an average of €200,000.

Rouen is not a major holiday centre, tending to concentrate more on industry than tourism, so the market is for long-term lets. In Rouen's old town, rental property can generate upwards of €600 a week for a two-bedroom property, while for four bedrooms you're looking at €1,323.

Key facts
■ **POPULATION** 102,000
■ **TAXES** Taxe d'habitation 6.53%,

taxe foncière 13.16%
■ **AIRPORT** Aéroport Rouen, Vallée de Seine, 76520 Boos, Tel: +33 2 35 79 41 00
■ **SCHOOLS** Contact the Rectorat de l'Académie de Rouen, 25 rue de Fontenelle, 76037 Rouen, Cedex, Tel: +33 2 35 14 75 00 for advice on education
■ **MEDICAL** Rouen University Hospital, 1 rue Germont, 76000 Rouen, Tel: +33 2 32 88 89 90
■ **PROS** A diverse and cultured city, Rouen combines industry and trade with a rich historical tradition ■ It offers a number of museums and churches, the tour de force being beyond doubt Notre-Dame cathedral ■ The majority of Rouen's streets are modern and sophisticated ■ As Rouen is a large city, there is an abundance of services and attractions
■ **CONS** As you leave the inner quartier, you come upon the sprawling industrial and dockyard areas ■ Rouen is covered only by French estate agents, who can have limited experience in dealing with foreign buyers.

CAEN

5 Caen is a history lover's dream, with its roots dating back to the relic of William the Conqueror, whose femur is held in the Abbaye aux Hommes. The city was heavily bombed during the Second World War, hence the post-war concrete mixed in with the 16th-century architecture. Learn more about the D-Day landings at the Caen Memorial and rekindle the spirit of the Norman Conquest at the ramparts of Caen castle, built by William in his early days as Duke of Normandy. One of Europe's biggest castles, it is also home to a fine art museum.

The surrounding lush landscape produces celebrated cheeses like Livarot, Pont L'Evêque and Camembert, and Caen's proximity to the coast ensures a ready supply of fresh seafood. This is also the place to live if you prefer the quiet life. Caen's beaches may not possess

Home to the world of property
Sky Channel 279, Virgin TV & www.realestatetv.tv

Real Estate TV gives you unprecedented access to the world's finest properties.

Experience an inspection trip from your living room, as we take you from the sun drenched coast of the Riviera through to the historic streets of Paris…

Living in the French Riviera, exclusively available on Real Estate TV. Also, coming soon to the channel, *Focus on France*.

To register for our French property finder service, call **0871 716 3901**.

the glitz, glamour and balmy weather of the Côte d'Azur but they have their own entirely different appeal, offering instead an unhurried lifestyle with scenic charm. Within the city, on rue St-Sauveur, a huge Friday market is held. The rue Froide and Caen's centre offer Parisian department stores.

Property in Caen has a quick turnover and, since tourism isn't a huge force in the area, the market is dominated primarily by the local French buyers. A large three-bedroom house with swimming pool situated just 10 minutes from Caen will tend to cost around €235,400, while a four-bedroom property will cost you an average of €318,000.

Rental prices in the city of Caen are much higher than in the surrounding countryside. Large cities such as Caen tend to attract long-term rather than short term rentals, and demand for rentals in the city comes mainly from the local market. Expect to generate between €475 a week for a one-bedroom property, reaching up to €2,000 for a five-bedroom house.

Key facts
■ **POPULATION** 117,000
■ **TAXES** Taxe d'habitation 5.37%, taxe foncière 11.88%
■ **AIRPORT** Caen Airport, Aéroport de Caen Carpiquet, 14000 Caen, Tel: +33 2 31 71 20 10
■ **SCHOOLS** Contact the Rectorat de l'Académie de Caen, 168 rue Caponière, BP 6184, 14061 Caen Cedex, Tel: +33 2 31 30 15 00 for advice on education
■ **MEDICAL** Central Hospital Caen, avenue Côte de Nacre, 14000 Caen, Tel: +33 2 31 06 31 06
■ **PROS** Caen is a dynamic and energetic yet pleasant and relaxing city ■ Easily accessible from the UK, it has its own port and airport ■ A bustling university city with many amenities and attractions ■ Ideal for a buyer who seeks a vibrant metropolis
■ **CONS** You may have to learn French to live and work here, as this is not a predominantly international city ■ Proximity to the city drives property and rental prices up substantially.

AVRANCHES

6 Avranches is a small rural town with tourist appeal, situated on a wooded hill in the La Manche département of Normandy, close to Mont-St-Michel and near the border with Brittany. A busy and historically important town, it serves as a convenient base for tourists who wish to visit the D-Day beaches while the city of Bayeux is just one hour away. There are regular traditional fêtes and daily local markets in the surrounding area, even on Sundays. The town commands fine views westward towards Mont-St-Michel, a renowned World Heritage site and France's second most popular tourist attraction after the Eiffel Tower. Avranches is surrounded by avenues which trace the ancient ramparts and hide a botanical garden.

There is a highly active British property market in and around Avranches and the prices are quite reasonable compared to the Calvados area and more industrial region of upper Normandy. The average price for a four-bedroom house is around €362,000. If you are looking for a property to restore, a small farmhouse can be purchased for around €120,000. The market has stayed busy for the past decade and most Britons prefer buying to renting as prices are so favourable. A two-bedroom house, ready to move it, can be purchased for around €217,000.

Avranches is located in an extremely active tourist area, with a buoyant holiday rental market. Proximity to Mont-St-Michel is a huge draw for tourists and the long-term rental market is cheap. However, properties tend to be rather shabby and not geared towards the foreign holiday market; they usually require a lot of work before moving in. The holiday rentals market is booming and runs between April and September, when a two-bedroom house rents for €589 a week.

Key facts
■ **POPULATION** 52,471
■ **TAXES** Taxe d'habitation 6.98%, taxe foncière 11.04%
■ **AIRPORT** Aéroport de Caen Carpiquet, 14000 Caen, Tel: +33 2 31 71 20 10
■ **SCHOOLS** Contact the Rectorat de l'Académie de Rennes, 96 rue d'Antrain, 35044 Rennes, Cedex, Tel: +33 2 99 28 78 78, Fax: +33 2 99 28 77 72 for advice on education
■ **MEDICAL** Centre Hospitalier Avranches-Granville, 59 rue Liberté, 50300 Avranches, Tel: +33 2 33 89 40 20, Fax: +33 2 33 89 41 25
■ **PROS** Located close to the port of Cherbourg and the coast ■ There is a highly active foreign community n An excellent, sunny climate
■ **CONS** The rental market tends to be rather quiet in the winter months.

DIEPPE

7 Dieppe, France's first seaside resort, has undergone a transformation in recent years. The port has shaken off its reputation as a visual eyesore, the ugly terminal buildings having been replaced by a breezy promenade. The seafront is now set back from the shore, creating space for a eye-pleasing expanse of manicured lawns, waterside restaurants and family play areas nearly 2km long.

Dieppe has long enjoyed its status as a destination for writers, musicians and painters. Visit the Café des Tribunaux, the favourite haunt of Renoir, Monet, Guy de Maupassant and Oscar Wilde. While in exile from England, Wilde came here to write his Ballad of Reading Gaol.

High on a cliff, the castle museum contains a collection of exhibits reflecting Dieppe's maritime history, including 16th-century ivory sculptures carved by local sailors, and a number of paintings by Picasso. There are plenty of fêtes throughout the year, including a kite festival and the Festival of the Flowers. Out of town, you

can see the birthplace of Guy de Maupassant at the Château de Miromesnil.

There has in the past been a fair amount of British interest in Dieppe due to the ease of access from the UK. In recent years, however, interest has slightly waned in the Dieppe area as the Normandy Riviera in Calvados and the Manche peninsula have become more developed, but a two-bedroom property on the outskirts of town remains an affordable proposition at around €197,000, while you are looking at an average of around €550,000 for a standard five-to-six bedroom house.

The rentals market here is healthy, but this is less of a holiday centre than it used to be. Prices are expensive compared to the lower Normandy area, and few foreign holidaymakers actually rent property here. If you have an average of €713 a week to spend then you can easily secure a four-bedroom property.

Key facts
■ **POPULATION** 36,000
■ **TAXES** Taxe d'habitation 24.13%, taxe foncière 57.08%
■ **AIRPORT** Aéroport de Caen Carpiquet, 14000 Caen, Tel: +33 2 31 71 20 10
■ **SCHOOLS** Rectorat de l'Académie de Rouen, 25 rue de Fontenelle, 76037 Rouen, Cedex,Tel: +33 2 35 14 75 00, Fax: +33 2 35 71 56 38
■ **MEDICAL** Hospitalier de Dieppe, avenue Pasteur, 76200 Dieppe, Tel:+33 2 32 14 76 76
■ **PROS** It used to be a thriving seaside resort for the French and English in the 19th century, and it retains much of its authentic charm today ■ It is still an interesting and attractive place to visit, and is highly accessible ■ Dieppe offers many attractions, both modern and historical ■ It is more welcoming than many of the neighbouring towns along the Seine-Maritime coast
■ **CONS** Property in the centre of Dieppe is expensive and most people buy in the surrounding areas ■ This town is less of a tourist resort than it is a thriving industrial and commercial port. ●

Property guide

Normandy has long been popular with British house hunters, particularly weekend home-owners and those commuting to Britain for work

MAISON DE LA FRANCE

Half-timbered houses in the historic city of Rouenslate roof and shutters

BUYERS ARE ATTRACTED TO NORMANDY BY THE wealth of affordable accommodation and the efficient transport links. Interest in the region is gaining momentum as more buyers are finding themselves squeezed out of the market in Brittany. Although most Britons favour the coastal resorts, cheaper properties, many in need of renovation, can be found inland.

Prices are still highly affordable compared to the rest of France, although costs do vary quite significantly within the region, tending to increase with proximity to Paris and the UK. For around €30,000 you can pick up a small characterful cottage in need of renovation. Spend €150,000 and you can buy a large, stone-built longère with plenty of land and outbuildings.

Cheaper properties abound in the ancient market town and popular tourist destination of Avranches, where properties offer good long-term investment opportunities. Pricier housing is located within the glamorous, lively resorts of Deauville, Trouville and the pretty port of Honfleur. Properties in central Rouen and Caen are expensive and the market is mainly driven by French buyers, this area having received little interest from foreign purchasers. High rates of turnover, however, make property in these locations a sound investment. Dieppe and its surrounds, on the other hand, offer affordable accommodation, a strong rental market, and excellent transport links to and from Britain, making it a popular location for UK investors. The Manche peninsula offers a plentiful supply of affordable accommodation and a buoyant rental market. Eure's proximity to Paris means that prices here are considerably higher than in outlying départements. The advantage of Eure is its accessibility to both the UK and French capitals. However, there are far fewer renovation properties available here than in the rest of Normandy. Bargain properties can be found in the Orne département which, as yet, remains relatively undiscovered by foreign investors.

Normandy offers an amazing array of property types ranging from farm buildings and timber-framed barns in teh more rural areas to town houses and apartments in urban areas, and châteaux, the most frequently occurring being the traditional longère (see side panel).

The rental market in this area is becoming flooded with holiday homes, and although there is still demand for accommodation, you may need to gear your property at a niche market, such as birdwatchers or British house hunters, in order to make a profitable turnover. A 2-bedroom beachside apartment sleeping up to six people yields an income of between €450 and €700 per week, while a 4-person gîte barn conversion brings in around €700 per week rising to €1,300 during the peak summer season. ●

LONGÈRE

■ A classic old style of property commonly found in Normandy as well as other parts of the Northwest. Some longères are hundreds of years old
■ These houses are traditionally built of stone
■ The roofs are characteristically slate or thatched and may feature timber roof beams
■ Longères are typically long and low, and some have no first floor
■ Many of these houses tend to have larger gardens than other property types
■ With the huge interest in reclaiming these long-abandoned properties in recent years, it is now becoming quite hard to find a genuine longère in need of restoration

WHAT CAN YOU GET FOR YOUR EUROS?

RENOVATED *LONGÈRE*

This is an extremely attractive and fully renovated property, located in Champ du Boult. Complete with a separate gîte perfect for rentals and outbuildings ideal for further conversion. The interior is designed in a traditional style and boasts exposed wooden beams and granite fireplaces. The property comes with three bedrooms and there is a large garden, perfect for enjoying summer evenings.

€262,000 CODE FPS

STONE-BUILT HOUSE

Located in Mesnil Clinchamps in the Calvados region of Normandy, this small, stone-built property currently has one bedroom but is ideal for expansion, with an adjoining outbuilding to renovate. Comprising of a large living room with kitchen area and an open fireplace there is also one bathroom. Complete wth a garage and a cellar this is a promising propery and ideal for DIY enthusiasts.

€86,750 CODE FPS

BARN TO RENOVATE

Situated near the town of St Pois with its numerous amenities, this stone-built barn is set in the countryside and offers excellent potential to create a large family home. Complete with 1.48 acres of land – perfect for the installing of a swimming pool – the setting of this property is ideal for those who seek a quiet rural bolthole. Once renovated this home offers excellent rental potential.

€87,000 CODE FPS

HABITABLE *LONGÈRE*

Easily accessible from the ferry ports this superb longère is situated only 1.5 kms from amenities. Comprising of a spacious living room with granite fireplace, exposed beams and stone walls, there is also a top-of-the-range fitted kitchen, one ground-floor bedroom and two bedrooms on the first floor. A large garage is situated in the barn, while other outbuildings offer wonderful conversion potential.

€195,800 CODE FPS

ELEGANT CHÂTEAU

An elegant 18th-century château with stunning views over the Normandy, this property has a living area of 400m2 and was beautifully restored in 2000. With many traditional features – including panelling, parquet floors and fireplaces – the château has numerous outbuildings and an artist's studio, and is set in 2.3 hectares of landscaped grounds with an uninterrupted view of the valley.

€820,000 CODE SIF

CHARACTERFUL COTTAGE

Situated in a rural location in the département of Calvados, this lovely stone cottage comes is only 20 minutes drive from the town of Vire. With one bedroom and a sitting room and dining area with fireplace and exposed beams, this is a cosy little cottage and ideal for a retired couple. Fully habitable, it comes with a small garden of 375 square metres and a private garage.

€92,000 CODE FPS

AVERAGE HOUSE PRICES NORMANDY

	2-bed		3-bed		4-bed		5/6-bed	
Deauville	€284,000	(£191,840)	€368,433	(£249,000)	€423,000	(£285,520)	€1,033,000	(£698,000)
Trouville	€183,200	(£124,000	€255,000	(£172,000)	€448,200	(£303,000)	€616,000	(£416,000)
Honfleur	€211,000	(£142,500)	€242,500	(£164,000)	€354,000	(£239,000)	€382,450	(£258,412)
Rouen	€200,000	(£135,000)	€237,000	(£160,040)	€277,400	(£187,400)	€407,000	(£275,000)
Caen	€210,000	(£142,000)	€235,440	(£159,100)	€318,100	(£215,000	€442,000	(£298,423)
Avranches	€217,000	(£147,000)	€295,000	(£199,322)	€362,000	(£245,000)	€550,300	(£372,000)
Dieppe	€197,000	(£133,000)	€239,000	(£161,220)	€293,000	(£198,000)	€406,050	(£274,400)

Nord-Pas-de-Calais & Picardy

Gothic cathedrals, rolling countryside and culture

JUSTIN POSTLETHWAITE

FACT BOX

- **POPULATION** 5,854,069 (+1.7% from 1990),
Nord-Pas-de-Calais: 3,996,588 (+0.8% from 1990);
Picardy: 1,857,481 (+2.6% from 1990)
- **UNEMPLOYMENT RATE** Nord-Pas-de-Calais: 13.4%;
Picardy: 11%
- **AVERAGE 4-BED HOUSE PRICE** €398,000
- **REGIONAL CAPITAL** Nord-Pas-de-Calais: Lille;
Picardy: Amiens
- **REGION SIZE** 31,789km²

Contents

Area profile

The closest area of France to Britain boasts busy, metropolitan cities, attractive seaside resorts and tranquil countryside

GETTING THERE

AIR Air France (0845 359 1000; www.airfrance.co.uk) flies to Paris Charles de Gaulle from where it is possible to get the train to Lille-Lesquin. **Lyddair** (01797 320000; www.lyddair. co.uk) flies to Le Touquet from Lydd. **Ryanair** (0871 246 0000; www.ryanair. com) flies to Paris Beauvais from Dublin and Glasgow.

SEA P&O (0870 520 2020; www.posl. com) and **SeaFrance** (0870 571 1711; www.seafrance.com) sail from Dover to Calais. **Norfolkline** (0870 870 1020; www.norfolk-line-ferries.co.uk) sails from Dover to Dunkirk. **Hoverspeed** (0870 240 8070; www.hoverspeed.co.uk) sails from Dover to Calais. **SpeedFerries** (0870 220 0570; www.hoverspeed. co.uk) sails from Dover to Boulogne.

ROAD From Calais take the A26 which runs through Pas-de-Calais and Picardy. The A1 runs from Arras to Picardy, while the A16 runs along the coast, linking the coastal resorts. The A16 and A25 also run from Calais to Lille. If you are flying into Paris, take the A16 to Amiens.

RAIL The Eurotunnel runs from Dover to Calais, and the **Eurostar** (0870 518 6186; www.eurostar.co.uk) runs from London Waterloo / Ashford Kent to Lille / Paris. The TGV network serves Lille and Calais; **Rail Europe** (0870 584 8848; www.raileurope.co.uk).

CLIMATE

NORD-PAS-DE-CALAIS		LONDON		NORD-PAS-DE-CALAIS		LONDON	
7	Dec	7		59	Dec	81	
8	Nov	10		63	Nov	78	
15	Oct	14		65	Oct	70	
19	Sep	19		58	Sep	65	
24	Aug	21		59	Aug	62	
23	Jul	22		63	Jul	59	
22	Jun	20		58	Jun	58	
15	May	17		50	May	57	
14	Apr	13		43	Apr	56	
8	Mar	10		43	Mar	64	
6	Feb	7		40	Feb	72	
7	Jan	6		46	Jan	77	

AVERAGE TEMPERATURE
(Celsius)

AVERAGE RAINFALL
(millimetres)

This long, thin region is one of France's smallest, the closest to the UK – Dover's white cliffs can be seen on clear days from the coast – and strongly influenced by Flanders in neighbouring Belgium whose Flemish style dominates the region's architecture. Nord-Pas-de-Calais is one of the wettest areas of France and receives the least sunshine, although temperatures are rarely extreme.

The northeast regions of Nord-Pas-de-Calais and Picardy are often overlooked by British homebuyers, although the hypermarkets are certainly not. Calais may not be the best introduction to France, but travel a little further and there is much to discover.

Flemish towns and the Opal Coast

Lille, the capital of Nord-Pas-de-Calais, is France's fourth largest city and just two hours from Waterloo on the Eurostar. Nominated as 2004's European City of Culture, Lille has benefited from the huge grants awarded with its title. Distinctly Flemish in flavour, the streets are dotted with bustling cafés and good shops. The coast is home to a number of small towns, the best of which is Le Touquet, with its dunes, pine forests and art deco tea rooms. Nord-Pas-de-Calais also has three large regional parks with a wealth of waterways and hiking trails.

Picardy's delightful and varied landscape has witnessed some of the worst battles ever, most notably the Battle of the Somme in the First World War. The region's largest city, Amiens, is home to France's largest Gothic structure, the Cathédrale de Notre-Dame, and it is situated in an area with many monuments. The coastal stretch is studded with small seaside resorts and sandy bays, and the south of the region is blessed with rolling hills, winding rivers and large forests.

The attractive coastline, known as the Opal Coast (Côte Opale), boasts long sandy beaches offering plenty of sporting opportunities such as kite-surfing and sand-yachting and numerous pretty resorts. Inland, the Flanders hills are dotted with windmills, several of which still produce flour from local grain, and lined with hop fields – beer (Artois is in the southwest) is the favourite tipple here. The region was the birthplace of France's manufacturing industry during the 19th century and also one of the country's main coalmining areas – local mines provided inspiration for Emile Zola's Germinal, one of the world's best-known 19th-century novels. Abandoned slagheaps have been imaginatively used for nature reserves and even a ski slope.

Nord-Pas-de-Calais has a history of wealth and prosperity, clearly reflected in the bourgeois architecture in many of the towns. Spanish and Italian touches are also apparent, a legacy of the area's vast trading influences during the Renaissance. Arras, Béthune and Lille boast particularly fine examples of narrow residential homes graced with elegant gables and slate-tiled roofs, reminiscent of the Flemish style. Arras also has a unique network of underground passages dating from medieval times.

FOOD AND DRINK

Many dishes from Nord-Pas-de-Calais and Picardy are rich in Flemish flavours and favour the liberal use of beer. Trademark dishes include flamiche (a sweet or savoury tart), commonly made with Maroilles cheese, and hochepot (a thick Flemish-style lamb ragout). Much of the fare features seafood – fish soup (caudière) and fish stews are favourites, and shellfish called coques, or poor man's oyster, are much loved too. Also well worth sampling are: carbonnade flamande (beef in beer); waterzooi (fish and vegetable stew); anguilles au vert (eels cooked with spinach and sorrel in white wine); andouillettes (sausages made from offal); and wild rabbit cooked with prunes or grapes. For a delicious dessert, try tarte à gros bords (a sweet custard flan), an Arras speciality. Maroilles cheese from Picardy is soft and tangy, often enjoyed with one of the region's smooth, fruity beers – in fact, this is the only part of France where more beer than wine is drunk.

JUSTIN POSTLETHWAITE

MAISON DE LA FRANCE

JUSTIN POSTLETHWAITE

Like Picardy, much of Nord-Pas-de-Calais has been used as a battleground, particularly during the First and Second World Wars. Arras and Albert, Cambrai, Loos and Neuve-Chapelle are synoymous with the First World War, while Dunkerque's beaches witnessed the evacuation of 350,000 Allied troops from 27 May to 4 June 1940.

The economy

Lille is France's second largest print and publishing centre, the third largest centre for the mechanical and electrical industries and the fourth largest food-processing site. Amiens, too, is a commerce-rich city and pharmaceutical production takes place in both Calais and Lille. Calais firm Nikko exports toys to Japan. The economy is also bolstered by British 'booze cruisers' who flock across the Channel with the hope of finding bargains in the hypermarkets of Calais.

Social groups

While some British buyers commute to southeast England from Nord-Pas-de-Calais, the region is primarily chosen for holiday homes or by those in business wanting easy access to London. Dutch and Germans are the main foreign buyers, especially civil servants working in Brussels, who find it cost-effective to commute from the region to Belgium, where the housing market is more expensive.

Only one in 10 British buyers chooses to buy on the coast, as most foreign interest is centred around inland locations, primarily within easy reach of the ports. The region's transport links to Britain have allowed buyers from southern England to purchase and enjoy weekend homes, creating a more expensive property market in the process. ●

ATTRACTIONS

■ Amiens's Notre-Dame cathedral

■ The busy Channel waters from Cap Blanc Nez and Cap Gris Nez

■ The Fine Arts Museum at Lille, second only to the Louvre

■ The Lille Braderie – the city's giant flea market held since the Middle Ages when servants were granted the right to sell their masters' unwanted belongings

■ The art deco La Piscine Museum of Art and Industry at Roubaix.

■ The Matisse Museum housed in the magnificent Palais Fénelon in Hainaut

■ Sportica, one of the country's largest and finest sports complexes

■ The beautiful valleys and forests in the Avesnois area

■ The battlefields of Nord-Pas-de-Calais and the museums

■ La Grande Place at Lille

PROFILE

MAISON DE LA FRANCE

Property hotspots

MAP KEY

- **5** Hotspot
- ○ Major town/city
- ✈ Airport
- ⛴ Ferry

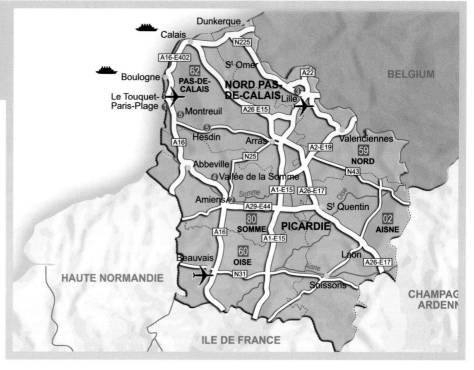

LE TOUQUET-PARIS-PLAGE

1 Reflecting its creation by the British a century ago, this sophisticated seaside resort was a magnet for wealthy celebrities who flocked here in the 1920s and 30s to play cricket and polo by day, then party by night. Marketed by the local tourist board as a 'four seasons' resort, throughout the year events from wine festivals to sports are held. The town is flourishing, thanks to the Channel Tunnel and Lydd Air's direct flights from Lydd in Kent, and many Britons commute daily to work in London. The beach, stretching for 11 kilometres, is ideal for sunbathers, while nature lovers can savour the Park of the Estuary, a signposted reserve stretching to 42 hectares, situated north of Le Touquet. A grandiose 1930s covered market draws shoppers every Thursday and Saturday, while the rue de Metz and rue St-Louis are lined with excellent speciality charcuteries, traiteurs and bakeries.

Inland from Le Touquet are the cheaper towns of Hesdin and Montreuil, which attract many who want to live in the Le Touquet area. Le Touquet itself is popular with Parisians escaping at weekends, and consequently this is an expensive area to buy in due to high demand; a four-bedroom house can cost an average of €675,000.

There are numerous tourist properties here. With a vibrant out-of-season rental market, rental properties cost from €565 a week for two bedrooms.

Key facts

- **POPULATION** 6,000
- **TAXES** Taxe d'habitation 7.83%, taxe foncière 9.70%
- **AIRPORT** Aéroport du Touquet, Côte d'Opale, 62520 Le Touquet-Paris-Plage, Tel: +33 3 21 05 03 99
- **SCHOOLS** École Active Bilingue Jeannine Manuel – École Internationale de Lille Métropole, 418 bis rue Albert Bailly, 59700, Marcq-en-Baroeul, Lille, Tel: +33 3 20 65 90 50
- **MEDICAL** Centre Hospitalier Docteur Duchenne, all. Jacques Monod, 62200 Boulogne sur Mer, Tel: +33 3 21 99 33 33
- **PROS** Le Touquet-Paris-Plage is an affluent area with a sophisticated atmosphere ■ Situated within two hours' drive of London ■ This is a very active resort, offering wide beaches, sand dunes and unique architecture
- **CONS** The resort is full in summer.

AMIENS

2 Picardy's largest city, Amiens, is a university city in the Somme département. It is renowned for its Gothic architecture, notably the Cathédrale de Notre-Dame, the biggest Gothic building in France. Construction started in 1218, when the citizens wanted a worthy monument to house what they believed to be John the Baptist's head.

The medieval quarter of St-Leu lies to the north of the cathedral with its network of canals. Buildings have been renovated into neat brick cottages, while the waterfront sparkles with restaurants and clubs. Each canal still functions as a waterway for the hortillonnages, a series of fertile market gardens reclaimed from the marshes created by the slow-flowing Somme river. Farmers travel about the canals in black punts, and a few still take their produce into the city by boat for the Saturday morning marché sur l'eau. Jules Verne, science-fiction writer and Amiens's most prominent former citizen, lived in the city from 1856 until his death in 1905. The Maison Jules Verne at 2 rue Charles Dubois has a model of a flying machine and the Nautilus.

Amiens caters for the local French market and is not popular with the foreign buyer. A three-bedroom house in Amiens starts at €230,000, and the city is affordable compared with much of the region.

Amiens caters mainly for long-term rentals. There are many business-connected rentals in this area, primarily from the French market. A weekly rental of a two-bedroom house would cost an average of €554.

Key facts

- **POPULATION** 132,000
- **TAXES** Taxe d'habitation 9.51%, taxe foncière 13.16%
- **AIRPORT** Aéroport de Beauvais, Service Chamco 60000, Beauvais, Tel: +33 3 44 11 46 66
- **SCHOOLS** École Active Bilingue Jeannine Manuel – École Internationale de Lille Métropole, 418 bis rue Albert Bailly, 59700, Marcq-en-Baroeul, Lille,

Tel: +33 3 20 65 90 50

▪ **MEDICAL** Centre Hospitalier Universitaire, place Victor Pauchet 2, 80080 Amiens, Tel: +33 3 22 66 80 00

▪ **PROS** Boasts a lively atmosphere, due to the presence of 25,000 students ▪ A vibrant, cosmopolitan city, excellent for those who desire a metropolitan lifestyle ▪ Amiens is affordable when compared with much of the region

▪ **CONS** Property turnover is very rapid in Amiens and it is primarily a French market ▪ British buyers don't tend to buy in Amiens unless it is for work purposes ▪ Many French estate agents prefer not to deal with the foreign market, but instead with the local French market.

LILLE

3 European Capital of Culture in 2004, Lille is France's fourth-largest city with plenty of stunning architecture, delectable food and drink, and sophisticated shopping. Lying in the Nord dépa tement, bordering Belgium, Lille combines a typically French atmosphere with a Flemish flavour.

Notable is the old quarter, Vieux Lille, which has been tastefully revived in Flemish style, in particular the Vieille Bourse, and the immense place du Général de Gaulle, called simply 'Grand Place' by locals. Don't miss the Musée des Beaux-Arts, or Fine Arts Museum, a classical and modern architectural gem, with its priceless collection of paintings from Goya to Rubens. There are plenty of good cafés and brasseries serving local fare like carbonnade (beef braised in beer) and mussels. The city's student population ensures that the streets are buzzing into the early hours. Cinemas and bars are found in the Halles district and old quarter, while the jazz scene is also thriving. Events in Lille include the September beer festival and the December Christmas markets.

Lille only attracts foreign buyers who seek to move to the area for employment purposes. Otherwise, the area is dominated by the locals.

This is not a tourist area and the market is therefore dominated by long-term rentals. Consequently Lille is dominated by the business market and by the local French market. Weekly rental rates are high, and a landlord can expect to earn an average of €650 for a two-bedroom house.

Key facts

▪ **POPULATION** 1,100,000

▪ **TAXES** Taxe d'habitation 7.83%, taxe foncière 9.70%

▪ **AIRPORT** Lille Airport, BP 227, 59812 Lesquin Cedex Tel: +33 3 20 49 68 68

▪ **SCHOOLS** École Active Bilingue Jeannine Manuel – École Internationale de Lille Métropole, 418 bis rue Albert Bailly, 59700, Marcq-en-Baroeul, Lille, Tel: +33 3 20 65 90 50

▪ **MEDICAL** Centre Hospitalier Régional Universitaire de Lille, avenue Oscar Lambret, 59037 Lille Cedex, Tel: +33 3 20 44 59 62

▪ **PROS** Lille is renowned for its dynamic shopping centres and abundance of retail outlets ▪ It has an extremely buoyant property market, albeit primarily a local French market

▪ **CONS** Lille is essentially a French market dominated by the French buyer, and is a city where the French live and work ▪ This is an expensive city in which to live.

THE FISHING LAKES OF THE SOMME VALLEY

4 Picardy is a haven for anglers, especially the lakes of the Somme and the Oise, with their rich flora and fauna. You can catch many different types of fish in this undiscovered area of France. For the invigorating country life, choose the Avesnois, close to the Ardennes. Situated in the southeast of the Nord département, at the very tip of Nord-Pas-de-Calais adjoining the Belgian border, this area is fondly referred to as 'little Switzerland', with its extensive network of rivers, canals and lakes making fishing, canoeing and other water sports popular.

A designated nature park, the Avesnois valleys and pine forests are interspersed with lush pastures and ancient walled towns. Val Joly at Eppe Sauvage is the largest lake north of Paris, with facilities including sailing, mini-golf and tennis. Many of the traditional arts and crafts of the Nord are still practised in this area. Le Quesnoy boasts more than three kilometres of perfectly preserved 17th-century fortifications, bearing witness to centuries of invasion.

Angling is an increasingly popular activity, and there is huge demand from the foreign market for angling businesses. A house in the Somme Valley costs from €93,000, while a four-bedroom home will set you back over €200,000. A fishing business near Calais costs from €400,000.

Key facts

▪ **POPULATION** Le Quesnoy 5,089, St-Quentin 69,287

▪ **TAXES** Taxe d'habitation 9.51%, taxe foncière 13.16%

▪ **AIRPORT** Aéroport du Touquet, Côte d'Opale, 62520 Le Touquet-Paris-Plage, Tel: +33 3 21 05 03 99

▪ **SCHOOLS** École Active Bilingue Jeannine Manuel – École Internationale de Lille Métropole, 418 bis Rue Albert Bailly, 59700, Marcq-en-Baroeul, Lille, Tel: +33 3 20 65 90 50

▪ **MEDICAL** Centre Hospitalier Universitaire, place Victor Pauchet 2, 80080 Amiens, Tel: +33 3 22 66 80 00

▪ **PROS** It can be an excellent and profitable business to purchase a fishing lake in Picardy ▪ The Avesnois regional park is a stunning natural park ▪ This is a must for those who love nature and outdoor or adventure sports ▪ A great area for those who desire to be close to southeast England

▪ **CONS** Prices are increasing all the time due to the rising demand from the British market.

MONTREUIL & HESDIN

5 At the heart of the historic Seven Valleys region, the town of Hesdin, with its bridges, red brick and white stone maisons de maître, is crossed by the rivers Canche and Ternoise. The focal points are the Town Hall, formerly the residence of Emperor Charles V's sister, Marie of Hungary, and the Wine Society. This is a good base for exploring the battle site and museum at Agincourt. Other attractions include the flower-decked village of Boubers-sur-Canche, and the Opal Coast, named after its white sandy beaches. The beautiful Hesdin forest stretches for more than 100 hectares, soaring above the Ternoise, Canche and Planquette valleys.

There is a good demand for short-term rentals in the area. Easy access means people come for short breaks, especially golfers. However, there is also high demand for hotels, rather than cottages or gites. Average income from a two-bedroom house will be about €524 a week.

Key facts

▪ **POPULATION** Montreuil 2,688, Hesdin 2,763

▪ **TAXES** Taxe d'habitation 7.83%, taxe foncière 9.70%

▪ **AIRPORT** Aéroport du Touquet, Côte d'Opale, 62520 Le Touquet-Paris-Plage, Tel: +33 3 21 05 03 99

▪ **SCHOOLS** École Active Bilingue Jeannine Manuel – École Internationale de Lille Métropole, 418 bis rue Albert Bailly, 59700, Marcq-en-Baroeul, Lille, Tel: +33 3 20 65 90 50

▪ **MEDICAL** Hôpital Rural, boulevard Richelieu 13, 62140 Hesdin, Tel: +33 3 21 86 86 54

▪ **PROS** A major focal point in Pas-de-Calais for the British buyer ▪ Located within 45 minutes to an hour of Calais, there is easy access to the UK

▪ **CONS** It is difficult to find a habitable home for less than E100,000. ●

HOTSPOTS

Property guide

The old town in Senlis, with its maze of narrow winding streets and medieval houses

PROPERTY GUIDE

COLOMBAGE HOUSES

- These elaborately timbered houses date back as far as the 15th century
- Traditionally, the timbers were morticed and pegged together with their riven sides exposed
- The spaces between the timber frames were most commonly filled with wattle-and-daub (a latticework of wooden stakes coated in sun- or kiln-baked clay), but some were filled with brick or rubble
- Plaster was applied to the exterior and interior walls which were then often lined with wainscoting (wooden panelling) to provide insulation and warmth
- Infilling the spaces created the characteristic half-timbered style, with the timbers of the frame being visible both inside and outside the building
- The roofs are traditionally tiled
- Many of the original buildings are still standing in the Rouen area

AVERAGE HOUSE PRICES IN THE REGION ARE €333,000, while the more exclusive properties can fetch upwards of €1,000,000. Nevertheless, this is still one of the cheapest areas in France, and prices remain competitive compared with Britain.

Government investment in Calais's run-down industry has reversed the migration trend and has attracted many new residents, which in turn has fuelled a surge in property prices. The attraction of new businesses to the area also puts added pressure on the market.

Foreign purchaser interest centres around the Seven Valleys area, including the Opal Coast, Montreuil, Hesdin and St-Pol-sur-Ternoise. There has been a sharp increase in demand for houses and prices are rising. So saying, for between €130,000 to €300,000 you can buy a traditional three- or four-bedroom family home in a picturesque village in the area – extremely good value compared with what you might buy in the UK.

Property prices in the chic coastal town of Le Touquet fetch premium rates, with apartments costing upwards of €250,000 and house prices starting at around €302,000. The price of three-bedroom houses averages €573,000, such is its popularity with Parisian weekenders, so there is little foreign interest in the Le Touquet-Paris-Plage area. Similar but much cheaper properties are available further inland, where a small, well-appointed farmhouse in a good location can be purchased for around €100,000. The Somme Valley is a particularly popular area and it is possible to buy a two-bedroom house here for as little as €130,000. The rental income generated from this area is also excellent thanks to the popularity of fishing holidays in the valley.

French buyers have pushed up prices in Amiens and Lille (European City of Culture in 2004), but there is still a good range of property available. A studio apartment sells for around €60,000 and family houses start at around €190,000 in Amiens and €188,000 in Lille for a two-bedroom property. With its own airport and Eurostar stop, Lille is highly accessible from London, Paris, Brussels and Luxembourg, and as such is a superb location for commuters – hence the higher prices, which show no sign of cooling.

The most common property type in the area is brick and colombage (half-timbering). A few new-builds are being constructed, but demand outstrips supply because the supply of renovation properties is drying up, and it can be cheaper to have a house built to spec. A studio in Picardy, for example, is currently available off-plan for around €80,000. ●

WHAT CAN YOU GET FOR YOUR MONEY?

MODERN VILLA

With six bedrooms and a spacious, well-maintained garden, this is a fabulous opportunity to purchase a modern villa. Situated on the edge of a village, this fully habitable property is close to the town of Boulogne and located in the region of Pas de Calais, close to the ferry ports. Complete with a garage, the villa is ideal for summer holidays with family and friends – or good for rentals.

€733,325 CODE VEF

GÎTE COMPLEX

Located in the Pas de Calais region, this fully habitable, high quality gîte complex offers nine bedrooms and is ideally located. Consisting of three comfortable cottages, all were recently built to provide spacious guest accommodation in a modern style. Each is fully self-contained, furnished and equipped to an exceptionally high standard with laundry room plus terrace and parking.

€559,325 CODE VEF

FARMHOUSE TO RESTORE

Charming partly renovated farmhouse set in a wonderful environment that benefits from panoramic views over the Canche Valley. Located close to Frevent with all its amenities, this house come with two bedrooms, one bathroom and has a loft ideal for conversion. With a garden of almost one acre and with central heating and electricity supplied to the property, this is a perfect holiday cottage.

€126,500 CODE FPS

RENOVATED HOUSE

Attractive detached property with guest cottage, set in 1.75 acres of grounds. With many original features such as marble floors, fireplaces, stained glass windows & oak panelling, the 400m2 living space comprises: Ground floor: entrance hall, living room, dining room, kitchen, study, 2 wc. First floor: 4 bedrooms, bathroom, wc, laundry room. Second floor: 4 bedrooms, bathroom, convertible loft, wc.

€808,780 CODE LAT

COUNTRY COTTAGE

Beautiful house with more than a quarter of an acre of garden bordering the Crequoise River. The property is comprised of: lounge with wood burning fireplace, study, veranda, fitted kitchen, four bedrooms, one en suite, two receptions, shower room, central heating, double garage and double glazing. It is situated in the beautiful Crequoise Valley and is close to local amenities.

€348,000 CODE LAT

LOVELY DETACHED HOUSE

Superb brick built detached house with outbuilding and over a third of an acre valley. Property comprises: Ground floor: entranceterrace, spacious living/dining room with insert fireplace, exposed beams & accesskitchen with exposed beams, bedroom with access to terrace, tiled bathroom + showermezzanine, 4 bedrooms, tiled bathroom + toilet. There's also double glazing and a wine cellar.

€318,000 CODE LAT

AVERAGE HOUSE PRICES NORD-PAS-DE-CALAIS & PICARDY

	2-bed		3-bed		4-bed		5/6-bed	
Le-Touquet-Paris	€302,215	(£204,200)	€574,000	(£388,000)	€675,000	(£456,000)	€710,122	(£480,000)
Amiens	€190,100	(£128,433)	€230,000	(£155,100)	€280,000	(£189,000)	€293,000	(f198,000)
Lille	€189,000	(£128,000)	€232,000	(£156,432)	€317,000	(£214,000)	€481,000	(£325,000)
Somme Valley	€139,000	(£94,000)	€190,500	(£129,000)	€200,420	(£135,420)	€238,120	(£161,000)
Montreuil & Hesdin	€133,000	(£90,000)	€218,000	(£147,300)	€281,200	(£190,000)	€305,000	(£206,030)

PROPERTY GUIDE

The *clear* choice for currency

- No fees or commission
- Achieve the best currency exchange rate
- Guarantee an exchange rate for up to two years
- Send your funds to any destination in the world safely and securely

 Foreign Currency Exchang

Telephone: 0800 783 4313/+44144 22 33 040

www.fcexchange.co.uk

Île-de-France

Paris and Versailles plus a wealth of rural delights

MAISON DE LA FRANCE

FACT BOX

- **POPULATION** 10,952,037
- **UNEMPLOYMENT RATE** 10.1%
- **AVERAGE 4-BED HOUSE PRICE** €1,665,000
- **REGIONAL CAPITAL** Paris
- **REGION SIZE** 12,008km²

Contents

Area profile

The closest area of France to Britain boasts busy, metropolitan cities, attractive seaside resorts and tranquil countryside

GETTING THERE

AIR Air France (084 5111; www.airfrance.co.uk), BMI (0870 264 2229; www.flybmi.co.uk), **British Airways** (0870 850 9850; www.britishairways.com), **easyJet** (0871 750 0100; www.easyjet.com) and **Flybe** (0871 700 0535; www.flybe.com) fly to Paris Charles de Gaulle. **Ryanair** (0871 246 0000; www.ryanair.com) flies to Paris Beauvais from Dublin and Glasgow. Air France flies to Paris Orly from London City.

SEA SeaFrance (0870 571 1711; www.seafrance.com) and **Hoverspeed** (0870 240 8070; www.hoverspeed.co.uk) sail from Dover to Calais. **P&O** (0870 520 2020; www.posl.com) sails from Portsmouth to Le Havre. **Speed Ferries** (0870 220 0570; www.hoverspeed.co.uk) sails Dover to Boulogne.

ROAD From Calais take the A16 south to Amiens then on to Paris. From Le Havre the A15 runs to Rouen, then the A14 takes you into Paris.

RAIL Eurostar (0870 518 6186; www.eurostar.co.uk) runs from London Waterloo to Paris Gare du Nord. SNCF runs to Versailles and Fontainebleau (www.sncf.com); Rail Europe (0870 584 8848; www.raileurope.co.uk)

METRO Paris has an easily navigable underground system. The métro is part of RATP, incorporating bus, métro RER trains and tramways to the city's outskirts.

CLIMATE

ÎLE-DE-FRANCE		LONDON		ÎLE-DE-FRANCE		LONDON	
7	Dec	7		50	Dec	81	
11	Nov	10		50	Nov	78	
16	Oct	14		55	Oct	70	
20	Sep	19		52	Sep	65	
25	Aug	21		62	Aug	62	
25	Jul	22		58	Jul	59	
23	Jun	20		52	Jun	58	
16	May	17		60	May	57	
15	Apr	13		50	Apr	56	
10	Mar	10		32	Mar	64	
7	Feb	7		42	Feb	72	
7	Jan	6		55	Jan	77	

AVERAGE **TEMPERATURE** (Celsius) AVERAGE **RAINFALL** (millimetres)

PARIS AND AND ITS ENVIRONS ARE KNOWN collectively as Île-de-France. The region's population is almost 11 million, nearly a fifth of the nation's total – remarkable, considering that France is the third largest country in Europe.

Glamorous and cosmopolitan, Paris is quite simply one of the world's great cities, both culturally and architecturally. Historically a haven for artists and writers from all over the world, the streets and expansive boulevards are lined with great cafés, bars and restaurants. The capital's architectural riches are manifold: Notre-Dame and Sacré-Coeur cathedrals, the Louvre and Musée d'Orsay, the Eiffel Tower, the Pompidou Centre – the list goes on and on.

Île-de-France is the wealthiest and most densely populated area of France and known as an island because of the network of rivers surrounding it.

The region provides a surprising mix of contrasts – city life at its most frenetic is within easy reach of oases of tranquillity contained within four natural parks; you can walk along the world's most exclusive boulevards and in lush forests; and you can admire ancient neolithic menhirs and the latest in modern architecture.

The crossroads of Europe

Paris has a long and proud history dating back 2,000 years. Conquered by Julius Caesar in 53 BC, Paris continued to flourish even in the Middle Ages and later became the scene of the storming of the Bastille during the French Revolution in 1789. Modern Paris

Putting on the glitz – the Champs-Élysées at night

owes its glorious architectural style and structure to Napoléon III's civic planner, Baron Haussmann, who removed the slums and laid out the elegant avenues, boulevards and parks. The city is divided into 20 arrondissements; they are organised numerically and spiral out of the centre clockwise.

Paris's strategic spot at the crossroads of Europe has been coveted by conquerors for centuries. The Parisii Celtic tribe were the first inhabitants to settle on the Île de la Cité, followed by the Romans and then the Frankish tribe, who declared Paris the capital of the kingdom of Gaul in the sixth century.

During the Middle Ages Paris enjoyed its first spell of prosperity when the river marshlands were drained to make the Right Bank and construction on key monuments such as Notre-Dame and the Louvre

FOOD AND DRINK

Although considered by many to be the world's gastronomic centre, Paris has very few dishes that it can claim as its own. Instead, the city's restaurants cater for a huge melting pot of culinary tastes and flavours. In addition to French eateries serving fantastic traditional and modern fare, there is a seemingly endless choice of international and ethnic cuisine, including North African, Vietnamese, Tibetan, Nepalese, Italian, Greek and Caribbean.

Two products that Paris is exceptionally proud of are Brie de Meaux, which has been made on the outskirts of Paris since the eighth century and now has AOC status, and Meaux mustard, originally cultivated by monks in the reign of King Charlemagne.

When it comes to drink, the choice is endless and best enjoyed at one of the numerous outdoor cafés. Pigalle is a low-budget red wine produced locally and targeted at tourists.

MAISON DE LA FRANCE

Fine dining capital of the world

ATTRACTIONS

- ■ Paris from the Eiffel Tower
- ■ The palace and gardens at Versailles
- ■ The Arc de Triomphe
- ■ Sacré-Coeur cathedral and Montmartre
- ■ A stroll round the Latin quarter
- ■ Notre-Dame cathedral
- ■ Window shopping down the Champs-Élysées
- ■ The Pompidou Centre – inside and out
- ■ A ride down the Seine on a bateau-mouche
- ■ The art museums – all tastes are catered for

started. Further splendour came during the Renaissance and in the 17th century when Louis XIV, the Sun King, nearly made the country bankrupt in his attempts to make Paris dazzle outsiders – hence the extravagant elegance of Versailles.

In the late 19th century the belle époque and its innovative Art Nouveau genre heralded the city's most influential period as Paris led the world in philosophy, art and science – as showcased in the International Exhibition in 1889, with the newly built Eiffel Tower its top attraction.

Today Paris continues its love affair with the latest in architecture and the city boasts several ultra-modern masterpieces such as the glass pyramid in the Louvre courtyard, the Pompidou Centre and the Opéra-Bastille.

The economy

A quarter of France's manufacturing industry is situated in Paris, and chemicals, pharmaceuticals, computer software and electrical equipment are all produced here. Paris is also an established centre of art, publishing, high-fashion clothes and jewellery; more than 8,000 foreign companies, including Esso, IBM, Kodak, Honda and Procter & Gamble, have headquarters in Paris. Galleries, bookshops, antique dealers and restaurants all dominate the 6th arrondissement, while La Défense business centre is home to ELF, Esso and IBM. East of Paris, Disneyland is a major employer.

Social groups

Like any cosmopolitan city, Paris is home to many nationalities, British and Irish among them. The capital also has large groups of immigrants from France's former colonies in Africa and Asia including Algerians, Senegalese and Vietnamese. ●

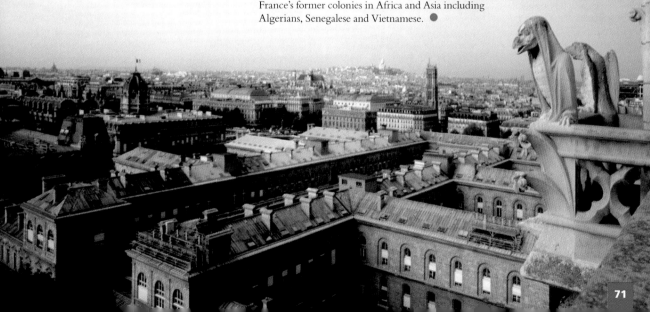

Property hotspots

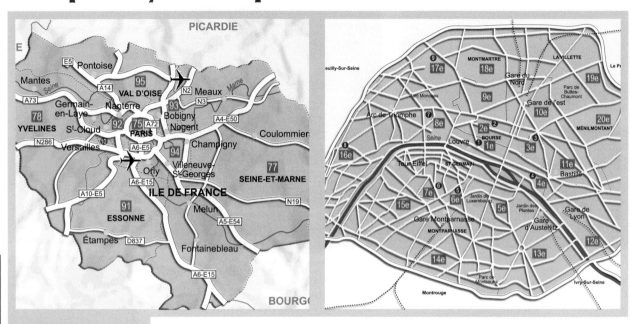

MAP KEY

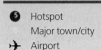

- **5** Hotspot
- Major town/city
- ✈ Airport
- ⛴ Ferry

ARRONDISSEMENT 1

1 Located on the Right Bank, the 1st arrondissement is the geographical and historical heart of the capital. The Louvre is here, and so are Les Halles and the Palais Royal. There are magnificent apartments for sale in blocks on the rue de Rivoli overlooking the Tuileries and Palais Royal gardens while renovated apartments are available near

Les Halles. Place Vendôme is another elegant area. Île de la Cité is home to some of the greatest sights – the Gothic Notre-Dame cathedral; Ste-Chapelle, with its spectacular stained-glass windows; and the Conciergerie, where Marie Antoinette was held prisoner. Spacious, quiet apartments with

high ceilings and thick walls are hidden behind the courtyards of a few select commercial façades. This is one of the most expensive property markets in Paris and you can easily pay millions for both apartments and houses. The starting price for a two-bedroom house in a Directoire building is over €651,000. Be aware that 18th- and 19th-century buildings cannot be altered in any way. The majority of buyers remain between 25 and 45 and although international demand has seen prices more than treble in 10 years, the market has stabilised.

The rental potential for this area is excellent. It is arguably the most popular arrondissement with tourists and the rental season here is year-round. Weekly prices for renting a two-bedroom apartment are around €638.

Key facts

- ■ **POPULATION,16,895**
- ■ **TAXES** Taxe d'habitation 5.88%, taxe foncière 6.65%
- ■ **AIRPORT** Paris Charles de Gaulle, BP 20101, F-95711, Roissy-Charles-de-Gaulle Cedex, Tel: +33 1 48 62 12 12,

Fax: +33 1 48 62 67 12
- ■ **SCHOOLS** Nearest: 8th and 7th
- ■ **MEDICAL** Clinique du Louvre, 17 rue des Prêtes, St-Germain l'Auxerrois, 75001 Paris; +33 1 53 40 60 60; www.cliniquedulouvre.com
- ■ **CLINIQUE** Mont-Louis, 8, 10 rue de la Foile, Régnaut, 75011 Paris; Tel: +33 1 43 56 56 56; www.clinique-mont-louis.fr
- ■ **PROS** There is a sense of community ■ A car is not necessary, because of the proximity to other arrondissements and the métro ■ Many roads are pedestrianised and it is a lively locale ■ It borders the nightlife and clubs of La Seinne and Le Marais
- ■ **CONS** The arrondissement becomes packed with tourists ■ The cost of living is high.

ARRONDISSEMENT 2

2 Primarily a business district and home to the Paris stock market (Bourse) and the Bibliothèque Nationale, the 2nd arrondissement is located between the Palais Royal and the grand boulevards. In the last couple of years, prices have increased here more than in any other area. Most Parisians tend to rent and buyers can occasionally

find a bargain apartment near the Bourse. Come the weekend, the district acquires a much more laid-back feel. You will find bargains in old-style shops among the maze of small alleys, while movie buffs can delight in cinemas along the boulevard des Capucines such as the Rex, an art deco building famous for its star-studded vault.

Gourmets may wish to visit Legrand, a family-run épicerie and wine merchant which has delighted Parisians since 1880, or you could dine at classic 1930s brasserie Vaudeville, an eatery popular with finance workers. This is the second most expensive district in Paris. You could acquire a south-facing three-bedroom apartment of 86m2 in a 17th-century building with exposed beams, fireplace, living room, equipped kitchen, bedroom overlooking a courtyard and basement parking from around €1,050,000.

The letting potential here is excellent, as there is no real end of season. The months from November to January are slightly cheaper, but on average the

HOTSPOTS

weekly rental price for a one-bedroom apartment is €517; you can double this figure for two bedrooms. It is primarily a business district, but there are also some tourist areas, so it offers a good mix of potential tenants.

Key facts
- ■ **POPULATION** 90,697
- ■ **TAXES** Taxe d'habitation 5.88%, taxe foncière 6.65%
- ■ **AIRPORT** Paris Charles de Gaulle, BP 20101, F-95711, Roissy-Charles-de-Gaulle Cedex; Tel: +33 1 48 62 12 12, Fax: +33 1 48 62 67 12
- ■ **SCHOOLS** Nearest: 8th
- ■ **MEDICAL** Centre de santé, Réaumur, 75002 Paris; Tel: +33 155 805 618
- ■ **PROS** A fabulous place to live; there is no need for a car here and it is easy to walk to the opera district in the nearby 9th arrondissement
- ■ **CONS** 18th- and 19th-century buildings that are listed in this locality cannot be changed in any way.

ARRONDISSEMENT 3 (LE MARAIS QUARTER)

3 The Marais quarter (3rd arrondissement) is a trendy area with a lively, cultural feel. It features the oldest buildings in Paris, some of which are medieval, while many 17th-century mansions nestle within this quiet, impressively preserved neighbourhood.

Originally, monks and knights settled in this arrondissement when it was just a patch of marshland and it was only at the beginning of the 17th century that the Marais began its reputation as a centre of luxury and regal elegance.

Generally high-priced with a few exceptions along the Right Bank, there are discreet cobbled lanes hiding courtyards, gardens, and grand, timbered apartments. There are also a few renovated offices, offering tall ceilings and huge windows. Many lesser-known museums like the Jewish Art and History Museum and Musée Carnavalet, which portrays Parisian history, are within walking distance. Few green open spaces exist, except for the exclusive place des Vosges.

Properties in the third have characteristically high ceilings and are generally smaller. Prices start at around €570,000 for a two-bedroom apartment but you can pay more than double this amount if you buy a place in a classic 19th-century Parisian building.

With excellent rental potential, purchasing property in this arrondissement is a surefire investment as prices are rising and rental income is high. Factors such as an apartment's decor can attract even higher fees in most areas, but especially in cosmopolitan areas such as this. The average weekly rental cost for a one-bedroom apartment is €575, while a two-bedroom apartment will earn the landlord around €703 per week, and three-bedroom homes almost €980.

Key facts
- ■ **POPULATION** 34,248
- ■ **TAXES** Taxe d'habitation 5.88%, Taxe foncière 6.65%
- ■ **AIRPORT** Paris Charles de Gaulle, BP 20101, F-95711, Roissy-Charles-de-Gaulle Cedex; Tel: +33 1 48 62 12 12, Fax: +33 1 48 62 67 12
- ■ **SCHOOLS** Nearest: 15th and 8th
- ■ **MEDICAL** Centre Médicio Social OSE, 106 rue Vieille du Tenyle, 75003 Paris; Tel: +33 1 48 87 87 85
- ■ **PROS** A quiet, dignified area where many 17th-century homes remain ■ The Picasso Museum and the Carnavalet Museum are located here, making it a great area for buying to let ■ The métro and proximity to central Paris make a car unnecessary ■ The 1st, 2nd, 4th, 10th and 11th arrondissements surround the 3rd, so there are incredible amenities on the doorstep in every direction
- ■ **CONS** A lively, extremely central area, there is always a lot of activity so buyers wanting a quiet life could find it all rather too noisy for their liking.

ARRONDISSEMENT 4 (JEWISH QUARTER)

4 The centre of the Marais is a fun, lively and mainly young area with a strong Bohemian flavour and it houses many trendy bars, shops, and restaurants. The rue des Rosiers is a centrepiece of Jewish lifestyle in Paris, while the Île St-Louis and the Île de la Cité are the oldest parts of Paris. Nestled between the Latin quarter and the Marais, leafy Île St-Louis has a tranquil village atmosphere and is especially popular with well-heeled Parisians and international residents. Past luminaries include Voltaire, Cézanne, Baudelaire, Helena Rubenstein and the Rothschilds.

Throughout the summer, the island's quay is the city's favourite sunbathing spot. In the north you'll find attractions such as the Pompidou Centre at the heart of the Beaubourg neighbourhood. To savour fine 17th- and 18th-century architecture, explore the neighbourhood from St-Gervais to St-Paul (between the rue St-Antoine and the rue de Rivoli) stopping by at the Musée de la Curiosité et de la Magie and the Maison Européenne de la Photographie. In this currently trendy area, prices have risen to match increased demand. Three-bedroom properties cost on average €1,640,000, and four-bedroom homes €1,681,000.

There is excellent rental potential, with no shortage of tourists renting here, so purchasing a property is a sensible investment, if a rather expensive one. November to January is considered a little quieter, but there is no firm end to the rental season. It is one of Paris's more expensive areas and a one-bedroom apartment here will generate an income of around €635 per week. A four-bedroom house will earn the owner more than €1,234 per week.

Key facts
- ■ **POPULATION** 30,675
- ■ **TAXES** Taxe d'habitation 5.88%, taxe foncière 6.65%
- ■ **AIRPORT** Paris Charles de Gaulle, BP 20101, F-95711, Roissy-Charles-de-Gaulle Cedex; Tel: +33 1 48 62 12 12, Fax: +33 1 48 62 67 12
- ■ **SCHOOLS** Nearest: 15th, 7th
- ■ **MEDICAL** Hôpital Hôtel Dieu, 1, place Pacuis Notre Dame, 75004 Paris; Tel: +33 1 42 34 82 34
- ■ **PROS** The historic heart of the city; its oldest landmarks, île St-Louis, île de la Cité, the St-Chapelle and Notre-Dame churches are here ■ Offers trendy designer boutiques, bars and restaurants and the Pompidou Centre ■ A strong alternative scene, with plenty of theatres
- ■ **CONS** A busy and noisy area, it is not to every buyer's taste, as this is where many Parisians come for their entertainment.

ARRONDISSEMENT 6 (ST-GERMAIN-DES-PRÉS)

5 Once the favourite haunt of Bohemians and intellectuals, this Left Bank neighbourhood has undergone regeneration and is now fashionably chic. Designer boutiques, art galleries and bistros like Polidor, which first served hearty food in 1845, can be found everywhere. Stop for coffee at Les Deux Magots, the place where Jean-Paul Sartre and Simone de Beauvoir spent their days writing, or relax in the Palais de Luxembourg gardens. St-Germain's legendary nightlife remains a major draw.

Buyers who appreciate period architecture will find some superb 19th-century properties in this district. Two-bedroom homes average over €852,000, and if you want four bedrooms expect to pay upwards of €1,953,000.

Alternatively there is the classic six- or seven-storey Haussmann mansion apartment, complete with wrought-iron balconies, railings and ornamental stonework. Close to the Jardin de Luxembourg you can find apartments with wood panelling and high ceilings but these sell at a premium and are primarily popular with foreign businessmen and well-heeled students.

As one of the top four tourist arrondissements, the area guarantees year-round rental income. One-bedroom apartments can be let for around €707 per week, while three-bedroom homes fetch around €1,330 per week.

Key facts

■ **POPULATION** 1999: 44,903
■ **TAXES** Taxe d'habitation 5.88%, taxe foncière 6.65%
■ **AIRPORT** Paris Charles de Gaulle, BP 20101, F-95711, Roissy-Charles-de-Gaulle Cedex; Tel: +33 1 48 62 12 12
■ **SCHOOLS** Nearest: 15th, as listed
■ **MEDICAL** Institut Arthur Vernes, 36 rue d'Assas, 75006 Paris; +33 1 44 39 53 00; www.institut-vernes.fr
■ **PROS** On the Left Bank, it is part of the famous Latin quarter and home to the Luxembourg Palace, art, antiques, bookshops and stylish boutiques ■ An up-and-coming, chic part of Paris following a makeover from its Bohemian roots, it is currently 'the' arrondissement ■ Posh boutiques, art galleries, theatres, nightclubs and restaurants are in plentiful supply ■ Near to the Eiffel Tower, in the 7th
■ **CONS** One of the most sought-after areas for buyers in Paris.

ARRONDISSEMENT 7

6 The 7th is one of the city's chic postcodes, with traditional, bourgeois character. Bordered to the north by the Seine with the 6th to the east and the 15th lying southwest, it is a draw for tourists. Here you will find the Musée d'Orsay with its Impressionist art collections, Les Invalides, where you can stroll along the impressive esplanade, and the Eiffel Tower. It's also home to the Assemblée

Nationale. This expensive, well kept area with chic apartments has a reputation for being quiet and safe; indeed, the French prime minister and several of the ministries are housed around Faubourg and St-Germain.

Grand and exclusive boulevard des Invalides has some beautiful architecture. Most of the period buildings are solid, handsome, and discreet, but there are modern exceptions.

The 7th is an expensive part of town and prices are higher than in the Marais. Two-bedroom properties here average over €587,000; four-bedroom homes nearly €1,628,000.

The rental potential is excellent as this is one of the top four tourist arrondissements. Returns will be high, but so will initila investment. With a year-round rental season, the average weekly letting price for a two-bedroom apartment is €724, while four-bedroom homes cost €1,070 per week.

Key facts

■ **POPULATION** 56,988
■ **TAXES** Taxe d'habitation 5.88%, taxe foncière 6.65%
■ **AIRPORT** Paris Charles de Gaulle, BP 20101, F-95711, Roissy-Charles-de-Gaulle Cedex; Tel: +33 1 48 62 12 12, Fax: +33 1 48 62 67 12
■ **SCHOOLS** Nearest: 7th, 15th
■ **MEDICAL** Hôpital de Jour 39, rue Varennes, 75007 Paris; Tel: +33 1 45 48 96 31
■ **PROS** The main highlights are the Eiffel Tower, the Musée d'Orsay and the Hôtel des Invalides, where Napoléon's tomb is located ■ Filled with dwellings and offices, this central location offers good employment opportunities ■ A central location, a car is not necessary ■ Attractions include Parc Georges Brassens, the swimming pool park Aquaboulevard and the Musée Rodin
■ **CONS** Very busy at weekends in the west side of the arrondissement which attracts lots of tourists ■ Fewer shops and cinemas than other areas.

ARRONDISSEMENT 8

7 This Right Bank arrondissement is the city's most expensive neighbourhood. Elegant hotels and first-class restaurants, such as the Buddha Bar, are here, along with the presidential Elysée Palace, the Champs-Elysées, the haute couture boutiques of the rue St-Honoré and palatial hotels like the George V and the Crillon.

In the area to the east, between the Champs-Elysées and place de la Madeleine, there is a mixture of 19th-century buildings interspersed with businesses. History buffs can visit place de la Concorde, the Luxor obelisk, and Église de la Madeleine for sculpture and architecture.

One of the most sought-after localities, this is a family-orientated part of Paris. It is also close to the lively 4th arrondissement, and yet it offers a tranquil retreat. Hugely sought after by international buyers, the 8th arrondissement is a quiet residential area and an excellent investment for those who can afford it. You can buy a two-bedroom property for €1,026,000 and a four-bedroom property for €1,122,000.

The best-sized property to let is a two-bedroom home and for higher rates it is best to go for short-term rentals. Two-bedroom apartments average €889 per week, but management costs can be high.

Key facts

■ **POPULATION** 1999: 39,303
■ **TAXES** Taxe d'habitation 5.88%, taxe foncière 6.65%
■ **AIRPORT** Paris Charles de Gaulle, BP 20101, F-95711, Roissy-Charles-de-Gaulle Cedex; Tel: +33 1 48 62 12 12, Fax: +33 1 48 62 67 12
■ **SCHOOLS** Nearest: 8th, as listed
■ **MEDICAL** Hôpital Européen Georges Pompidou, 20 rue Leblanc, 75908 Paris Cedex 15; www.hbroussais.fr/HEGP/

■ **PROS** Encompasses the Champs-Elysées, the Arc de Triomphe, the Elysées Palace, the Madeleine Church and the avenue Montaigne and Faubourg St-Honoré fashion houses ■ The traditional Paris, it features the more residential, Haussmann-style buildings ■ A car is unnecessary, as there is excellent public transport
■ **CONS** Tourists from all over the world flock here ■ Surrounding cafés, bars and restaurants are fearsomely expensive to frequent.

ARRONDISSEMENT 16

8 This residential area – formerly the village of Passy – runs west from the Arc de Triomphe out to Bois de Boulogne, the city's huge, rambling park where many locals run or ride horses. It is another area of expensive property, with large apartments both old and modern. In the west of the arrondissement there is little street life so it is quiet at night. Further west, the district of Neuilly is similar and ideal for buyers seeking tranquillity.

Literary lovers can visit the apartment of Balzac, who wrote the Comédie Humaine. Close by, the Musée Marmottan boasts the largest number of Monet paintings in the world.

Geographically the largest arrondissement, the 16th is very smart. Property is frequently owned and let by insurance companies and a growing number of Middle-Eastern purchasers are buying here. With more residential emphasis than in other arrondissements, classic Haussmann buildings can sell for many millions of euros. The older areas with very quiet avenues are located in the south and east near the Trocadéro, and apartments here cost slightly more than the area's average. On the whole, two-bedroom houses average just over €678,000, while four-bedroom homes cost around €1,447,000.

With good rental potential, prices are slightly lower than in other areas. Short-term rentals are better value and two-bedroom properties are the most popular. One-bedroom flats average just over €570 per week, while two-bedroom apartments fetch €700.

Key facts

∎ **POPULATION** 161,817
∎ **TAXES** Taxe d'habitation 5.88%, taxe foncière 6.65%
∎ **AIRPORT** Paris Charles de Gaulle, BP 20101, F-95711, Roissy-Charles-de-Gaulle Cedex; Tel: +33 1 48 62 12 12, Fax: +33 1 48 62 67 12
∎ **SCHOOLS** Nearest: 16th, 8th, as listed
∎ **MEDICAL** Centre Médical Edouard Rist, 14, rue Boileau, 75016 Paris; Tel: +33 1 40 50 52 00
∎ **PROS** The locale of wealthy Parisians ∎ The Bois de Boulogne and Trocadéro are here (home to government institutions) ∎ Near the Trocadéro, the Musée de la Marine and the well known Musée de l'Homme
∎ **CONS** This quiet locality would not suit every purchaser or tenant ∎ Not much nightlife.

ARRONDISSEMENT 17

9 This diverse district contains several residential areas, including the upmarket western part near the Arc de Triomphe. It is generally a chic area, but smaller and more accessible than the 16th, sharing Monceau park with the 8th. Many embassies are based here. Areas like the place des Ternes have a lively feel to them while the Marché des Moines, one of the cheapest markets in the capital, rubs shoulders with luxury boutiques such as Kenzo, Armani and Louis Vuitton. This is a quiet area after office hours, although you can visit the Palais des Congrès which hosts various exhibitions. Most buildings are 19th-century and have bigger rooms than in most other arrondissements.

The quiet residential area between Portes de Champerret and Maillot is ideal for brand new two-bedroom properties, while prices in the Arc de Triomphe and Parc Monceau area to the west are higher, as are areas near to Neuilly in the north.

In this arrondissement short-term lets offer the best value. Two-bedroom properties offer the best investment for those buying to let, fetching on average about €801 per week. There is no real end of season here, although November to January tends to be slightly cheaper than the rest of the year. However, be aware that there are high management costs associated with short-term lets.

Key facts

∎ **POPULATION** 161,138
∎ **TAXES** Taxe d'habitation 5.88%, taxe foncière 6.65%
∎ **AIRPORT** Paris Charles de Gaulle, BP 20101, F-95711, Roissy-Charles-de-Gaulle Cedex; Tel: +33 1 48 62 12 12, Fax: +33 1 48 62 67 12
∎ **SCHOOLS** Nearest: 16th, 8th
❂∎☀ **17TH**
∎ **MEDICAL** Centre Médico-Physique, 174, rue Courcelles, 75017 Paris; Tel: +33 1 45 74 75 15
∎ **PROS** One of the more wealthy areas ∎ A growing number of international foreign buyers ∎ Smaller than the 16th, it has a sense of community ∎ A lively outlook; it has great restaurants, packed bars and some amazing nightclubs
∎ **CONS** High management costs for short-term lets ∎ Some areas are very quiet, which could deter tourist tenants.

VERSAILLES

10 Situated in département 78, Versailles is undoubtedly best known for the sumptuous palace created by Louis XIV to glorify his reign as the Sun King. Yet Versailles is also a stylish suburb with elegant homes and easy access to the city

centre by means of the train. It is well served by the Paris D10 and A13 autoroutes, but far enough out to feel a world away from the life of the city.

Versailles will be especially attractive to those property buyers who are happy to trade off a daily commute in return for plenty of spacious parkland. King Louis XIV was a great patron of the arts, so the area is well served by theatre, festivals and fêtes that dominate the cultural calender.

Characterised by its 17th- and 18th-century buildings, a market, shops and the Rive Gauche railway station with routes into central Paris, the Left Bank St-Louis area of Versailles is the oldest quarter, and has been regenerated over the past decade. Filled with exclusive boutiques, it's a desirable locality.

The average four-bedroom home costs around €971,000 but you can pay a lot more for period homes. Two-bedroom properties sell for an average of €596,000, and a good choice for families is the peaceful, leafy area of Gatigny. However, take time to look around as you'll find some cheaper properties for sale, along with some much more expensive ones.

Rental potential in this area is average. Lets are mostly long-term lets and renters are

generally people who work in the city. A small apartment on a long-term basis is cheaper than in central Paris, attracting young marrieds. Two-bedroom apartments average around €801 per week.

Key facts

∎ **POPULATION** 85,726
∎ **TAXES** Taxe d'habitation 4.80%, taxe foncière 4.60%
∎ **AIRPORT** Paris Charles de Gaulle, BP 20101, F-95711, Roissy-Charles-de-Gaulle Cedex; Tel: +33 1 48 62 12 12, Fax: +33 1 48 62 67 12
∎ **SCHOOLS** British School of Paris, 38 quai de l'Ecluse, 78290 Croissy-sur-Seine; Tel: 33 1 34 80 45 90; Lycée International of St-Germain-en-Laye (American School) rue du Fer à Cheval, BP 230, 78104 St-Germain-en-Laye; Tel: +33 1 34 51 74 85
∎ **MEDICAL** Clinique Internationale du Parc Monceau, 21 rue de Chazelles, 75017 Paris; Tel: +33 1 48 88 25 25; www.cinique-monceau.com
∎ **PROS** An oasis of history, a select and glamorous area ∎ More peaceful than the centre ∎ The avenue de la Reine, or Queen's Avenue, is a beautiful place to live ∎ Good local amenities and new shopping centres ∎ A vibrant community in itself
∎ **CONS** Taxis from the centre are expensive ∎ Traffic jams between Paris and Versailles are common ∎ The RER (suburban train system) can take up to an hour to reach central Paris. ●

Property guide

In recent years, price rises in the capital have been among the steepest in France, with prices forecast to continue rising at 10 per cent per annum

This region offers excellent appreciation and superb rental return

HAUSSMANN APARTMENTS

- Erected in the 19th century, these six-storey stone-built apartment blocks are built in a neoclassic style and resemble elongated 18th-century townhouses
- Continuous ironwork balconies wrap around the third and sixth floors
- They are characterised by their mansard roofs which typically have two slopes on each of the four sides
- The roof's lower slope is steeper than the one above, is almost always covered in slate and was traditionally decorated with slates of different colours and shapes. The roof usually has dormer windows set in it
- The upper slope is not usually visible from ground level
- The beautiful internal features typically include parquet flooring, cornices, open fireplaces and marble mantelpieces

ALTHOUGH PRICES ARE HIGH, THERE ARE STILL affordable properties to be found in up-and-coming areas, such as Ménilmontant in the 11th arrondissement, the Buttes aux Cailles in the 13th and areas of Belleville and the Parc des Buttes-Chaumont in the 19th. The thriving 9th, and Montparnasse in the not-so-glitzy 14th, also feature affordable properties, while Montmartre, in the 18th, has some of the cheapest prices in the city. Basically, the old adage location, location, location is key to prioperty purchase in this thriving metropolis; there are bargains to be found in mosty arewas if you have the time and the patience to search and wait, but generally prices reflect the amount ot which a particular district is currently considered 'fashionable'. While this can make prices seem incongruous in some areas, it is be a good indicator of where to look for investment portential.

The avenue de Clichy and Batignolles areas in the 17th have seen major price rises. Classic Haussmann-style buildings left in their original state and not divided into apartments dominate the 16th and command high prices. Haussmann apartments in the 8th, 16th and 17th sell at a premium rate. More expensive are the 1st and 2nd arrondissements, where non-French purchasers form about seven per cent of the buyers. This figure is doubled in the more desirable 6th, 7th, 16th and parts of the 17th.

Neuilly, Boulogne, St-Cloud and Levallois to the west of Paris are peaceful suburbs, popular with families and central Parisian workers. The town of Versailles, home of Louis XIV's grand palace, is a beautiful, lively town, with stunning townhouses. Accommodation is more spacious and includes a garden for the same price as some Parisian apartments. As such, it's a popular rental location with Parisians.

Foreign property investors tend to favour Paris's Haussmann apartment blocks. However, for those who prefer more modern-style accommodation, there are plenty of contemporary, well-built apartment blocks with balconies, lifts and underground parking.

With the serious shortage of Parisian rental accommodation, and apartments in Paris costing, on average, 50 per cent less than London flats, purchasing an apartment in the French capital could be a sound long-term investment. Rents vary from one arrondissement to another, but you can expect average weekly yields of €800 for a two-bedroom apartment, with significantly higher yields for properties situated within the 1st and 2nd arrondissements. ●

WHAT CAN YOU GET FOR YOUR MONEY?

PARISIAN TOWNHOUSE

Located in the elegant and centrally located St Germain district of Paris this four-bedroom, three bathroom property dates from the 1880s. Giving out onto a charming paved courtyard, this is a fabulous townhouse with bags of potential and masses of character. Ideal as a rental property – you could generate excellent returns – or for those seeking to relocate to Paris for work purposes.

€4,888,000 CODE SIF

CENTRAL APARTMENT

This is a two-bedroom, two-bathroom and two reception room apartment, situated within walking distance of Faubourg St Honor. Located near the Place Beauvau, this is a typical Parisian apartment with a living area of 148 square metres. On the second floor of an 1860s building, the apartment boasts attractive period decorations including beautiful mouldings and fireplaces.

€1,100,000 CODE SIF

LUXURIOUS VILLA

Located only a few minutes from Paris, near the Marne River, this luxurious house has all the amenities one could desire. Built in 1993, with a total surface of 940 square metres – plus 160 square meters of balconies and terraces – the majestic triple reception hall comes with impressive marble designs and columns. The kitchen is particularly modern, equipped with all mod cons, while there are five bedrooms.

€4,680,000 CODE FPS

MAISON DE MAITRE

This charming 14th century property is located in a charming village only 15 minutes from La Defense and Paris. With 300 square metres of habitable space arranged over four floors and surrounded by grounds of almost an acre, this property comes with a swimming pool, outbuildings and a guest house of 115 square metres. This fine maison was completely renovated in 2002.

€895,000 CODE SIF

EXCEPTIONAL PROPERTY

Set in a very pretty village and enjoying lovely views, this is a beautiful Château resting on the River Seine. This exceptional property has been totally renovated over a period of 10 years without losing any of it's authenticity. The two buildings enclose a large courtyard, and there is ½ an acre of garden. The largest building is the barn which is 350 years old and was part of the nearby Château until the Revolution.

€1,751,000 CODE FPS

RENOVATED WATERMILL

This superb property is located in the area of Rambouillet and only 70kms from the centre of Paris. Formerly a water mill it is set in beautiful gardens and grounds of 3.7 acres and the property benefits from being surrounded by countryside – ideal situation for those interested in horse riding. The main house, which is thatched, comprises three bedrooms and there are many outbuildings to convert.

€728,000 CODE FPS

AVERAGE HOUSE PRICES ÎLE-DE-FRANCE

	2-bed		3-bed		4-bed		5/6-bed	
Arrondisement 1	€439,801	(£650,905)	€477,642	(£706,910)	–		–	
Arrondisement 2	–		€1,050,109	(£709,533)	–		–	
Arrondisement 3	€569,688	(£384,911)	€856,390	(£578,642)	€3,160,553	(£2,135,509)	–	
Arrondisement 4	–		€1,639,683	(£1,107,894)	€1,680,721	(£1,135,622)	€2,341,552	(£1,582,130)
Arrondisement 6	€852,233	(£575,833)	€1,722,287	(£1,163,707)	€1,953,386	(£1,319,855)	–	
Arrondisement 7	€586,742	(£396,447)	€1,441,553	(£974,022)	€1,628,105	(£1,100,071)	€5,901,383	(£3,987,421)
Arrondisement 8	€1,025,603	(£692,974)	€898,211	(£606,899)	€1,122,317	(£758,322)	€2,429,108	(£1,641,289)
Arrondisement 16	€677,693	(£457,901)	€1,335,283	(£902,218)	€1,446,731	(£977,521)	€3,770,874	(£2,547,888)

Champagne-Ardenne

Picturesque 16th-century Troyes and Champagne

MAISON DE FRANCE

Contents

FACT BOX

■ **POPULATION** 1,342,363
■ **UNEMPLOYMENT RATE** 10.5%
■ **AVERAGE 4-BED HOUSE PRICE** €255,260
■ **REGIONAL CAPITAL** Châlons-en-Champagne (formerly known as Châlons-sur-Marne)
■ **REGION SIZE** 25,600km²

Area profile

A hi-tech boom and eager EU civil servants are looking to put plenty of fizz into Champagne's housing market

GETTING THERE

AIR AirFrance (0845 359 1000; www.airfrance.co.uk), **British Airways** (0870 850 9850; www.britishairways.com), **BMI Baby** (0870 264 2229; www.bmibaby.com), BMI (0870 6050 555; www.flybmi.com), **easyJet** (0871 750 0100; www.easyjet.com) and **Flybe** (0870 567 6676; www.flybe.com) all operate flights from various UK airports to Paris, where connections are available via air, rail and road to Champagne-Ardenne. For northern Champagne-Ardenne, Brussels-South Charleroi may be more convenient than Paris, and Ryanair flies to Charleroi from Dublin and Glasgow.

ROAD The A26 runs from the ferry port at Calais straight through to Reims. Change on to the N43 at Arras for Charleville-Mézières. From Paris the A4 goes straight to Reims, and the N51 runs from Reims to Épernay.

RAIL TGV trains serve Reims, while SNCF services operate from Paris Gare de l'Est and Reims, Châlons-en-Champagne, Troyes and Charleville-Mézières. You could take the **Eurostar** (0870 518 6186; www.eurostar.co.uk) to Lille-Europe and from there SNCF services to Champagne-Ardenne. For all rail enquiries and more details about local services, contact **Rail Europe** (0870 584 8848; www.raileurope.co.uk).

CLIMATE

CHAMPAGNE-ARDENNE		LONDON			CHAMPAGNE-ARDENNE		LONDON	
6.2	Dec	7			58	Dec	81	
9.6	Nov	10			58	Nov	78	
15	Oct	14			66	Oct	70	
19	Sep	19			43	Sep	65	
35	Aug	21			58	Aug	62	
24	Jul	22			66	Jul	59	
23	Jun	20			53	Jun	58	
15	May	17			53	May	57	
14	Apr	13			48	Apr	56	
8.9	Mar	10			48	Mar	64	
5.6	Feb	7			38	Feb	72	
6.2	Jan	6			46	Jan	77	

AVERAGE TEMPERATURE
(Celsius)

AVERAGE RAINFALL
(millimetres)

THE CHAMPAGNE-ARDENNE REGION IN THE northeast of France is the home of the famous sparkling wine, which has been produced here since the 17th century.

Four départements make up the Champagne-Ardenne region: Ardennes, Marne, Aube and Haute-Marne. The north is dominated by the dense forests, rolling hill country and lakes and gorges of the Ardennes Massif, stretching into neighbouring Belgium. In the lower reaches of the region, the land gets flatter and is criss-crossed by rivers and canals. Huge expanses of vineyards dominate the chalky, undulating plains that make up much of Marne and Aube. Where the soil is unsuitable for grape cultivation, vineyards give way to vast stretches of wheat and cabbages.

Champagne moments

Capital of the region is Reims, just two hours' drive from Paris. This handsome city, with its wide avenues and a wealth of parks, is home to one of France's finest buildings – the magnificent Gothic Cathédrale Notre-Dame, a UNESCO World Heritage Site. Its façade is adorned with over 2,000 stone figures, 56 of which depict French monarchs, all of whom were crowned in Reims, according to tradition. The city's Old Town has typically narrow streets, and Reims is a friendly city with a lively, youthful feel.

South of Reims is Épernay, the centre for Champagne production where some of the most famous marques, including Moët & Chandon, with its 30 kilometres of cellars, are to be found. Most cellars are open to the public, so visitors can learn about the intricate Champénoise process and, of course, taste the finished product.

To the southeast of Reims, across the plains, Châlons-en-Champagne – formerly Châlons-sur-Marne – is dominated by the St-Étienne cathedral which stands on the edge of one of the many canals that flow through the centre.

Further south, into the Aube département, lies the most beautiful city in the region, Troyes, with its narrow streets, well preserved half-timbered houses and wonderful Gothic Cathédrale St-Pierre-et-St-Paul and Basilica St-Urbain. It also has a small modern art museum that's worth the detour. The most southerly département is Haute-Marne, home to the feudal town of Chaumont, which has some impressive Renaissance architecture.

Champagne-Ardenne's countryside has much to offer, too. In the hilly and densely forested north, where the Ardennes stretch into south Belgium, visitors can indulge in birdwatching, nature walks, fishing, and watersports such as canoeing and sailing on the various lakes in the region and on the river Marne. The route touristique du Champagne is a pleasant drive through many hectares of vineyards,

FOOD AND DRINK

Champagne-Ardenne's world-famous tipple enhances the flavour of many dishes, notably coq au Champagne (chicken in Champagne). Since the region shares a border with Belgium, many Flemish tastes have permeated the local gastronomy. Flamiche is a flan made with leeks, cream and eggs. Endive flamande is made by wrapping the vegetable in ham and adding white sauce. Chaudrée is a hearty fish stew, while potée Champenoise is a favourite dish of smoked ham, sausage and cabbage. Troyes is known for its spicy tripe sausages (andouillettes). Ardennes is most famous for its quality smoked hams (jambons d'Ardenne), but other specialities include game, fresh trout and pike. Sweets are unfussy, but delicious nonetheless. Mouth-watering gaufres are butter-rich waffles enjoyed with sugar and fresh cream. Biscuits de Reims are scrumptious paper-thin macaroons. Naturally, Champagne is the region's main draw, but many other wines are produced, including the still red, Bouzy.

MAISON DE LA FRANCE

If you want to sample some of the world's finest Champagnes head for Épernay

ATTRACTIONS

■ Go fishing on the three Lacs de la Forêt d'Orient

■ Don't miss historic Reims and its stunning Cathédrale Notre-Dame

■ Explore Troyes with its Gothic and Renaissance churches, cathedral and St-Urbain Basilica

■ Visit the imposing fortified château of Sedan

■ Visit Champagne maisons and vineyards in and around Reims and Épernay, including Mumm, Moët & Chandon, Mercier, Krug and Castellane

■ Look out for windmills along the canals in the north of the region

■ Nature-lovers should head to the Parc Naturel Régional de la Montagne near Reims

■ Go on a 4x4 tour through the Ardennes forests

and southwest of Reims, the Parc Naturel Régional de la Montagne de Reims offers lots of interesting trails, and some unusual botany to boot.

As in many regions in northern France, the weather is extremely variable. Champagne-Ardenne is certainly slightly colder than the south, but the summers are mostly warm and dry.

The economy

Wine and Champagne (including Moët & Chandon, Mercier and Krug) production has driven the economy of this region, specifically in Épernay and Reims, since the 16th century. However, hi-tech industries are now developing in Reims and Charleville-Mézières on the industrial park, the Centre régional d'innovation et de transfert de technologie. Tourism is also increasing in Reims and the Champagne-producing areas, while the region's lush countryside is an ever-popular destination for tourists.

Social groups

The northern part of Champagne-Ardenne – Charleville-Mézières in particular – attracts a lot of Belgian buyers because of the commutable distance to Brussels. Much of the region is also just an hour by rail from Paris and this attracts many Parisian commuters. British buyers looking for a bargain tend to stay away from the 'Champagne triangle' encompassing Reims, Épernay and Châlons-en-Champagne. ●

Property hotspots

MAP KEY

⑤ Hotspot
○ Major town/city
✈ Airport
⛴ Ferry

CHARLEVILLE-MÉZIÈRES & SURROUNDS

1 The Ardennes département of the Champagne-Ardenne region is formed by deep, thickly wooded valleys, which are magnificent in any season, and it is traversed by the winding Meuse and Semoy rivers. The capital is Charleville-Mézières, formed nearly 40 years ago from two competing communities. Charleville is the birthplace of the poet Rimbaud; Mézières, the original town, was founded in 899 AD.

The town is now the world capital of puppetry, hosting a week-long puppet festival every three years in September. In the 17th-century Vieux Quartier, christened the 'new town', visit the Ardennes Museum; the Notre-Dame of Hope Basilica; and the Musée Rimbaud, housed in a windmill near place Ducale, with an entire room dedicated to the young poet. A short distance away lies Sedan, site of the largest fortified château in Europe.

With more than 150,000 hectares of oak, beech and ash, the surrounding forests of the Ardennes provide plenty of hunting for wild boar and game. Local specialities reflect forest treasures, such as game cooked in wild juniper, and red turkey terrine with bacon salad.

Charleville-Mézières and its surrounds is a popular area with foreign buyers as it is inexpensive. With prices ranging from just over €132,000 for a two-bedroom house to around €216,000 for a home with four bedrooms, property prices are way below the national average.

Tourism is one of the main growth industries in the Ardenne area, and rental property is expensive. Tourists are mainly French, Dutch and Belgian, with increasing numbers of Britons. The average rental for a two-bedroom house currently stands at €450 per week.

Key facts

■ **POPULATION** 58,092
■ **TAXES** Taxe d'habitation 7.68%, taxe foncière 12.02%
■ **AIRPORT** Reims-Champagne Aéroport, 51450 Bétheny, Tel: +33 3 26 07 15 15
■ **SCHOOLS** Association des Amis de l'Enseignement International de Reims siège social, Chaussée Bocquaine, 51100 Reims, Tel: +33 3 26 05 15 83
■ **MEDICAL** Centre Hospitalier, Général de Manchester, 45 avenue de Manchester, Charleville-Mézières, Tel: +33 3 24 58 70 70
■ **PROS** Foreign buyers are mainly from Luxembourg, Denmark and Brussels ■ More English buyers are being drawn here by the many fermettes to renovate, complete with parcels of land ■ The perfect destination for families pursuing outdoor activity holidays and an ideal region for nature lovers
■ **CONS** Proximity to Brussels makes this area more expensive, with many civil servants buying property ■ It is essential to have a grasp of the language if moving here, as there are few British.

REIMS & ÉPERNAY

2 In the heart of Champagne, home to the vineyards of the Pinot Noir and Pinot Meunier grape varieties, historic Reims owes its fame not only to Champagne, but also to its numerous UNESCO treasures. The 13th-century Cathédrale Notre-Dame is a Gothic masterpiece. It houses a collection of renowned statues, and was on several occasions a coronation site for the kings of France. Even older is the Abbaye St-Rémi, half-Romanesque, half-Gothic in style, and comparable in size to the Notre-Dame-de-Paris.

Beneath the city and its suburbs are 240 kilometres of cellars cut into the chalk. During the bombing of the Second World War, the citizens of Reims sheltered there, but now the cellars house more than a billion bottles of Champagne. Property buyers have the pick of the Champagne trail from Reims to Épernay, which covers 70 kilometres of Champagne's villages and the vineyards between. On the left bank of the Marne valley, Épernay rivals Reims as a Champagne producer, boasting over 100 kilometres of cellars. If you prefer outdoor pursuits, boating on the Marne takes you past endless vineyards.

Buyers are prepared to pay high prices to live in the area, and interest from Paris has further increased prices. The average cost of a five-bedroom property in the area is nearly €353,000, while two-bedroom houses start at over €166,000.

This area is very popular with

SOMEPLACE ELSE

The Champagne-Ardenne region is gloriously rural and a riot of natural colours and fragrances

tourists as the Champagne route is centred around Reims and Épernay. Half the tourists here are French, but there are also a number of British, Belgian and German visitors. A two-bedroom property will generate an average of €525 a week, while a four-bedroom will earn €806.

Key facts

■ **POPULATION** 218,358
■ **TAXES** Taxe d'habitation 7.68%, taxe foncière 12.02%
■ **AIRPORT** Reims-Champagne Aéroport, 51450 Bétheny, Tel: +33 3 26 07 15 15
■ **SCHOOLS** Association des Amis de l'Enseignement International de Reims siège social, Chaussée Bocquaine, 51100 Reims, Tel: +33 3 26 05 15 83
■ **MEDICAL** Centre Hospitalier Universitaire de Reims, rue Général Koenig, 51100 Reims, Tel: +33 3 26 78 78 78
■ **PROS** Just an hour from Paris, Reims is a popular destination and easily accessible n It is rich in culture and history ■ Épernay is less inspiring but is home to the Champagne industry, with many

cellars located in the avenue de Champagne ■ Reims offers many smart townhouses and apartments ■ Most buyers are French, many moving here for work, not just to relocate or retire
■ **CONS** Huge demand in the Reims market pushes up prices ■ Easy access from Paris to Reims also makes property very expensive.

CHÂLONS-EN-CHAMPAGNE

3 The capital of the Marne département, formerly known as Châlons-sur-Marne, is historically linked to Attila the Hun. Not just a Champagne centre, Châlons also produces beer, textiles and electrical equipment, and fortunately has retained its medieval architecture. Running parallel to the Marne, the Châlons canals are spread through an area known as the Left Bank, with many stone bridges and old cafés. Close to place Monseigneur Tissier is the town hall, which is one of the grandest buildings in

the city. Also here is the famous church of Notre-Dame-en-Vaux, which is a UNESCO World Heritage site. Notre-Dame is surrounded by charming stone houses and the Gothic cathedral of St-Étienne. Le Petit Jard, situated between two of the canals on the south side of town, is a peaceful riverside garden. Nearby, the little town of St-Ménéhould has contributed to the world food with its recipes for pigs' feet and carp. Just 8km from Châlons, Champagne tastings take place at the Joseph Perrier estate.

In the countryside around Châlons, a two-bedroom property costs over €160,000, or €200,000 for a three-bedroom property. Châlons-en-Champagne receives mainly French visitors, but many tourists come between spring and autumn. Holiday rentals are very expensive, and rentals are generally long term rather than holiday lets. Despite there being little demand for seasonal rentals,

many people are buying to let here, and the market will grow. A weekly rental in a two-bedroom property will generate an average of €480.

Key facts

■ **POPULATION** 48,000
■ **TAXES** Taxe d'habitation 6.10%, taxe foncière 6.48%
■ **AIRPORT** Reims-Champagne Aéroport, 51450 Bétheny, Tel: +33 3 26 07 15 15
■ **SCHOOLS** Association des Amis de l'Enseignement International de Reims siège social, Chaussée Bocquaine, 51100 Reims, Tel: +33 3 26 05 15 83
■ **MEDICAL** Centre Hospitalier de Châlons-en-Champagne, 51 rue du Commandant Derrien, 51000, Tel: +33 3 26 69 60 60
■ **PROS** Foreign tourism is on the increase, and particularly from Britain ■ The area within a 5km radius of Châlons is very popular for buying property ■ There are excellent access routes
■ **CONS** There is a shortage of renovation properties ■ Increasing demand for property is pushing up already high prices even further. ●

Property guide

Thriving employment markets in Charleville-Mézières and Reims make them ideal for relocators looking for the real French experience

MAISON DE LA FRANCE

Rolling hillsides covered in vineyards provide the backdrop for many of Champagne-Ardenne's villages

ALTHOUGH PRICES ARE RISING THROUGHOUT the region, properties in Champagne-Ardenne are still relatively inexpensive compared to the UK. You should, however, expect to pay more the nearer you get to Brussels in the north and Paris in the west. The region has not yet attracted much interest from British house hunters – the main influx is from Benelux. In and around the heart of Champagne, prices are higher due to Parisian purchasing power – a four-bedroom house in countryside around Verzy is about €435,000.

With Reims and Épernay only an hour from Paris by TGV, the market has soared in the last few years. A family house in Épernay costs around €350,000;

the same in Reims buys a house but no garden. Tourism and the wine industry have made Reims one of the region's priciest spots, yet demand for relocation still makes the area a sound investment. Demand far outstrips supply, so the shortage of rental properties has created a landlords' market. Épernay is also a prime buy-to-let area, with about 300,000 visitors a year, many of them British and American. Property prices start at upwards of €200,000.

Civil servants from Brussels have pushed prices up in Charleville-Mézières where four- and six-bedroom houses cost between €216,000 and €307,000. Brussels commuters have also bolstered prices in Châlons-en-Champagne, where prices range between €160,000 and €300,000. Increasing numbers of foreign visitors plus city regeneration plans give Châlons-en-Champagne similar long-term buy-to-let value.

For long-term letting, Reims, Charleville-Mézières and Épernay are the best locations, but short-term seasonal letting is growing in Reims. Charleville and Bogny-sur-Meuse offer tourist letting markets with high rents and a long season. A two-bedroom country cottage near Épernay can yield €375 to €1,000 per week. Reims and Épernay feature elegant three-storey townhouses and smart apartments, and the surrounding countryside has a good selection of stone-built maison de village at reasonable prices. Or you could splash out on a 16th-century château for the princely sum of €1.25m. ●

MEDIEVAL TROYES TOWNHOUSES

- Troyes, ancient capital of Champagne, was constructed so that the layout of its historic town centre resembled a Champagne cork
- Troyes is considered to be the only place where you can see a complete medieval town built from wood
- The city is renowned for its ancient half-timbered houses, many of which now hover above the modern, bustling shops below them at street level
- The unique style of these houses is characterised by oak beams and brightly painted walls which are filled with wattle and daub
- These tall, narrow townhouses are usually three storeys high
- The gable end of the building faces in the direction of the street

PROPERTY GUIDE

WHAT CAN YOU GET FOR YOUR EUROS?

DETACHED HOUSE

Fully restored and habitable this detached property is in good condition and comes with a garden. Located in a small village in the Haute-Marne region, this property dates back to the 19th century and comes with one bedroom and one bathroom, and is arranged over two floors. With a plot of 195 square metres and a private garage, this is a real bargain. It's possible to convert the loft into a second bedroom.

€25,000 CODE FIR

BAROQUE-STYLE HOME

This charming property, built in 1745, has been fully renovated and offers 280 square metres of living space over two floors. With three reception rooms, four bedrooms and three bathrooms, there is also a separate cellar and an attic suitable for conversion. Outside there is an outbuilding with a tower and pigeonnier, and the whole plot is set in 2,500 square metres of well-manicured gardens.

€602,000 CODE SIF

TRADITIONAL FARMHOUSE

This great terraced farmhouse comes with plenty of land and was formally a cheese dairy. Situated in the Bourbonne area, the farmhouse come with two bedrooms and one bathroom and dates back to 1860. The house offers a private garage and sits in a plot of 1,323 square metres. Inside there are many traditional features such as a fireplace and wooden floors, while outside there are outbuildings to convert.

€40,000 CODE FIR

ELEGANT CHÂTEAU

Situated in Haute Marne, this elegant 18th century chateau comes with a number of outbuildings – including a caretakers apartment and stables – and also benefits from having a lake in its grounds. The property contains five reception rooms, 11 bedrooms and six bathrooms. Set in more than 5 hectares of gardens and woodland, and boasting a total of 690 square metres of living space, it also comes with a pool.

€1,219,000 CODE SIF

COUNTRY RESIDENCE

This charming property is set within landscaped gardens of 2,600 square metres. This fully restored family home offers more than 340 square metres of living space, and comes with four bedrooms, two bathrooms and a fully equipped kitchen. With bags of character, it also offers a guest cottage and a garage with wine cellar. In a country setting, this house is only 1¼ hours from Paris.

€568,421 CODE FRA

PERFECT FAMILY HOME

This is a lovely, traditional-style house located in a small town in the Aube. Only 5km from the medieval town of Troyes which offers numerous shops, restaurants and a train station, the property is also within easy reach of the nearby Parc de la Forêt de l'Orient with lakes, where you can enjoy fishing, boating or just relaxing. The property offers three bedrooms and one bathroom and an exterior workshop.

€205,000 CODE FRA

AVERAGE HOUSE PRICES CHAMPAGNE-ARDENNE

	2-bed	3-bed	4-bed	5/6-bed
Charleville-Méziéres	€132,420 (£89,500)	€210,000 (£140,000)	€216,000 (£146,000)	€307,000 (£207,435)
Reims & Épernay	€166,000 (£112,000)	€240,225 (£162,314)	€289,084 (£195,327)	€353,310 (£239,000)
Chalons-en-Cham	€160,183 (£108,232)	€199,000 (£134,500)	€261,100 (£176,410)	€294,000 (£199,000)

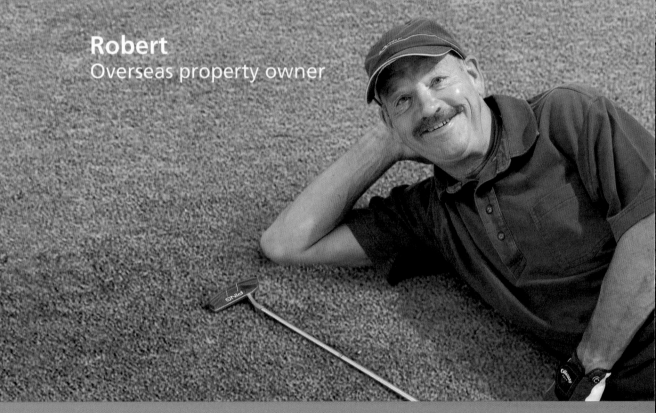

Alsace, Lorraine & Franche-Comté

Strasbourg, the Vosges mountains and Germanic

FACT BOX

■ POPULATION 5,161,580
■ UNEMPLOYMENT RATE Alsace: 8.9%; Lorraine: 10.2%;
Franche-Comté: 9.1%
■ AVERAGE 4-BED HOUSE PRICE €290,337
■ REGIONAL CAPITAL Alsace: Strasbourg; Lorraine: Metz;
Franche-Comté: Besançon
■ REGION SIZE 48,033km²

Contents

Area profile

Bordering Germany and Switzerland, these regions offer a very different cultural and architectural experience…

GETTING THERE

AIR Air France (0845 084 5111; www.airfrance.co.uk) flies directly from Gatwick to Strasbourg. For the northern Lorraine area, it is easier to fly with **Ryanair** (0871 246 0000; www.ryanair.com) to Brussels-South Charleroi; Ryanair flies from Dublin and Glasgow to Charleroi.

ROAD The A26 runs from the Calais ferry port to Reims, and from there the A4 continues to Metz and Strasbourg. From Metz take the A31 south to Nancy and, for Besançon, follow the A26 from the Channel ports, or the A5 from Paris to Troyes, continuing on the A5 and the A31 for Dijon, changing to the A39 and then the A36. From Paris, the A4 runs through Reims to Metz and Strasbourg.

RAIL TGV services (www.tgv.co.uk) operate between Paris Gare de l'Est, and Nancy, Metz and Strasbourg. TGV services also operate between Paris Gare de Lyon and Besançon, while the **Eurostar** (0870 518 6186; www.eurostar.com) runs from the UK to Lille, where TGV services continue to Besançon. From Lille-Flandres there are direct train services to Metz. For all enquiries and more details on local services, contact **Rail Europe** (0870 830 2008; www.raileurope.co.uk).

THIS NORTHEASTERN CORNER OF FRANCE offers a different taste of the country, with Germanic influences abounding in language, gastronomy and architecture, from the quaint half-timbered houses of Alsace to the wooden chalets of Franche-Comté. While Franche-Comté in the south shares its boundary with Switzerland, Lorraine and Alsace share much of their eastern borders with Germany, and at various times in their history have been under German rule.

Neighbouring influences

Lorraine is the largest but least known of the three regions that make up this area. Its countryside is generally flat, although it gets hillier to the east as flat fields give way to the tree-covered mountainsides of the Vosges that dominate the north of Alsace.

Many of Lorraine's towns and cities were destroyed in the two world wars of the last century, as evidenced by the poignant memorials and military cemeteries around the small town of Verdun, scene of the First World War's bitterest and bloodiest battle in which hundreds of thousands of men died.

Elsewhere, visitors to Lorraine come to discover the handsome and appealing cities of Nancy and Metz and the fortified town of Toul. Nancy is characterised by grand 18th-century boulevards, buildings and palaces and some fabulous Art Nouveau architecture, while Metz, 50 kilometres further north, has a stunning Gothic cathedral with

Chagall windows. The triangle of land between Nancy, Metz and Verdun encompasses the Lorraine Regional Park – 2,000 square kilometres of forests, streams and lakes.

The Alsace region is separated from Lorraine by the Vosges mountains and from Germany by the Rhine. At various times in its history, Alsace has been ruled by Germany, and this is reflected in its architecture, language and traditions.

Regional capital Strasbourg has for centuries been a crossroads, linking northern Europe with Mediterranean Europe. It's a cosmopolitan city, home of the European Parliament and the European Court of Human Rights, while the ancient Grand Île area is a World Heritage site. Strasbourg is known for its sandstone Cathédrale Notre-Dame and the pretty half-timbered houses that overhang the canal in the Old Town.

If you can put up with the hordes of tourists, the Route du Vin (stretching from Marlenheim in the north to Thann in the south) takes in castles, forts, endless terraced vineyards and picture-postcard towns and villages as it winds its way south for 170 kilometres, skirting the southern Vosges to the west and the Rhine to the east.

The countryside gets more rugged further south in the Franche-Comté region, where the Jura mountains offer opportunities for hiking and paragliding in summer and skiing in the winter. There is some beautiful scenery to discover in the Parc Natural Régional du Haut-Jura, while

CLIMATE

	ALSACE, LORRAINE & FRANCHE-COMTÉ	LONDON		ALSACE, LORRAINE & FRANCHE-COMTÉ	LONDON
Dec	5	7	Dec	41	81
Nov	8	10	Nov	40	78
Oct	15	14	Oct	43	70
Sep	21	19	Sep	56	65
Aug	26	21	Aug	69	62
Jul	24	22	Jul	56	59
Jun	23	20	Jun	74	58
May	16	17	May	74	57
Apr	14	13	Apr	48	56
Mar	9	10	Mar	36	64
Feb	5	7	Feb	36	72
Jan	5	6	Jan	33	77

AVERAGE TEMPERATURE (Celsius)   **AVERAGE RAINFALL** (millimetres)

FOOD AND DRINK

The cooking of this region is, unsurprisingly, heavily influenced by German cuisine, with many local dishes featuring pickled cabbage and pork – such as choucroute, white cabbage marinaded in beer, served with sausage, bacon and pork and often accompanied by a huge glass of beer. The locals enjoy a host of savoury pies and tarts, the most famous being quiche Lorraine. Another local favourite is the pizza-like tarte Flamande (a thin layer of pastry topped with cream, onion and bacon, cooked in a wood-fired oven). Meat and fresh fish stews are also enjoyed regularly, with baeckeoffe (a stew of marinated meat and vegetables) being a particular favourite.

The local wines also have strong German influences. White Rieslings, some outstanding, are most popular. Spicy and aromatic Gewürztraminer is most typical of Alsace and goes well with sauerkraut, sausages, spicy dishes and the Alsatian cheese Munster; it even makes a decent dessert wine. The region also manufactures much of the country's beers – Strasbourg is home to Kronenbourg.

MAISON DE LA FRANCE

PROFILE

ATTRACTIONS

■ Don't miss the annual Foire des Vins held every August in Colmar, where the town comes alive with food and drink stalls, concerts, free street entertainment and fireworks displays

■ The Christmas markets of Strasbourg, Mulhouse, Colmar and Metz are an experience not to be missed

■ Head to the Jura mountains in Franche-Comté for some outdoor activity and nature-watching opportunities

■ Wonder at the futuristic architecture of Le Corbusier's Notre-Dame-du-Haut chapel, north of Besançon

■ Indulge in the local food and drink specialities: locally brewed beers, crisp white wines and choucroute garnie

■ Wander round the medieval centre of Strasbourg and see the magnificent Gothic cathedral

■ Visit the Kronenbourg brewery in Strasbourg to get a flavour of the local beer

■ Take time out to visit the poignant war memorial in Verdun, where hundreds of thousands of soldiers were killed in the First World War

■ View the region from the water by taking one of the many boat cruises along the river Rhine

historic architecture – namely the Renaissance Palais Granvelle and the 12th-century Cathédrale St-Jeancan – can be sought out in the region's capital, Besançon, a lively city with a large student population. East of Besançon is the citadel town of Belfort, while to the north is the quirky Chapelle Notre-Dame-du-Haut designed by Le Corbusier.

The economy

The economy of this area is wide and varied: Lorraine is home to some of France's largest petrochemical and plastics factories and telecommunications centres, while Alsace is split between the civil servant Mecca of Strasbourg and the business of wine making and export. Franche-Comté is known for its production of spectacles. Strasbourg, by contrast, gets much of its income from politics-related business and finance. Service and tertiary industries provide a lot of employment in these regions – 58 per cent of workers are employed in the service industry. Agriculture, chemicals and plastics are also major industries. More than half of France's toys and 80 per cent of the country's eyewear is produced in Franche-Comté's Jura département. The telecoms industry is big in Metz – the Technopole Metz 2000 base is a big employer.

Nancy and Strasbourg, too, are centres of commerce and industry. For this reason the area is great for people looking to work in any of these industries, but other job seekers could struggle.

Social groups

The region as a whole has lots of German and Swiss residents; much of Alsace is German-speaking. Strasbourg has a multinational population because of its wealth of large European institutions. ●

Property hotspots

MAP KEY

- ⑤ Hotspot
- ● Major town/city
- ✈ Airport
- ⚓ Ferry

STRASBOURG

1 Flanking the Franco-German border, Strasbourg is the base of the European Union and the European Court of Human Rights, with a truly cosmopolitan air. Also a UNESCO World Heritage site, Strasbourg has a medieval centre with a maze of cobbled squares, half-timbered houses and meandering canals. The pink sandstone Gothic Cathedral of Notre-Dame displays a rich tapestry of carved doorways, gargoyles and a rose window.

The historic Grande Île is encircled by waterways. A guided walk from its western corner through Petite France shows the French and German influences that shaped the Old Town, where millers, tanners and fishermen lived. Narrow streets with half-timbered houses are criss-crossed by canals, with the watchtowers of the Ponts Couverts, part of the 14th-century fortifications, and the Vauban Dam, built to protect Strasbourg from attack, standing by. For an insight into Alsace life, do not miss the Musée Alsacien. In December, Strasbourg's famous Christmas market draws crowds from far and wide.

Many foreigners have chosen to make Strasbourg their home, particularly Germans, so prices are high; a two-bedroom house will sell for over €407,000.

The rentals market is also strong. The presence of international students creates a long-term lets market, while there is also good demand from holiday-makers – many tourists visit for the Christmas market, and Strasbourg is a tourism magnet. A landlord can earn an average of €428 per week from a two-bedroom property.

Key facts

■ **POPULATION** 267,051
■ **TAXES** Taxe d'habitation 6.97%, taxe foncière 6.35%
■ **AIRPORT** Strasbourg International Airport, 67960 Entzheim, Tel: +33 3 88 64 67 67
■ **SCHOOLS** Lycée International des Pontonniers, 1 rue des Pontonniers, 67081, Tel: + 33 3 88 37 15 25, www.scolagora.com/ponto/Site_Web
■ **MEDICAL** Centre Hospitalier Universitaire, 1 place de l'Hôpital, 67000, Tel: +33 3 88 11 67 68
■ **PROS** Main demand from the French and German market, with some international appeal ■ A prominent and wealthy industrial city ■ Accessible and central for the rest of Europe
■ **CONS** Property and land very expensive compared with the rest of France ■ Proximity to the border increases demand and prices ■ Huge demand for renovation property, which is scarce due to a lack of migration.

METZ & NANCY

2 Metz, just 65 kilometres from the German border, became part of France in 1552, but then fell under German occupation from 1870 to 1918 and once again during the Second World War.

Ochre stone lends warmth to its Renaissance buildings. Leafy paths trace the Roman and medieval ramparts, and follow the Seille and Moselle rivers. Late Gothic stained glass and additions by Marc Chagall adorn the Cathedral of St-Étienne, the third highest in France. In place de la Comédie is the oldest working theatre in France, while another gem, the Arsenal, built under Napoléon III, is now a concert hall.

Upstream lies the university town of Nancy, the historical capital of Lorraine, founded at a European crossroads. Its famed place Stanislas, created by the Polish exiled King Stanislas Leszczynski, is one of Europe's finest with many beautiful churches. A two-bedroom house costs from €232,000; a five-bedroom home over €413,000.

The rental market is stable in Metz, if expensive. Metz attracts many tourists, and both cities are popular rental areas, so this is a very good area for investment. Peak season runs from early July until August, with rental activity up to the end of September. A two-bedroom property would yield €571 a week.

Key facts

■ **POPULATION** 233,328
■ **TAXES** Taxe d'habitation 5.81%, taxe foncière 6.47%
■ **AIRPORT** See Strasbourg
■ **SCHOOLS** Rectorat de l'Académie de Nancy-Metz, rue Philippe-de-Gueldres 2, BP13, 54035 Nancy, Tel: +33 3 83 86 20 20
■ **MEDICAL** Hôpital Clinique Claude Bernard, 97 rue Claude Bernard, BP45050, 57072 Metz, Tel: +33 3 87 39 66 66 ■ Centre Hospitalier Universitaire, 29 avenue Maréchal de Lattre de Tassigny, 54000 Nancy, Tel: +33 3 83 85 85 85
■ **PROS** Both cities are culturally and architecturally rich ■ There is high demand from Luxembourgers for cheap property ■ Apartments in both city centres are very popular
■ **CONS** The city centres are prohibitively expensive ■ There's an enormous demand for renovation properties on the outskirts of the cities, but with limited property available on the market.

THE VOSGES

3 The stunning mountainous Vosges in western Alsace present a panorama of high forests, lakes, gorges and waterfalls. Two regional parks, one in the south – covering the Vosges massif from the valley of Ste-Marie-aux-Mines to the edge of Belfort and Luxeuil-les-Bains – and a northern one featuring a forest at its centre, are excellent for outdoor pursuits.

In Haut Alsace, the Ballons des Vosges are dominated by a series of rounded peaks or ballons. This land of the marcaires (mountain farmers), tending their herds on moorland pastures, boasts geological splendours, with large quartz and feldspar crystals in its granite. Notable are the eroded volcanic hills of Petit Ballon and Grand Ballon.

Gérardmer is a popular southern Vosges resort, offering skiing in the winter and its lake for activities in summer. Between the southern Vosges and the northern reaches of the Jura mountains, attractive Belfort has a restored old town. Dominated by a fortified castle and Bartholdi's red sandstone lion marking the city's resistance to siege during the Prussian War, Belfort is known for its antiques market.

Property here is limited while demand is high, so prices are rising. Expect to pay around €197,000 for a habitable two-bedroom property.

The Vosges region boasts a year-round rental season, mainly for outdoor holiday-makers. With growing tourist interest in the area, mostly from the French, winter is currently the most popular season, especially for skiing and winter sports. An excellent rental and investment area, especially for short-term rentals, Gérardmer is the area's main draw, where a two-bedroom property will generate an average of €408 per week.

Key facts

■ **POPULATION** 100,065
■ **TAXES** Taxe d'habitation 6.97%, taxe foncière 6.35%
■ **AIRPORT** See Strasbourg
■ **SCHOOLS** Rectorat de l'Académie de Besançon, rue de la Convention 10, 25030 Besançon Cedex, Tel: +33 3 81 65 47 00, www.ac-besancon.fr
■ **MEDICAL** Centre Hospitalier de

Belfort-Montbéliard, 14 rue Mulhouse, 90000 Belfort, Tel: +33 3 84 57 40 00
■ **PROS** Excellent for outdoor activities, such as climbing and mountain biking ■ Forested mountains, lakes and wine routes stretch along the Rhine from Strasbourg ■ Belfort is popular with international buyers, particularly the Germans and Dutch, but the French remain the main buyers ■ Property prices are relatively affordable
■ **CONS** There is a limited supply of sought-after renovation properties.

BESANÇON

4 The ancient, attractive grey-stone capital of Franche-Comté lies between Alsace and Burgundy on the northern edge of the Jura mountains, encircled by a bend in the river Doubs. Having first begun as a Gallo-Roman city, Besançon then absorbed different identities as a Spanish settlement, and then it became a provincial town.

The city is the birthplace of artificial silk, or rayon, and it counts among its native sons the pioneering Lumière brothers and epic novelist Victor Hugo.

Located on the banks of the Moulin St-Paul canal, in the heart of the town, the attractive Besançon Port accommodates pleasure boats, house boats and floating hotels. Sampling its waterside charms by barge is a must, passing through tunnels dug under the 19th-century citadel via the lock of the St-Paul windmill. There are plenty of lively and inexpensive riverside restaurants, cafés and bars near place Battant.

Property in Besançon is currently affordable, although this is likely to change as demand continues to increase. Prices are further fuelled by the limited number of renovation properties available. Currently a two-bedroom property would set you back around €190,000.

This area is largely ignored by foreign tourists, making for a

slow rentals market. It's therefore difficult to rent property out seasonally. The winter rentals market is particularly poor, as peak season here is between May and September, when foreign tourists visit, primarily from Germany and America. A two-bedroom property rents from €403 a week.

Key facts

■ **POPULATION** 125,000
■ **TAXES** Taxe d'habitation 7%, taxe foncière 9.70%
■ **AIRPORT** See Strasbourg
■ **SCHOOLS** Rectorat de l'Académie de Besançon, rue de la Convention 10, 25030 Besançon Cedex, Tel: +33 3 81 65 47 00, www.ac-besancon.fr
■ **MEDICAL** Hôpital Universitaire St-Jacques, 2 place St-Jacques, 25030 Besançon Cedex, Tel: +33 3 81 66 81 66
■ **PROS** There are good bargains to be found in this area, especially for those seeking winter rather than summer holiday homes ■ Prices are on the increase, but property is still good value for money ■ Investment is good
■ **CONS** Property prices are higher than average ■ Growing demand + dwindling supply is causing prices to rise ■ There is a lack of renovated properties and properties to renovate.

LONS-LE-SAUNIER, HAUT-JURA & VALLÉE DES LACS

5 Close to the Swiss border, the Haut-Jura and Doubs départements share an exceptional setting in a regional park that is full of opportunities for winter sports enthusiasts and nature lovers in the summer.

At altitudes ranging from 800 to 1,600m and just an hour from Geneva, Haut-Jura is the most authentic of French mountain ranges, with villages nestling at the foot of its valleys. The Transjurassienne, the cross-country ski race, attracts thousands of participants from all over the world. St-Claude, the largest city, lies close to the ski resort of Les Rousses and has

a history of pipe making and diamond cutting, while Morbier is renowned for its cheese.

Haut-Doubs often experiences harsh winters, though summers are pleasant. Distilleries throughout the region produce excellent apéritifs and liqueurs.

This is a very popular area with foreign buyers and it is typified by the colourful houses and swathes of rustic villages and hills. You can pick up a habitable two-bedroom property in this region from around €141,000, while a three-bedroom property will set you back €214,000 and a four-bedroom home around €272,000. If you've got a large family or want to rent a property to more people, five-bedroom houses average just under €335,000.

The town of Lons-le-Saunier attracts a lot of short-term rental interest, and much rental income is generated by the popular Jura ski resort, Les Rousses. The main rental season runs from May to September, prices ranging from €588 for a two-bedroom property to €1,040 for five bedrooms.

Key facts

■ **POPULATION** 43,601
■ **TAXES** Taxe d'habitation 8.46%, taxe foncière 15.58%
■ **AIRPORT** Geneva International Airport, PO Box 100, CH1215, Geneva 15, Tel: +41 2 27 17 71 11
■ **SCHOOLS** Rectorat de l'Académie de Besançon, rue de la Convention 10, 25030 Besançon Cedex, Tel: +33 3 81 65 47 00, www.ac-besancon.fr
■ **MEDICAL** Hospitalier Général de Lons-le-Saunier, 55 rue du Docteur Jean-Michel, 39000 Lons-le-Saunier, Tel: +33 3 84 35 60 00
■ **PROS** The mountains attract winter sports and nature lovers ■ Prices are relatively low ■ Most demand is French, but increasingly German and British
■ **CONS** Renovation properties are in demand, but rare, while local demand makes international buys difficult ■ Proximity to Geneva and Brussels is driving up prices. ●

HOTSPOTS

Property guide

Properties in Lorraine are very reasonably priced and are larger than average for France, yet the region is still not very popular with foreign buyers

The towns and villages of Alsace boast a wealth of timber-fronted properties

A LOW COST OF LIVING, EXCELLENT TRAVEL links, and relatively few tourists and international residents make this area ideal for those wishing to escape the hubbub. Metz and Nancy's prices have increased dramatically in the past five years, and demand continues to outstrip supply. Four-bedroom houses average €300,000.

Alsace has a booming property market with little opportunity to snap up renovation bargains, although most homes are generously proportioned. Prices are above average because of Alsace's superb central location within Europe. Its vibrant regional capital, Strasbourg, has a bustling student and tourist population, with excellent rental prospects. Despite the high price tag of €604,000-plus for a five or six-bedroom home in the centre, the constant influx of well-to-do workers ensures good profit margins – properties in the Orangerie district go for premium prices. A one-bedroom house sleeping two will earn around €695 to €995 per week.

Property prices in Franche-Comté are above average, though the area is not hugely popular with foreign buyers. A three-bedroom house close to the Jura retails from €200,000, while a four-bedroom farmhouse in need of repair can be purchased for under €100,000. With regular Swiss and German visitors, there is very good investment potential in the area as a whole. A three-bedroom chalet close to Lake Chalain sleeping up to six people can be rented out for €300 to €700 per week.

If short-term holiday lets are your aim, Metz and Strasbourg's Christmas markets provide a good winter rental market. The Jura is gîte country. For winter gîtes, Metabief and Les Rousses are developing ski resorts, where populations double in winter. Haut-Doubs is a big draw because of its winter sports potential. Besançon's prices are increasing, but accommodation still offers reasonably good value, with five to six-bedroom homes averaging €328,000. The Velotte district is very exclusive and buyers are now paying premium prices for new executive homes in Besançon. ●

TYPICAL PROPERTIES

- The predominant architectural styles in the region are stone and half-timbered
- Stone houses in towns such as Sauverne and Wissembourg use local red sandstone
- Nancy in Lorraine is famous for its stunning Art Nouveau architecture, the influences of which can be seen in decorative details such as stained glass
- In the Jura you will find long and low alpine chalets, built from timber and stone, and featuring slate roofs

ALSATIAN ARCHITECTURE

- The medieval villages of Alsace are renowned for their timber-fronted, colourfully painted properties, with flower pots and boxes
- Flat-tiled, gabled roofs are steeply sloping, and have chimneys at each end
- Houses are built on raised stone foundations, and walls are timber built

WHAT CAN YOU GET FOR YOUR MONEY?

BUSINESS OPPORTUNITY

Located in Haute Saone this listed 18th-century Chateau comes with a large parcel of land and is bordered by a river. Offering six reception rooms, 12 bedrooms and 12 bathrooms, the property also carries land totalling 2.9 hectares. There are also two separate gîtes, several outbuildings and a caretaker's house within grounds partly bordered by a river, making this ideal as a gîtes or chambres d'hote business.

€1,300,000 CODE SIF

CHÂTEAU IN THE JURA

This 18th-century Château has 600 square metres of living space which is arranged over two floors. A unique feature are the two towers adorning the property, while there is ample attic space that could be easily converted. The property is set at the edge of a village between Dole and Besancon, with pretty views, and has nine bedrooms, three bathrooms and three hectares of land.

€1,100,000 CODE SIF

WATERFRONT HOME

This château was built in 1830 on the remains of a medieval chateau destroyed in the Revolution. Situated at the edge of a village in a dominant position with a wonderful views, the property has a living area of about 1500 square metres and stands in grounds of about 3.8 hectares through which runs a large river. There are eight reception rooms, five bedrooms and two bathrooms and 9.39 acres of land.

€1,155,600 CODE SIF

DETACHED PROPERTY

This four-bedroom detached property comes with around 0.39 acres of land and is situated Lons-Le-Saunier in the Jura. Fully habitable the property comprises of a spacious lounge, kitchen with all mod cons, two bathrooms and a private garage. Located in a verdant region, there is plenty for the outdoor enthusiast to do and this is perfect for this who love the countryside. All amenities to hand.

€271,200 CODE FPS

FARMHOUSE WITH GÎTE

With seven-bedrooms and two bathrooms this farmhouse is located near Baccarat and comes with a separate gîte and 8.6 acres of land. Inside there is a spacious living Room and modern kitchen while on the first floor there is a workshop of 60 square metres and plenty of storage space. The gîte offers one bedroom and has a separate entrance and the whole property enjoys views over the valley.

€498,750 CODE FPS

MODERN STONE FARMHOUSE

Offering 110 square metres of living space and with an attic to convert, this modern house requires some work to render it fully habitable. Situated in Lons-le-Saunier in the Franche-Comté, the kitchen has been recently renovated, there is a large living room of 57 square metres complete with a woodburning stove and new tiles and insulation has been installed. With grouns totalling nearly one and a quarter acres.

€171,200 CODE FPS

AVERAGE HOUSE PRICES ALSACE-LORRAINE & FRANCHE-COMTÉ

	2-bed	3-bed	4-bed	5-bed
Strasbourg	€407,596 (£275,403)	€309,772 (£209,306)	€445,158 (£300,783)	€603,665 (£407,882)
Metz & Nancy	€232,315 (£156,970)	€280,378 (£189,445)	€299,794 (£202,564)	€412,835 (£278,943)
The Vosges	€196,623 (£132,854)	€206,764 (£139,706)	€249,665 (£168,693)	€262,608 (£177,438)
Besancon	€190,113 (£128,455)	€251,497 (£169,931)	€273,094 (£184,523)	€328,340 (£221,852)
Lons-le-Saunier	€141,448 (£95,573)	€214,114 (£144,672)	€272,274 (£183,969)	€335,153 (£226,455)

PROPERTY GUIDE

The Loire

France's grandest river and most stunning châteaux

COMITÉ RÉGIONAL DU TOURISME ET DES LOISIRS

FACT BOX

- ■ **POPULATION** 5,662,390
- ■ **UNEMPLOYMENT RATE** 9%
- ■ **AVERAGE 4-BED HOUSE PRICE** €312,000
- ■ **REGIONAL CAPITAL** Pays-de-la-Loire: Nantes; Centre: Orléans
- ■ **REGION SIZE** 71,232km²

Contents

Area profile

The Loire is France's longest river, along whose banks sit magnificent châteaux and stunning rolling countryside

PROFILE

GETTING THERE

AIR AirFrance (0845 084 5111; www. airfrance.co.uk), Flybe (0871 700 0535; www.flybe.com) and **GB Airways** (0870 551 1155; www.gbairways.com) all fly to Nantes from Gatwick. **Ryanair** (0871 246 0000; www.ryanair.com) flies to Tours, La Rochelle and Poitiers from Stansted. **British Airways** (0870 850 9850; www.britishairways.co.uk) flies to Nantes from Heathrow.

ROAD Take the A26 from Calais and continue on to the A16-E40 and then the A16 and A26. From there follow the A16-E402 to Rouen, taking the A28 on to the A28-E402 at junction 23. From Le Havre the A13-E46 runs down to Rennes, and the N137 or the A81-E50 continues on into the Pays de la Loire. From Paris the A10-E6 runs into the centre and continues on to the south of the region, and the A11-E50 then runs on into Pays-de-la-Loire.

RAIL Rail Europe (0870 584 8848; www.raileurope.co.uk) operates TGV services to Le Mans, Angers, Nantes, Poitiers, La Rochelle and Angoulême from Paris Gare Montparnasse.

THE LOIRE IS FRANCE'S LONGEST RIVER AND it cuts through two of the country's most beautiful regions: Centre and Pays-de-la-Loire. Both are rich in history and between them they boast fertile farmland, stunning medieval and Renaissance châteaux, and the magnificent Loire river itself. Tourists flock to the region's medieval châteaux and plentiful vineyards, and UNESCO has designated the long stretch between Sully-sur-Loire and Chalonnes a protected World Heritage Site.

The Loire boasts contrasting landscapes. The west is characterised by extensive flat plains, marshlands with sandy beaches – the nine kilometres of white sands at La Baule are among the best in Europe – and a rocky wild coast at Le Croisic. The islands of Yeu, with its white houses with blue shutters reminiscent of the Cyclades, and Noirmoutier, accessible at low tide by a pedestrian causeway, lie off the coast at Beauvoir. Inland are rolling hills and hedgerows – like Normandy – and the Loire valley is rich in woodland and corn and sunflower fields. This is a region of rivers and there are some 400 kilometres of navigable waterways.

Orléans, capital of the Centre region, is famous for its association with Joan of Arc who liberated it in 1429. Much of the centre's historic Roman architecture remains intact and there are some excellent museums here and a Gothic cathedral. Further southwest is Tours, a large, cosmopolitan university city with wide, attractive avenues and boulevards lined with busy cafés.

Pays-de-la-Loire is where the National Equestrian School is located, at Saumur, and the beautiful

surroundings provide great horseriding country. Saumur is also famous for its huge caves where wine is stored and mushrooms are grown (almost 70 per cent of France's button mushrooms are produced here). Northwest of Saumur is Angers, a Roman city that sits above the Maine river. Its majestic 13th-century château houses the historic L'Apocalypse, a tapestry that illustrates the last book in the Bible.

Along the region's coastline there are picturesque fishing ports, small seaside resorts and sloping sandy beaches. Les Sables-d'Olonne is a cheerful port with a large fish market that supplies the town's wealth of seafood restaurants. Pays-de-la-Loire's capital is Nantes, a large and lively university city with splendid botanical gardens. It too has its own grand Gothic cathedral.

Legacy of the Middle Ages

In common with much of central France, the Loire reached prosperity in the Middle Ages when many of the finest buildings were constructed. Gothic architecture prevails and the best examples include St-Étienne cathedral at Bourges, one of the country's largest churches and a stunning example of the High Gothic style, and the Notre-Dame cathedral at Chartres, one of Christianity's main shrines with its mismatched towers and magnificent stained-glass windows. The Loire was home to the Plantagenets whose kingdom included Scotland and the Pyrenees, and Henry II of England, father of Richard the Lionheart and King John, who held his court at Angers.

Many of the region's hundreds of châteaux were built during this time, although most were expanded

CLIMATE

	THE LOIRE	LONDON		THE LOIRE	LONDON
Dec	8	7	Dec	64	81
Nov	12	10	Nov	62	78
Oct	17	14	Oct	60	70
Sep	22	19	Sep	58	65
Aug	24	21	Aug	60	62
Jul	25	22	Jul	52	59
Jun	23	20	Jun	52	58
May	16	17	May	60	57
Apr	17	13	Apr	42	56
Mar	11	10	Mar	44	64
Feb	8	7	Feb	56	72
Jan	9	6	Jan	60	77

AVERAGE TEMPERATURE (Celsius)

AVERAGE RAINFALL (millimetres)

FOOD AND DRINK

Pork, fowl, game, and seafood form the basis of a wide range of delectable dishes from the Loire. Freshwater fish is often served with beurre blanc, a melted butter sauce flavoured with shallots and wine vinegar. Sold in charcuteries throughout Touraine, rillons de Tours are crispy hunks of pork. A favourite dish from Berry is poulet en barbouille, chicken braised with carrots and onions in brandy and wine. Fresh produce is plentiful, especially asparagus. Tasty desserts include tarte tatin (a caramelized apple tart), crémets d'Anjou (whipped cream and egg whites), and clafoutis (batter pudding with cherries). Fine goat's cheeses include Crottins de Chavignol and Valençay.

Chilled Rosé d'Anjou or Rosé de Touraine is a popular afternoon tipple, and excellent sparkling wines include Vouvray Pétillant, Saumur Mousseux and Crémant de Loire. Other local drinks include bernache, this year's grape juice as it starts to ferment, and fruit brandies.

MAISON DE LA FRANCE

ALL PHOTOS MAISON DE LA FRANCE

ATTRACTIONS

- ■ The city of Nantes
- ■ The old quarter at Le Mans
- ■ The Côte Sauvage at Le Croisic
- ■ Azay-le-Rideau château, and its son et lumière
- ■ A river cruise down the Loire
- ■ The Apocalypse tapestries in Angers château
- ■ The shell-covered doorways in L'Île Penotte, the old quarter in Les Sables-d'Olonne
- ■ Chambord château
- ■ Saumur's champagne cellars
- ■ Chartres cathedral and old quarter

and embellished during the Renaissance when local and foreign artists vied with each other for the nobility's patronage. Many châteaux have beautiful formal gardens, a hallmark of this period, and most are set in woodland to allow easy access to hunting grounds. The Loire's best known châteaux can be found at Amboise, where the fortress perches on a cliff top over the river; Angers – one of the oldest châteaux; Azay-le-Rideau, almost totally surrounded by the river Indre and considered to be the most beautiful; Chambord, the largest and most spectacular, boasting no fewer than 440 rooms and a unique double staircase reputedly designed by Leonardo da Vinci; and Chenonceau, perhaps the most exquisite.

The economy

A landscape of forests, small towns and villages

dotted along the Loire's river particularly lends itself to gîte tourism. However, the celebrated wine industry – with wines ranging from Sancerre and Pouilly Fumé in the east of the region to Muscadet in the area around Nantes – together with agricultural production still offers a stable support to the region's economy. Industry and commerce in the major cities of Le Mans and Nantes are strong supporters of the economy.

Social groups

Parcay-les-Pins stands out because of its almost 40 per cent British home ownership. However, the rest of the region is generally made up of the French. ●

PROFILE

Property hotspots

MAP KEY

- **5** Hotspot
- Major town/city
- ✈ Airport
- ⛴ Ferry

VENDÉE COAST

1 The Vendée combines coastal areas, grasslands and lush bocage countryside. With near-white sand stretching for 250 kilometres, safe bathing and gently sloping beaches, the Vendée coast is an ideal location for families.

Les Sables-d'Olonne is a fishing port where cheerfully painted villas lead on to a long bistro-lined promenade. Famous for its quayside fish market, this popular resort also has a large indoor food market, designer boutiques and exclusive eateries. Inland, La Roche-sur-Yon, once an isolated village, has become the principal town in the Vendée, and locals are proud of their theatre and the National Stud. The town is flanked by countryside and the Yon river provides a natural north/south divide between La Roche-sur-Yon and Pays Yonnais.

This is a popular, easily accessible area with a healthy rentals and property market. A modern four-bedroom villa in Les Sables-d'Olonne starts at €295,000, while a two-bedroom house in La Roche costs from around €150,000. There are plenty of tourists to generate rental income in Les Sables-d'Olonne and with good long-term rental potential in La Roche-sur-Yon, the Vendée coast is an excellent investment. Average rents are €614 per week for a two-bedroom property.

Key facts
- **POPULATION** 68,992
- **TAXES** Taxe d'habitation 8.19%, taxe foncière 16.76%

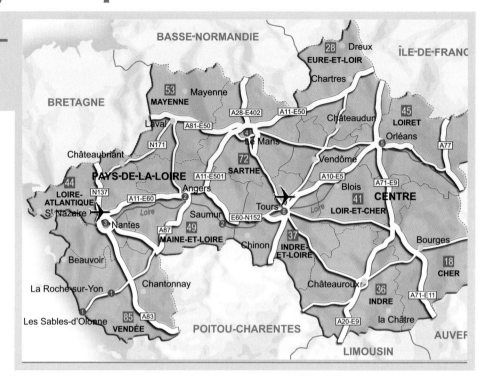

AIRPORT Nantes-Atlantique Airport, 44346 Bouguenais Cedex, Tel: +33 2 40 84 95 33
SCHOOLS Cité Scolaire Internationale Grand Air, Lycée et Collège de Grand Air, 77 avenue du Bois d'Amour, 44500 La Baule Escoublac, Nantes, Tel: +33 2 40 11 58 00
MEDICAL Centre Hospitalier Côte-de-Lumière, 75 avenue d'Aquitaine, 85119 Les Sables-d'Olonne, Tel: +332 51 21 85 85
PROS Easily accessible, the Vendée is well served by the N160 and nearby TGV links ■ Popular with permanent relocators ■ Plenty of activities to be enjoyed ■ Good weather
CONS A predominantly French-speaking area n Summer crowds.

SAUMUR & ANGERS

2 Saumur is an historic wine-making city built into the chalky white tufa stone so characteristic of the Loire valley. Its stunning clifftop château houses magnificent decorative arts and horse museums. Horse lovers should try to catch a display by the Cadre Noir at the National Horse and Riding School.

Angers, further west, occupies a site above the Maine river. During Roman times it served as a crossroads for routes from Rennes, Nantes and Tours. Today it is known for its castle and Gothic architecture, and for flowers, wines, liqueurs and umbrella production.

Saumur and Angers are major tourism centres, with great potential for those buying to let. Properties are cheaper than in neighbouring Brittany and hugely attractive to buyers and investors who now spill over into the Loire region – the cheapest properties start at around €110,000 for a farmhouse needing renovation.

Angers has a buoyant property market, with excellent transport links drawing people to the area. Prices range from €131,000 for a two-bedroom property to €370,000 for five bedrooms.

This is a good area for investment, with huge demand for rentals. There is more long-term than short-term demand in Angers. The average price for a two-bedroom property is €534 per week.

Key facts
- **POPULATION** Saumur 31,443, Angers 151,279
- **TAXES** Taxe d'habitation 6.08%, taxe foncière 9.35%
- **AIRPORT** Nantes-Atlantique Airport, 44346 Bouguenais Cedex, Tel: +33 2 40 84 95 33
- **SCHOOLS** Cité Scolaire Internationale Grand Air, Lycée et Collège de Grand Air, 77 Avenue du Bois d'Amour, 44500 La Baule Escoublac, Nantes, Tel: +33 2 40 11 58 00
- **MEDICAL** Centre Hospitalier de Saumur, route de Fontevraud, 49400 Saumur, Tel: +33 2 41 53 30 30, www. ch-saumur.fr
- **PROS** Good weather and attractive surroundings ■ Angers is extremely cosmopolitan, with a large foreign population and a strong British community ■ Excellent transport links
- **CONS** Unreliable market prone to

oscillating prices n With little commercial industry, Angers relies on agriculture ■ Huge competition in the rental market.

NANTES

3 Nantes lies in northwest France at the intersection of the Loire, Erdre, and Sèvre rivers. It is officially part of the Loire region, yet many of the residents of this former capital of Brittany regard themselves as Brétons. The Château des Ducs de Bretagne, with its striking 14th-century tapestry, occupies a central place in the city.

Although France's seventh biggest city is geared towards innovation, encapsulated by resident Jules Verne in his novels, the Old Town features many historical gems. Its fine cathedral, half-timbered mansions and Musée des Beaux-Arts are well worth a look. Pleasure steamers regularly leave from the quays to explore the Muscadet vineyards.

A relatively new property hotspot, Nantes is both a technological and research centre. The market is dominated by local buyers rather than second-home buyers and investors. Non-locals tend to settle in the surrounding countryside. Although prices have risen steadily in the region, property remains affordable and a two-bedroom house will cost around €248,000.

There is a good long-term rentals market. A two-bedroom property in Nantes averages €554 per week.

Key facts
■ **POPULATION** 150,605
■ **TAXES** Taxe d'habitation 6.50%, taxe foncière 6.24%
■ **AIRPORT** Nantes-Atlantique Airport, 44346 Bouguenais Cedex, Tel: +33 2 40 84 95 33
■ **SCHOOLS** Contact Rectorat de l'Académie de Nantes, 4 rue de la Houssinière, BP 72616, 44326 Nantes, Tel: +33 2 40 37 37 37 for advice
■ **MEDICAL** Hôpitaux dy CHU de

Nantes, 1 place Alexis Ricordeau, 44000 Nantes, Tel: +33 2 40 08 33 33
■ **PROS** Excellent business and employment prospects ■ Cosmopolitan city popular with relocators ■ Excellent transport links, with cheap flights from the UK ■ Attractive old town
■ **CONS** Some ugly and modern architecture ■ Not a major tourist destination so the buy-to-let market is limited ■ The commuter belt including Sautron, Clisson, Haute Goulaine and Baine Goulaine is popular but pricy.

LE MANS

4 Le Mans, synonymous with motor racing, has a beautiful old quarter with medieval cobbled streets and half-timbered houses. Cyrano de Bergerac with Gérard Depardieu was filmed in the shadow of the glorious Cathédrale St-Julien. The car museum – part of the 24-hour race circuit complex – is well worth a visit.

The property market here is buoyant due to the influx of Parisian buyers. The city is very industrialised and consequently not a popular location for foreign buyers. A four-bedroom house will cost around €280,000.

Key facts
■ **POPULATION** 150, 605
■ **TAXES** Taxe d'habitation 7.64%, taxe foncière 10.74%
■ **AIRPORT** Aéroport Tours Val de Loire, 40 rue de l'Aéroport, 37100 Tours, Tel: +33 2 47 49 37 00
■ **SCHOOLS** Contact the Rectorat de l'Académie d'Orléans-Tours, 21 rue Saint Étienne, 45043 Orléans Cedex 1, Tel: +33 2 38 79 38 79
■ **MEDICAL** Centre Hospitalier Régional du Mans, 194 avenue Rublillard, 72000 Le Mans, Tel: +33 2 43 43 43 43
■ **PROS** Perfect for commuting to Paris ■ One of the cheapest areas in the Loire
■ **CONS** Le Mans is very industrial and not traditionally popular with relocators to the Loire or for holiday rentals ■ The city has limited tourist appeal n People tend to buy on the outskirts or in the surrounding countryside.

ORLÉANS

5 Orléans, capital of the Centre region, is famous for Joan of Arc who liberated the city in 1429; each year on 8 May the city expresses its gratitude to the Maid of Orléans with parades and displays of medieval pageantry. Although many of the old buildings of the city were destroyed during the Second World War, huge reconstruction efforts have been made since then to recover the city's former splendour. Highlights include Cathédrale Ste-Croix, Musée des Beaux-Arts, Natural Science Museum, and Maison de Jeanne d'Arc.

A two-bedroom property will set you back around €220,000, a four-bedroom property more like €290,000. Orléans draws many tourists and is within commuting distance of Paris, so there's a healthy rentals market.

Key facts
■ **POPULATION** 150,605
■ **TAXES** Taxe d'habitation 5.26%, taxe foncière 8.28%
■ **AIRPORT** Aéroport Tours Val de Loire, 40 rue de l'Aéroport, 37100 Tours, Tel: +33 2 47 49 37 00
■ **SCHOOLS** Contact the Rectorat de l'Académie d'Orléans-Tours, 21 rue St-Étienne, 45043 Orléans Cedex 1, Tel: +33 2 38 79 38 79
■ **MEDICAL** Centre Hospitalier Régional d'Orléans, 1 rue Porte Madeleine, BP 2439, 45032 Orléans Cedex 1, Tel: +33 2 85 14 44 4
■ **PROS** Easy access to Paris, so commuting is easy ■ Pleasant Loire microclimate ■ Plenty of historic tourist attractions ■ Many employment and educational opportunities
■ **CONS** Concerns over the inconsistent nature of the rental market.

TOURS & THE TOURAINE

6 Tours was the capital of France under the reign of Louis XI. Today it acts as a gateway to Touraine, with its

remarkable châteaux and the Loire vineyards – it's known as the 'garden of France' for its fruit, flowers and red wines.

Elegant Tours Old Town abounds with Renaissance and neoclassical architecture. Nearby is the exquisite Château de Chenonceau, also known as the 'ladies' castle' because its history was shaped by so many women, including Catherine de Medici.

The property market is becoming increasingly healthy in this popular area of the Loire. There are many châteaux for sale, and property at the high end of the market can be more expensive than in other parts of the Loire – much of the demand is from the local French market.

With the increase in budget flights to this delightful area, international interest is also increasing, and you can still pick up cheaper homes at the low end of the market. A two-bedroom property will cost you around €181,000; three bedrooms upwards of €254,000.

Key facts
■ **POPULATION** 132,820
■ **TAXES** Taxe d'habitation 6.32%, taxe foncière 7.92%
■ **AIRPORT** Aéroport Tours Val de Loire, 40 rue de l'Aéroport, 37100 Tours, Tel: +33 2 47 49 37 00
■ **SCHOOLS** Contact the Rectorat de l'Académie d'Orléans-Tours, 21 rue St-Étienne, 45043 Orléans Cedex 1, Tel: +33 2 38 79 38 79
■ **MEDICAL** Hôpital Bretonneau, 2 boulevard Tonnellé, 37044 Tours, Cedex 9, Tel: +33 2 47 47 47 47 www.chu-tours.fr
■ **PROS** Probably the most popular tourist area in the Loire, with UNESCO World Heritage status ■ A large university population and thriving café culture ■ Excellent transport links ■ A growing foreign (particularly British) community in Chinon and Loches
■ **CONS** Azay-le-Rideau and Langeais, in the Touraine, have few foreign buyers ■ Some French is essential ■ The Touraine is fairly quiet, which might not suit everyone. ●

HOTSPOTS

Property guide

The Loire, made up of the Pays-de-la-Loire and Centre regions, is a favourite destination of second-home owners avoiding the saturated market of Brittany

A pigeonnier in the Sarthe département of the Loire

TYPICAL PROPERTIES

- Small medieval chateaux in varying states of repair can still be bought
- Building materials and construction types vary considerably. Northern properties tend to have granite or schist, or even half-timbered (colombage) facades, and slate roofs. Grey stone tends to give way to cream-coloured limestone or tufa (tuffeau), while slates are replaced by terracotta roofs towards the South
- A typical rural property is the longère – a long low building, sometimes thatched, incorporating a former stable
- Typical of the Vendée are single-storey houses with terracotta roofs and pretty blue wooden shutters, set amongst pine trees
- Modern apartments are popular both in seaside resorts and towns
- Leaseback of new properties is a growing market. Approached with caution, this can be a good investment in desirable locations

CONSIDERABLE PRICE VARIATIONS IN THE region reflect its size and diversity. The Vendée, to the south, is very popular with second-home buyers and those planning to retire to the area. Here, property tends to be more modern and more expensive towards the coast. Further north, on the Loire–Atlantique coast, the chic resort of La Baule has seen a huge demand for properties with sea views, although two-bedroom apartments can be found for around €150,000.

Inland, a recent influx of Parisians has pushed prices up in urban centres such as Nantes (ranked the most attractive city in France), Angers and Tours and the neighbouring countryside. In Orléans, in the Centre region, a city-centre maison bourgeoise valued at €300,000 reflects the popularity of cities within reach of Paris. In spite of this, with property currently averaging €120,000 overall, the Centre region prices rank only seventh in France. This makes rural properties here a particularly good investment, especially with the current rise in the market due to a trend of the French towards relocating to the countryside. And when, as predicted, demand stabilises due to French buyers reaching their borrowing limit, its popularity as a holiday destination should keep things buoyant.

With an appreciation of 12.99 per cent from 2005 to 2006, properties in the Pays-de-la-Loire averaged €135,610 during the first half of 2005. In the Vendée, a house similar to the one valued at €300,000 in Orléans, but with an additional house to renovate, has a price tag of €214,800 - higher than the area average. Here again, rural properties represent the best value.

Short-term rentals remain dynamic, generally increasing towards the coast. The seasonal weekly rent for a small apartment in La Baule is €900. Inland, rural cottages or gîtes can still command a good seasonal income. Of two similar two-bedroom cottages in the Touraine, the one with a pool commands high-season weekly rents of E900, nearly double its near neighbour's. A gîte sleeping seven in the Vendée, with pool, makes €1,100 in peak season; larger gîtes rent out at €1,500 or more.

A recent flood of rental properties released by local first-time buyers has dampened demand in the long-term rentals market, although there is still a shortage of medium to large rural properties for rent, increasing their investment value. Meanwhile, year-round investment returns of well over E1,000 per week explain the high demand for properties in exclusive La Baule. ●

WHAT CAN YOU GET FOR YOUR MONEY?

SUPERB CHÂTEAU

With 35 hectares of land, nine bedrooms, four bathrooms and five reception rooms, this 19th century château is truly unique. Offering bags of charm this property offers many original features and is situated between Angers and Saumur, to the east of Anjou. Arranged over three floors and with 500 square metres of living space the property is in perfect condition and comes with a pool.

€1,292,880 CODE SIF

PETIT CHÂTEAU

This charming petit Château dates from the 18th century and is situated in attractive wooded grounds of approximately five hectares. only 20 kms to the east of Orleans, the property is well situated for the Autoroute and is only 120 kms from Paris. An 18 hole golf course is within five minutes drive of the property which has an enclosed swimming pool, games room and nine bedrooms.

€602,000 CODE SIF

CHÂTEAU WITH LAKES

Only 30 minutes from Nantes and located in the northeast of the Loire Atlantique, this 19th century chateau offers two lakes, various outbuildings and more than 44 acres of land. The property itself has 900 square metres of living space and has a staggering 20 bedrooms, ten bathrooms and seven reception rooms. Perfect as a small business or hotel, the grounds also offer stables, garages and barns.

€1,608,000 CODE SIF

UNIQUE MANOR HOUSE

Situated near Segre, this is a very rare manor house dating back to the 15th century and in excellent condition throughout. Set on approximately five acres of land, complete with access to the river and private boat dock, this is an exceptional family house with room for further development. The property comes with four bedrooms and many unique features such as a bread oven.

€620,000 CODE FRA

RENOVATED LONGÈRE

This village property is located in Vienne, between Monts-sur-Guesnes and Richelieu. The renovated longère has three bedrooms, a traditional finish with a fireplace, hexagonal floor tiles and exposed beams, while outside there are outbuildings and a large garden. Set in 1,700 square metres of grounds complete with a well, this is the ideal location for a family home, being close to Poitiers.

€294,250 CODE FRA

DELIGHTFUL LONGÈRE

Situated only ten minutes from Chateaubriant this three-bedroom longere is set on land of 3,000m². There are many original feature within the property, such as the wood-burning fireplace, but there are also a number of modern touches such as the patio and built in wardrobes. The first floor offers a balcony and small sun room and it is here that you'll find the master bedroom.

€282,000 CODE FRA

PROPERTY GUIDE

AVERAGE HOUSE PRICES THE LOIRE

	2-bed		3-bed		4-bed		5-bed	
Vendée Coast	€149,961	(£101,325)	€257,937	(£174,282)	€295,308	(£199,533)	€410,028	(£277,046)
Saumur & Angers	€193,453	(£130,712)	€278,555	(£188,213)	€296,467	(£200,316)	€369,521	(£249,677)
Nantes	€247,752	(£167,400)	€286,304	(£193,449)	€371,588	(£251,073)	€568,574	(£384,172)
Le Mans	€183,135	(£123,740)	€207,001	(£139,866)	€279,768	(£189,033)	€351,729	(£237,655)
Orléans	€218,760	(£147,811)	€230,766	(£155,923)	€289,273	(£195,455)	€436,018	(£294,607)
Tours	€180,759	(£122,135)	€254,373	(£171,874)	€338,214	(£228,523)	€446,140	(£301,446)

Burgundy

Vineyards, world-renowned wine and culture

MAISON DE LA FRANCE

FACT BOX

- **POPULATION** 1,610,067
- **UNEMPLOYMENT RATE** 8.9%
- **AVERAGE 4-BED HOUSE PRICE** €227,000
- **REGIONAL CAPITAL** Dijon
- **REGION SIZE** 31,592km²

Contents

Area profile

Burgundy is wine country and is the perfect destination for pleasure-seekers, food fans and those who love the outdoors

PROFILE

GETTING THERE

AIR Air France (0845 0845 111; www.airfrance.co.uk) flies to Lyon from Heathrow. **British Airways** (0870 240 0747; www.britishairways.co.uk) and **Flybe** (01392 366 669; www.flybe.com) fly to Lyon from Heathrow. **easyJet** (0870 600 0000; www.easyjet.com) flies to Lyon from Stansted. **Ryanair** (0871 246 0000; www.ryanair.com) flies to St Étienne from Stansted.

ROAD From Calais the A26 leads you down to Reims and on to Troyes, from where the A5 takes you into Burgundy. The A6 from Paris will take you straight to the heart of Burgundy, passing through Sens, Auxerre, Beaune, and finally Mâcon. The A43 also runs south from Lyon through Burgundy and on into the Rhône-Alpes.

COACH Eurolines (0870 514 3219; www.eurolines.com) operates coach services to Chalon-sur-Saône, Dijon and Mâcon.

RAIL From Paris there is a direct TGV link to Dijon. Contact **Rail Europe** (0870 584 8848; www.raileurope.co.uk) for details.

LYING AT THE HEART OF FRANCE, BURGUNDY (Bourgogne in French) is a peaceful region renowned for its historic architecture, abundance of Michelin-starred restaurants and the production of fine wines, primarily in the Côte d'Or ('Hills of Gold'), where most of the esteemed Burgundy vineyards are found, the best ones occupying the south-facing chalky hillsides.

Burgundy is quite a long way from the coast and its climate tends to attract those after a cooler, less Mediterranean feel, although summers can be hot and showery. Autumn, when the grapes are harvested, is the most pleasant time of year, when warm, sunny days show off the beautiful landscape to the full. This is especially so in the rural La Puisaye area where there are gentle, rolling hills and long, tree-lined waterways – perfect for cyclists or walkers.

Wealth, wine and power

The riches of Burgundy date back to the Middle Ages, when the Dukes of Burgundy ruled over an empire that stretched through northeast France and up into Flanders, and included lands in Spain and Portugal. Dijon, capital of Burgundy and of Côte d'Or département, boasts impressive townhouses, elaborate churches and the grand Palais des Ducs. Home of the famous mustard, Dijon has an exclusive air, although it's a friendly, sociable place.

Nearby Beaune's main attraction is the 15th-century hospice, Hôtel-Dieu, a stunning example of Burgundian architecture, with multicoloured,

Burgundy is renowned for its architecture

patterned roof tiles and carved wooden balconies. Each year since 1885, on the third Sunday in November, the Hospices de Beaune charitable wine auction has been held in its grounds, the region's 45 vineyards auctioning their new wines before a select audience to raise money to support the hospital. The ceremony is lavish and shows off the finest Burgundy food and wine, while the amount paid for each wine is used as an indication of the quality.

Other examples of medieval richesse can be found in the Gothic cathedral of Auxerre on the Yonne river, the outstanding Château d'Ancy-le-Franc, the Renaissance Palais Ducal in Nevers and the convent in Mâcon, which now houses a collection of Renaissance French and Flemish paintings. The area has much older roots though, as evidenced by the 10th-century abbey in Cluny, and the Roman remains at Autun.

CLIMATE

BURGUNDY		LONDON		BURGUNDY		LONDON	
11	Dec	7		62	Dec	81
15.4	Nov	10		64	Nov	78
19.7	Oct	14		58	Oct	70
24.2	Sep	19		67	Sep	65
25.7	Aug	21		65	Aug	62
27.2	Jul	22		51	Jul	59
23.7	Jun	20		62	Jun	58
18	May	17		86	May	57
19.5	Apr	13		52	Apr	56
12.2	Mar	10		53	Mar	64
9.4	Feb	7		53	Feb	72
10	Jan	6		59	Jan	77

AVERAGE TEMPERATURE (Celsius)

AVERAGE RAINFALL (millimetres)

FOOD AND DRINK

Burgundy is a gastronome's delight and it is here that you will find some of France's best food and wine. The region's signature dish is the classic boeuf Bourguignon stew, followed closely by coq au vin (chicken in red wine). Burgundy boasts the largest, most flavoursome snails (escargot) in France and the exquisite Chaource and Époisses cheeses. The world-famous Dijon mustard adds piquancy to many local dishes. Morvan is known for its ham, pork and kidney dishes. Other regional favourites are oeufs en meurette (eggs poached in red wine with bacon, onions and mushrooms) and jambon persillé (ham and parsley in a meat-wine gelatin). Speciality foods include boar, mushrooms, crayfish and quail. The region produces some of France's finest wines, most notably great red and white Burgundies made from the Pinot Noir (red) grape and the Chardonnay (white) grape. Chablis, one of France's most sophisticated whites, is probably the best-known of the Chardonnay wines.

MAISON DE LA FRANCE

Burgundy's snails are considered France's finest

ATTRACTIONS

■ Head for the remarkable Roman remains at Autun

■ Drink a glass of chilled Chablis in the town where it is produced

■ In Dijon, seek out the patterned tiled roofs, sip a kir (an aperitif made with white wine and locally produced cassis, a blackcurrant liqueur) and take home some mustard

■ Join the Burgundy wine trail by following the Saône south from Dijon, taking in Côte de Nuits, Côte de Beaune and Mâcon vineyards

■ Don't miss the Hôtel-Dieu in Beaune, a stunning 15th-century hospice

■ Join the swimmers, kayakers and rowers on the river Saône, or take one of the many luxury barge cruises on offer

■ Visit the hilltop town of Vézelay with its 12th-century basilica and narrow cobbled streets

■ Don't leave Burgundy without tasting its most famous dish, boeuf Bourgignon

■ Visit an Époisses producer and see how this local cheese is washed in Burgundy wine during the five to eight weeks that it is matured

The Economy

Burgundy's main income derives from the region's expanses of vineyards – directly and indirectly. Although Burgundy does manufacture a range of industrial products, industry accounts for only a quarter of the working population and this remains an ultimately rural region, with much of the land given over to arable farming in the absence of vineyards. The region's vineyards, cultural heritage and gastronomic delights also generate a healthy income from tourism, which is on the up, especially in the cities of Dijon and Beaune. Thanks to low-cost flights into the region, these are becoming popular city break destinations for British visitors, as well as Italians, Swiss, Germans and Dutch.

Social groups

Due to its relative isolation, Burgundy has never been a favoured area for the foreign property market, which is surprising given the high standard of living the area offers. The property market increased by approximately 12 to 17 per cent in 2005, partly through British interest, but also due to Dutch and Belgian buyers.

There aren't that many British inhabitants here, given that most British buyers seek a Mediterranean climate and prefer to be nearer the coast. Those drawn to Burgundy tend to be motivated as much by its culture, history, cuisine and wine as for its affordable property. This being the case, the area tends to be frequented more by couples seeking a sophisticated and peaceful retirement.

Property hotspots

MAP KEY

5 Hotspot
○ Major town/city
✈ Airport
⛴ Ferry

HOTSPOTS

CÔTE D'OR

1 Côte d'Or is Burgundy's most famous winemaking region, and consequently experiences a huge tourist interest. Its capital, Beaune, is well located for exploring the vineyards. A tourist draw in its own right, the old quarter is graced with a picturesque central square and the Hospices de Beaune, first created after the Hundred Years' War. In a region associated with the traditional boeuf Bourguignon, which has long been famous outside Burgundy, Charolais beef and top-quality goat's cheese, there are many dishes prepared en meurette, in a red wine and bacon sauce. Beaune also has the finest French restaurants, such as Ma Cuisine, a bistro with a 12-page wine list.

The best-known villages in the area include Meursault, Puligny-Montrachet and hillside hamlet Chassagne-Montrachet. The sleepy village of Meursault, with its medieval church and Romanesque houses, is home to Château Meursault, one of Burgundy's top wines.

The Côte d'Or is one of the most expensive and popular locations in which to buy in the region and consequently prices in and around Beaune are above the national average. Most buyers are French locals with the occasional foreign buyer. However, the region is experiencing greater foreign interest and prices have risen appreciably in the towns.

This area is popular with the foreign market, and guarantees rental income. Côte d'Or offers at least a seven-month

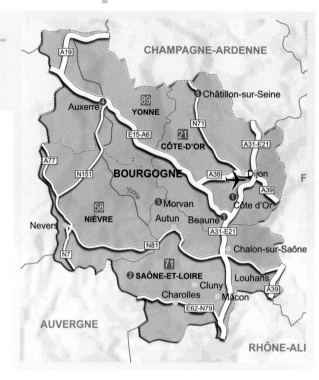

rental season, as September and November are months jam-packed with various wine festivals and auctions. A two-bedroom property can earn an average of €678 per week, while a three-bedroom property earns €922.

Key facts
■ **POPULATION** 506,755 (Beaune 21,923)
■ **TAXES** Taxe d'habitation 19.46%, taxe foncière 34.81%
■ **AIRPORT** Dijon-Bourgogne Aéroport, 21601 Longvic Cedex, Tel: +33 3 80 67 67 67
■ **SCHOOLS** Contact the Rectorat de Dijon, 51 rue Monge, 21033 Dijon, Tel: +33 3 80 44 80 00
■ **MEDICAL** Medical Centre Hospitalier Philippe le Bon, avenue Guigone de Salins, 21200 Beaune, Tel: +33 3 80 24 44 44
■ **PROS** Ideal region for those seeking an authentic French environment ■ Côte d'Or is the commercial and cultural epicentre of Burgundy
■ **CONS** Far from the coast, this is not a family area n Property is limited

and difficult to get hold of ■ Market is controlled by the wealthy Parisian second-home buyer.

SAÔNE-ET-LOIRE (CLUNY AND MÂCON)

2 Not hugely popular with foreign buyers, and boasting more cattle than people, Saône-et-Loire is extremely rural. There are, however, a number of traditional villages, sustained by the prosperous wine and tourist trade, amid the verdant hills of this historic region. As beautiful as it is though, do not think of buying in this region unless you know what you are letting yourself in for. Life here is very different to city living.

Mâcon is a vibrant tourist town situated on the banks of the river Saône, only one hour from Geneva. There is an influx of Austrian and German buyers keen to take advantage of the town's cheap property and

picturesque surroundings. Ideal for sporting and leisure holidays, this is also a perfect spot for those seeking to start a bed-and-breakfast business.

Cluny is another draw for the foreign buyer, with Cluny Abbey being the region's primary tourist destination. This highly attractive and traditional village is home to the elite higher education institution, the Grande École des Ingénieurs. The region is ideal for an investment property and tourist-based business. Predictions are that this is an area destined to blossom, and although prices are on the increase and you are looking at over €203,000 for a two-bedroom property, the region remains cheaper than many in France, but surprisingly is one of Burgundy's more expensive.

Burgundy does not offer the strongest of rentals markets, making this an unhealthy investment for those seeking to buy-to-let, at least in the short term. The season is short, and lets here are mostly short term holiday lets. A three-bedroom property can earn you €745 a week.

Key facts
■ **POPULATION** 543,700
■ **TAXES** Taxe d'habitation 21.50%, taxe foncière 35.71%
■ **AIRPORT** Dijon-Bourgogne Aéroport, 21601 Longvic Cedex, Tel: +33 3 80 67 67 67
■ **SCHOOLS** Contact the Rectorat de Dijon, 51 rue Monge, 21033 Dijon, Tel: +33 3 80 44 84 00
■ **MEDICAL** Centre Hospitalier les Chanaux, boulevard de l'hôpital, 71018 Mâcon Cedex, Tel: +33 3 85 20 30 40/77/69
■ **PROS** Lots of sporting and leisure activities to enjoy ■ The region is known throughout the world for its wines, with a number of vineyards offering tastings ■ An attractive region for those seeking the real culture and history of Burgundy
■ **CONS** Not much for children to do ■ This is primarily a rural area, not ideal for those seeking an active city lifestyle.

MORVAN REGIONAL PARK

3 True to its Celtic name 'Morvan', meaning black mountain, this regional park is bursting with spectacular scenery. Created in 1970 to protect its cultural and natural heritage, Morvan is one of France's least densely populated areas, but is within easy reach of many tourist destinations, such as the tiny, walled town of Vézelay with its Romanesque abbey, La Madeleine. For centuries the park served as a backdrop for ghostly folk tales and now many activities are focused around the forests, hills and lakes, including canoeing, mountain-biking and potholing.

To the northeast of the park lies Saulieu, an ancient market town which is well worth visiting for its 17th-century basilica with animal motifs, and the bible that once belonged to Emperor Charlemagne. Saulieu also has a reputation for fine dining, championed by the late, world-renowned chef, Bernard Loiseau, whose refined cuisine made the Côte d'Or into one of France's most prestigious restaurants. His signature dish – sautéed frogs' legs in puréed garlic and parsley – is still on the menu, and the restaurant is now run by Loiseau's protégé, Patrick Bertron.

Properties in the Morvan Regional Park are less expensive than in other areas of Burgundy owing to the park's distance from major wine areas and its seasonal nature. However, the area is experiencing price hikes, although it is still possible to buy a renovations project for €130,000. There are more foreigners than locals buying in the area, which pushes demand up. Expect to pay, on average, €187,000 for a three-bedroom property.

Morvan is a busy holiday area, especially during the peak rental season from April to September. The surroundings are pleasant and there are many outdoor activities to attract potenital renters. An average four-bedroom gite will range in price from €470 per week to €690 a week.

Key facts
- **POPULATION** 34,405 (Saulieu 2,835, Vézelay 507)
- **TAXES** Taxe d'habitation 23.51%, taxe foncière 39.76%
- **AIRPORT** Dijon-Bourgogne Aéroport, 21601 Longvic Cedex, Tel: +33 3 80 67 67 67
- **SCHOOLS** Contact the Rectorat de Dijon, 51 rue Monge, 21033 Dijon, Tel: +33 3 80 44 84 00
- **MEDICAL** Centre hospitalier de Saulieu, 2 rue Courtépée, 21210 Saulieu, Tel: +33 3 80 90 55 05
- **PROS** An affordable area in which to live, and an excellent area for a second home ■ This is a healthy investment area ■ Perfect for nature lovers seeking a rural retreat
- **CONS** During the winter season the area becomes rather isolated, with less of a community feel ■ This is not a recommended family area due to the lack of suitable activities and isolation.

AUXERRE

4 Situated to the southeast of Paris, Auxerre overlooks the Yonne river and was once the capital of Burgundy. This is the land of the Auxerrois wine routes, where Chablis, the first of the great Burgundy whites, is produced.

Auxerre is celebrated for its Gallo-Roman remains, while its red-brown roofs frame the Gothic spires of the Cathedral of St-Étienne. The Romanesque bell tower of the former abbey of St-Germain is another popular draw.

Property is significantly cheaper on the outskirts of Auxerre than it is in the centre, or in the expensive Côte d'Or wine region and the capital, Dijon. However, many Parisians own holiday homes here and in recent years this has encouraged price hikes, rendering it one of Burgundy's more expensive areas. Just 30 minutes from Auxerre, you can buy a fully habitable four-bedroom house from around €234,000 and a two-bedroom one from around €125,000.

Although the region is not known for its rentals market, there is potential for lettings.It can be difficult to secure seasonal rentals in Auxerre; the market is primarily geared to long-term local rentals.

Key facts
- **POPULATION** 37,600
- **TAXES** Taxe d'habitation 25.15%, taxe foncière 34.93%
- **AIRPORT** Dijon-Bourgogne Aéroport, 21601 Longvic Cedex, Tel: +33 3 80 67 67 67
- **SCHOOLS** Contact the Rectorat de l'Académie de Dijon, 51 rue Monge, BP 1516, 21033 Dijon Cedex, Tel: +33 3 80 44 84 00, Fax: +33 3 80 44 84 88
- **MEDICAL** Centre Hospitalier d'Auxerre, 2 boulevard de Verdun, 89011 Auxerre, Tel: +33 3 86 48 48 48, www.ch-auxerre.fr
- **PROS** The Yonne département is easily accessible from Paris
- **CONS** This is a cooler area than south Burgundy, with a much milder climate.

CHÂTILLON-SUR-SEINE

5 Located to the east of Auxerre, between Champagne and Burgundy, this picturesque town is positioned on a rocky outcrop overlooking the river Seine. As a newly discovered market, it offers excellent scope for foreign investors seeking an as yet untapped area.

Châtillon-sur-Seine is a quiet town, boasting an extremely attractive old quarter and a wealth of interesting architecture. It lacks the lush vegetation and rolling hills of southern Burgundy but has a number of interesting features. Among them is the 'Treasure of Rix', an exquisite hoard of pre-Roman archaeological finds, including 6th-century golden tiaras and a four-wheeled Roman chariot. The area also offers fishing and many other outdoor activites.

In terms of property prices, Burgundy remains one of France's cheapest regions, despite experiencing one of the highest percentage increases in recent years. Châtillon-sur-Seine is very affordable with prices roughly between 10 and 20 per cent cheaper than those in the rest of Burgundy.

A two-bedroom property currently costs an average of €140,000 but predictions state that within five years these properties will have appreciated dramatically. Currently, investment opportunities are ideal with it being possible to purchase a habitable three-bedroom home for an average of €172,000.

As the town is not a hugely popular tourist attraction, it may be difficult to generate much rental income. It is possible to rent a three-bedroom cottage from €215.

Key facts
- **POPULATION** 6,900
- **TAXES** Taxe d'habitation 19.26%, taxe foncière 33.97%
- **AIRPORT** Dijon-Bourgogne Aéroport, 21601 Longvic Cedex, Tel: +33 3 80 67 67 67
- **SCHOOLS** Contact the Rectorat de Dijon, 51 rue Monge, 21033 Dijon, Tel: +33 3 80 44 84 00
- **MEDICAL** Hôpital Général, 3 rue du Faubourg Raines, 21000 Dijon, Tel: +33 3 80 29 30 31
- **PROS** This is a relatively new hotspot so it a good time to invest ■ A quiet area, ideal for those seeking a peaceful rural retreat
- **CONS** There is little of interest in the area ■ The town and landscape have been described as austere. ●

HOTSPOTS

Property guide

Burgundy's future looks good, with investors attracted by the wealth of value-for-money properties available

JUSTIN POSTLETHWAITE

PROPERTY GUIDE

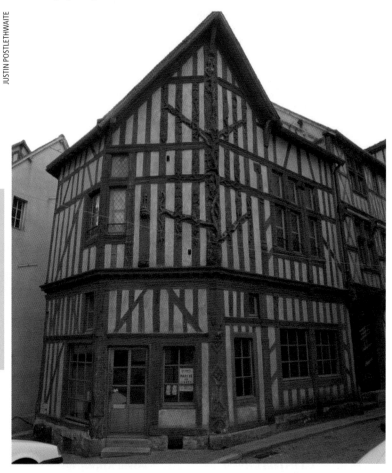

Half-timbered townhouse in Yonne

WINE-GROWER'S HOME (MAISON VIGNERONNE)

- ■ The maison vigneronne was typically built from local stone, but if this was scarce brick or daub on a timber structure was used instead
- ■ The main entrance to the house was via a gallery on the first floor or a raised ground floor called the galerie mâconnaise
- ■ The timbered houses were usually only one storey high although lofts are sometimes converted and dormer windows installed
- ■ A separate doorway on the ground level provides access to the cellar
- ■. The roof was typically covered in flat terracotta tiles and sloped on four sides
- ■ A colonnade running along the front of the house under the curved edge of the roof shelters the walls from harsh weather conditions
- ■ The side roofs were often extended to create a shelter for a storage area

HOUSE PRICES IN BURGUNDY HAVE RISEN by an average of 12 per cent in the last few years, although some regions have recorded increases of 15 to 17 per cent, while in certain areas, such as Côte Chalonnaise and Chablis, prices have soared by as much as 40 per cent. Despite this, Burgundy has a plentiful supply of traditional houses at affordable prices. A converted stone barn in need of refurbishment could cost you as little as €60,000 (although the price reflects the amount of work that will need to be done before it becomes habitable), while for around €120,000 you could find a four-bedroom farmhouse with outbuildings. Generally, a good-sized home full of character, with a minimal amount of work necessary, will cost you an average of €227,000.

As far as renovation projects go, most were snapped up over 10 years ago when people first became interested in Burgundy, but there are still some decent farmhouses to be found for around €100,000. Those with higher budgets might prefer a fabulous manor house in need of refurbishment, which could be yours for around €230,000.

Properties in the northern areas of Burgundy, such as Auxerre, are expensive due to the influx of Parisians now seeing the areas as perfect for their holiday-home, and the fact that the climate is slightly cooler than in southern Burgundy. Côte d'Or and its environs offer few real value-for-money properties because the high demand and scarcity of land for new developments keep prices on an upwards spiral. The market here is fast-moving and renovation properties are hard to find. The best value for money exists to the west of the Côte d'Or, towards the border with Central France. For this reason, foreign investors often purchase property outside the wine region, in cheaper areas such as Morvan and Auxois, or Autun where a four-bedroom villa with pool and large garden costs €415,000. The lively city of Dijon is pricy and attracts mainly French house hunters and investors.

The short-term rental market is stable and offers solid investment opportunities. Therefore, as expected, holiday homes can yield high rates of return. The income from a house sleeping four to six people, for example, averages between €650 and €1,200 per week.

The region's property styles vary according to location. Most common is the maison vigneronne, which dominates the wine-growing areas. In Charollais to the west, large farmhouses are built from pink granite, whereas homes in Morvan are traditionally built from dark-grey granite. ●

WHAT CAN YOU GET FOR YOUR MONEY?

CHARACTERFUL FARMHOUSE

On the border between Burgundy and the Jura, this two-bedroom farmhouse is located near Poligny. A single-storey renovated property, it is set on grounds of 2.5 acres and resides in a quiet village, only 2.5kms from all amenities and 12 kms from the motorway. There is plenty of opportunity to expand this property. Situated in a peaceful location, the house is only 100 kms away from the ski slopes.

€210,000 CODE FRA

CHARMING CHÂTEAU

Located in the Saone et Loire département this charming small 18th-century château offers its owner three reception rooms, five bedrooms and three bathrooms. Enjoying over one hectare of mature gardens, this property comes with a living area of 450 square metres and is set in a very quiet hamlet, with shops close by. In good condition the château has a pool, a separate guest house and outbuildings.

€680,000 CODE SIF

MAGNIFICENT MAISON

2This superb property, comes complete with a separate caretakers house, a swimming pool and numerous outbuildings ideal for conversion. Residing in nearly two hecatres of grounds, the property has five reception rooms, eight bedrooms and four bathrooms. Dating from the 17th century and offering some 480 square metres of living space, it offers many attractive period features.

€1,284,000 CODE SIF

DETACHED PROPERTY

Detached property dating from 1880 with 3.6 acres of land and various outbuildings, bordering a canal. 280m2 accommodation comprises: Tiled entrance hall with wc, kitchen with fireplace, utility room, lounge with fireplace, dining room with fireplace, 2 bedrooms, both with fireplaces, bathroom. First floor: 6 bedrooms. Situated in a quiet village with amenities, 20 mins TGV station.

€330,000 CODE LAT

FORMER PRESBYTERY

Former Presbytery set in quarter of an acre (1000m2) garden. The property comprises: Entrance hall, living room, kitchen with dining area, 2 bedrooms, bathroom. 18m2 converted attic, vaulted cellar. Benefits from electric heating, original features including stone tiled floor, fireplace & oakwood staircase. Bread oven. Situated in the centre of Morvan, 10 minutes from Saulieu.

€180,000 CODE LAT

LAKESIDE LUXURY

This house has loads of potential, and could be many things to many people – just let your imagination run wild! Built in about 1850 and located in a lovely village in the Charollais hills, it offers habitable accommodation in one part of the building and the mill itself, which is partly renovated. There are a total of four bedrooms and glorious views over the surrounding lake.

€239,785 CODE VEF

AVERAGE HOUSE PRICES BURGUNDY

	2-bed	3-bed	4-bed	5-bed
Cote d'Or	€192,392 (£129,995)	€188,217 (£127,174)	€243,070 (£164,237)	€408,993 (£276,347)
Saone-et-Loire	€203,366 (£137,410)	€263,811 (£178,251)	€268,449 (£181,385)	€299,580 (£202,419)
Morvan Regional Park	€115,311 (£77,913)	€187,103 (£126,421)	€199,532 (£134,819)	€328,342 (£221,853)
Auxerre	€125,390 (£84,723)	€190,486 (£128,707)	€234,167 (£158,221)	€248,200 (£167,703)
Château sur Seine	€139,596 (£94,322)	€172,301 (£116,420)	€189,959 (£128,351)	€441,654 (£298,415)

MGK Consulting S.A

BUY WITH PEACE OF MIND

MGK Consulting offer complete assurance and personal service from first contact to the completion of the sale.

Are you looking for a castle?
An exceptional luxury property?
Or a vineyard in France?

MGK Consulting will welcome you, guide you and advise you.

MGK Consulting SA
REAL ESTATE AGENT
17 rue des Pierres du Niton
1207 - GENEVE - SWITZERLAND

Telephone +41 022 786 2870 Fax +41 022 786 2860
Email mgk@mgkconsulting.ch

www.mgkconsulting.ch

Poitou-Charentes

Beautiful wetlands, great beaches and hours of sun

CREDIT?

FACT BOX

■ **POPULATION** 1,640,068
■ **UNEMPLOYMENT RATE** 9.5%
■ **AVERAGE 4-BED HOUSE PRICE** €309,000
■ **REGIONAL CAPITAL** Poitiers
■ **REGION SIZE** 25,790km²

Contents

Area profile

There is plenty to discover in Poitou-Charentes, from unspoilt villages and poplar-lined canals to an abundance of seafood

GETTING THERE

AIR AirFrance (084 5111; www.airfrance.co.uk) flies from Gatwick to Nantes via Paris Charles de Gaulle. **GB Airways** (0870 551 1155; www.gbairways.com) flies to Nantes from Gatwick. **Ryanair** (0871 246 0000; www.ryanair.com) flies to Tours, La Rochelle and Poitiers from Stansted. **Flybe** (0871 700 0535; www.flybe.com) flies to La Rochelle from Belfast, Birmingham, Edinburgh, Glasgow and Southampton.

ROAD Take the A26 from Calais and continue on to the A16-E40 and then the A16 and A26. From there follow the A16-E402 to Rouen, taking the A28 on to the A28-E402 at junction 23. From Le Havre the A13-E46 runs down to Rennes, and the N137 or the A81-E50 continues on into the Pays-de-la-Loire. From Paris the A10-E6 runs into the centre and continues on to the south of the region, and the A11-E50 then runs on into Pays-de-la-Loire. From there the N137 runs through Nantes, where it becomes the A83 and continues on into Poitou-Charentes. From there the A10 runs north and south through the region with the N149 running east into Poitiers.

RAIL Rail Europe (0870 584 8848; www.raileurope.co.uk) operates TGV services to Le Mans, Angers, Nantes, Poitiers, La Rochelle and Angoulême from Paris Gare Montparnasse.

THIS IS ONE OF THE COUNTRY'S QUIETEST AND least spoilt regions where much of the countryside remains as it was when the region was inhabited by the Celts, more than two millennia ago. In the north, on the border with the Loire, are the unique Marais Poitevin marshlands, crisscrossed with small canals set among market gardens and verdant pastures. The 'Green Venice' is scattered with traditional thatched homes with dried-mud walls and the main means of transport is by wooden punt.

The Poitou-Charentes region is sandwiched between Pays-de-la-Loire and Aquitaine on the Atlantic coast. It encompasses the port city La Rochelle, the region's capital Poitiers and the small town of Cognac, the spiritual home of brandy.

Boasting nearly 500 kilometres of beautiful coastline and a clement climate, Poitou-Charentes attracts tourists from spring through to autumn. Inland, the beautiful wooded valleys are dotted with vineyards that provide the grapes for the famous Cognac, much of which is exported to the UK and Japan. The region's canals, wetlands and walking trails attract canoeists, hikers and cyclists alike.

The coastline is protected by four islands, the most popular of which – Île de Ré – attracts thousands of tourists to its beaches in the summer months. Île de Ré actually gets more hours of sunshine than any other part of France bar the Mediterranean. Both Île de Ré and Île d'Oléron are attached to the mainland by long toll bridges. Over half of France's oysters are farmed in the Marenne-Oléron basin and seafood is naturally one of the region's culinary specialities.

La Rochelle is a charming port with a wealth of

seafront restaurants and an expanding university. For centuries, it was one of France's most prominent Atlantic ports with strong trade links with North America. Today, the town experiences an influx of mostly well-to-do French holiday-makers in July and August, and although the town itself doesn't have any beaches, many visitors get their sunbathing fix by crossing to the beaches of Île de Ré.

Poitou-Charentes is a region rich in history and the attractive town of Saintes is home to some of France's most important Roman remains – the imposing Germanicus arch built in 18 AD, the amphitheatre, which once seated 15,000 spectators and where summer festivals are held annually today, and the Roman baths form an impressive testimony to the Roman occupation of the area.

Historical heritage
It was during the Middle Ages that Poitou-Charentes reached the height of its splendour.

The region forms part of the pilgrims' way to the shrine of St James in Santiago de Compostela in northwest Spain and over 600 monuments in the area are part of this legacy. There are fine examples of Romanesque architecture, with its hallmark of ornate stonework, throughout the region, including the Notre-Dame-la-Grande cathedral at Poitiers (also one of Europe's oldest religious buildings with its fourth-century St-Jean baptistry); St Peter's cathedral in Angoulême, with its stunning Romanesque façade; the graceful frescoes in the abbey church in St-Savin; Châteliers abbey on the Île de Ré; and the 12th-century hospice in Pons, a UNESCO monument.

CLIMATE

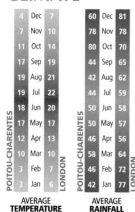

POITOU-CHARENTES		LONDON
4	Dec	7
7	Nov	10
11	Oct	14
17	Sep	19
19	Aug	21
19	Jul	22
18	Jun	20
17	May	17
12	Apr	13
10	Mar	10
3	Feb	7
3	Jan	6

AVERAGE TEMPERATURE
(Celsius)

POITOU-CHARENTES		LONDON
60	Dec	81
78	Nov	78
80	Oct	70
44	Sep	65
42	Aug	62
44	Jul	59
50	Jun	58
50	May	57
46	Apr	56
58	Mar	64
46	Feb	72
42	Jan	77

AVERAGE RAINFALL
(millimetres)

FOOD AND DRINK

Seafood is one of the region's specialities, with moules à la mouclade (mussels marinated in wine or cooked in cream) and oysters (eaten raw with lemon juice or shallot-flavoured vinaigrette, or hot in a cream sauce) frequently top of the menu. Other favourites are fish soup with white wine and snails served with herbs, butter and more wine. The region produces top-quality meats including Poitou-Charentes lamb, from Montmorillon and Confolens, and succulent beef. An unexpected local delicacy sold by some butchers is beaver-meat sausages. Dishes from the Marais-Poitevin feature boiled eels (bouilliture d'anguilles), kid with green garlic, leg of mutton, ham, snail sauce and haricot beans (mojettes). The hot, sunny climate produces some of the world's juiciest melons; other produce includes goat's cheese and top quality butter. Cognac is the region's major claim to fame; strict criteria govern which brandies can bear the name. Other drinks include Pineau de Charentes, a blend of eau-de-vie and grape must.

MAISON DE LA FRANCE

ALL PHOTOS POITOU-CHARENTES COMITÉ RÉGIONAL DE

Poitou-Charentes was also a frontier land during the Hundred Years' War and a highly fought over possession during the Napoleonic wars when the British navy lay siege to the coastline. Around a dozen fortresses line the coast including the unique star-shaped fortifications on the islands of Aix, Madame and Oléron. The imposing oval-shaped stone Fort Boyard, constructed with enormous difficulty on the sea bed, is perhaps the best known castle in the area. Even the Tour de la Lanterne lighthouse at La Rochelle was used as a defensive building and housed many foreign prisoners whose graffiti on the inner walls makes interesting reading.

The economy

Agriculture is the region's major economic driving force. Chauvigny has a number of small paper mills and its porcelain factories provide employment for many. Cognac's heart and soul revolve around the production of its namesake, brandy. Angoulême in Charente continues its tradition of paper mills, although on a smaller scale than previously, while tourism is a developing strand of the economy. There are now 75 restaurants in the city. Tourism, together with mussel and oyster fishing, forms the mainstay of Île de Ré, while La Rochelle is supported by fishing, tourism and commerce.

Social groups

Saintes, Angoulême and Charente are favourites with British relocators, and purchases here offer excellent investment opportunities. To the west of Poitiers, Chauvigny, Bellac, L'Isle Jourdain, St-Savin, Montmorillon and Bussière-Poitevine are prime holiday-home localities, especially popular with British tourists. ●

Focus on Charente

A fertile river valley with both rural villages and sophisticated towns, the Charente is the ideal relocation destination

THE CHARENTE VALLEY IS PATTERNED INTO fields of verdant farmland and numerous vineyards that gracefully divide the rolling hills. Cognac originated here in a quieter, more rural time, but now the country idyll rubs shoulders with classy shops, restaurants and newly built villas that attest to the area's increasing wealth. Very popular with British buyers looking to relocate permanently instead of buying a second home, this western département between Bordeaux and the Loire valley features great stretches of sandy Atlantic beaches while, inland, several large rivers (including the Charente) run through peaceful wooded valleys.

The capital of Charente is the walled city of Angoulême, home to the annual World Music Festival. The city's most famous museum, the Centre National de la Bande Dessinée, celebrates cartoon characters from around the world – everything from Astérix to Peanuts. Housed in a former brewery elegantly modernised with contemporary glass extensions, the museum safeguards and displays some 4,000 original drawings.

Prosperous Cognac is, predictably, the base of the main Cognac houses. The oldest, Martell, was

"Although most of Cognac's attractions are connected with the drink that bears its name, there are many other sites to visit"

founded by a former smuggler and although most of the city's attractions are connected with the drink that bears its name, there are many other sites to visit. The château ruins, for example, are the birthplace of King François I while the town's museum contains an exhibition on the history of the region's wine-making industry. Cognac is also well known for its annual detective film festival.

House prices tend to increase westwards in the region, although they are still cheaper than in the Dordogne. The typical Charentaise house is made from stone and timber, with an ochre-tiled roof. Recently, the département has seen a 15 per cent increase in prices but, despite this, a two-bedroom property will cost only around €193,000. ●

CHARENTE FACTS

■ Charente is home of the most exclusive of brandies, Cognac

■ Angoulême houses a naval academy founded by Louis the Unavoidable (Louis XVIII) which is over 150km from the coast

■ In 1806 the 77-year-old General Resnier became the world's first hanglider pilot, launching himself from the ramparts of Angoulême and soaring over the Charente river

■ Each July, Cognac hosts the Blues Passion festival, a blues festival that attracts over 40,000 followers

Charente has many unspoilt villages to relocate to

ESSENTIALS

■ **POPULATION** Angoulême 103,746, Cognac 27,042
■ **TAXES** Taxe d'habitation 25.05%, taxe foncière 57.28%
■ **AIRPORT** Limoges/Bellegarde Airport, 87100 Limoges; Tel: +33 5 55 43 30 30

KEY FACTS

■ **SCHOOLS** Bordeaux International School, 53 rue de Laseppe, 33000 Bordeaux; Tel: +33 5 57 87 02 11
■ **MEDICAL** Centre Hospitalier, rue Montesquieu,16100 Cognac; Tel: +33 5 45 36 75 75
■ **RENTALS** The tourism market here is very healthy and buoyant, offering an excellent return on your investment   Good to average market, rental period up to four months a year   Demand is intermittent from Easter to end of October, but winter lets are possible   The average weekly rental from a two-bedroom property is €590
■ **PROS** Cheap renovation properties, with a two-bedroom house costing from €100,000   A wealthy area; Angoulême is a lively town   Charente is the second sunniest region in France   A four-bedroom property is affordable at around €309,000 but prices are expected to rise and have already done so by 15%, making this a good time to invest
■ **CONS** Few habitable properties and poor employment prospects   Growing popularity means rising prices   Angoulême and south Angoulême are very expensive   Some prices have doubled due to foreign interest   This is a very rural area so may not be ideal for families with small children   If you can't speak French living here may be hard.

Property hotspots

MAP KEY

⑤ Hotspot
◯ Major town/city
✈ Airport
⛴ Ferry

ÎLE DE RÉ & LA ROCHELLE

1 La Rochelle is an unspoilt Atlantic seaside town in Charente-Maritime, with a historic centre and waterfront protected from redevelopment and traffic.There are four distinct neighbourhoods: the 17th to 18th-century centre; the Les Minimes marina development; the residential and industrial inner suburbs; and Île de Ré.

Within the triangle of place de Verdun, the Porte Royale and the Tour de la Lanterne is the historical centre where most of La Rochelle's architectural treasures lie, such as the military Tour St-Nicolas, which provides a beautiful view of the Vieux Port. You'll also find the Musée du Nouveau Monde, the Musée des Beaux-Arts and the Port des Minimes, an enormous marina.

Île de Ré benefits from the Gulf Stream and year-round warmth. The north is a haven of oyster farms, salt marshes, wildlife sanctuaries and great stretches of unspoiled beaches. The east is more residential, with villages such as St-Martin or Ste-Marie and their whitewashed cottages with brightly painted shutters. Here you can buy a two-bedroom maison de village to renovate for €235,000, or a five-bedroom townhouse for more like €486,000.

Île de Ré does not offer year-round rentals but La Rochelle University ensures regular long-term tenants, while tourism brings good short-term summer rentals. A one-bedroom flat can make €352 per week, while a four bed can make €849.

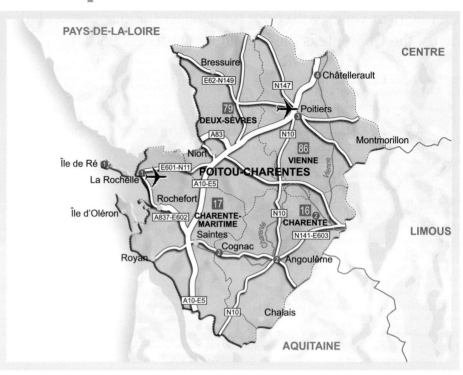

Key facts

■ **POPULATION** 96,555
■ **TAXES** Taxe d'habitation 6.15%, taxe foncière 5.32%
■ **AIRPORT** La Rochelle-Île de Ré Airport, rue du Jura, 17000 La Rochelle, Tel: +33 5 46 42 30 26
■ **SCHOOLS** Cité Scolaire Internationale Grand Air, Lycée et Collège de Grand Air, 77 avenue du Bois d'Amour, 44500 La Baule Escoublac, Nantes, Tel: +33 2 40 11 58 00
■ **MEDICAL** Centre hospitalier de La Rochelle, rue du Docteur Schweitzer, 1700 La Rochelle, Tel: +33 5 46 45 50 50, www.ch-larochelle.fr/
■ **PROS** Coastal resorts are popular ■ Property in St-Martin-de-Ré is also popular and La Rochelle has a busy, and therefore stable rental market ■ Île de Ré enforces a two-storey height limit, plus tiled roofs, whitewashed walls and green shutters on all buildings ■ There are some very good transport links to most major cities
■ **CONS** An influx of Parisian second-home buyers have raised prices substantially ■ Île de Ré is quiet in winter but very busy (500,000 visitors) in the summer season

CHARENTE

2 For information on Hotspot 2, the Charente region, see the special feature on page 115.

POITIERS

3 Overlooking the Clain and Boivre rivers, Poitiers was seat to the dukes of Aquitaine and has tempted capture by many past conquerors from Joan of Arc to Richard the Lionheart.

It boasts a thriving university, stunning Romanesque Notre-Dame Cathedral and lively nightlife. Open spaces are plentiful; the 18th-century Parc de Blossac, with its elegant, terraced limestone gardens, is set on the town's ramparts. Unusual events take place throughout the year with a dog fair and the Colla Voce festival of music for organ and voice.

On the outskirts of the city is Futuroscope, the futuristic theme park set in more than 50 hectares devoted to giant screens, 3D cinemas, circular cinemas and other state-of-the-art audiovisual spectacles. Space Station 3D recounts the daring in-orbit assembly of the International Space Station. At night the finale is a fantastic laser light show with fireworks.

A two-bedroom, semi-detached townhouse on four levels close to the cathedral starts at €162,000. If you're looking for a home to renovate, try Thénezay, a small market town just 30 minutes from Poitiers. For around €230,000 you can acquire a large four-bedroom house with traditional features and a garden. In the quiet village of Vivonne, large homes dating from 1880, in local hand-dressed stone with brick vaulted ceilings and stained-glass windows sell from around €200,000.

The rentals market is fairly healthy, although lets tend to be more long term. Average weekly rents for Poitiers and the

Poitou-Charentes boasts some stunning beaches along the Atlantic coast like this one at Fouras

surrounding area are €841 for a two-bedroom property, while a four-bedroom property can generate €2,210 a week.

Key facts

■ **POPULATION** 1999: 83,500

■ **TAXES** Taxe d'habitation 6.08%, taxe foncière 7.10%

■ **AIRPORT** Poitiers-Biard Aéroport, Biard, 86000 Poitier, Tel: +33 5 49 30 04 40

■ **SCHOOLS** Cité Scolaire Internationale Grand Air, Lycée et Collège de Grand Air, 77 avenue du Bois d'Amour, 44500 La Baule Escoublac, Nantes, Tel: +33 2 40 11 58 00

■ **MEDICAL** Centre Hospitalier Universitaire de Poitiers, 2 rue de la Miletrie, 86021Poitiers, Tel: +33 5 49 44 44 44

■ **PROS** Good rail links and cheap flights from London Stansted ■ Excellent climate ■ The Vendée coast is just 90 minutes away and ski resorts are two hours to the west ■ Bellac, Montmorillon, St-Savin, Chauvigny, L'Isle-Jourdain and Bussière-Poitevine are increasingly popular with foreign buyers ■ **CONS** Once one of the cheapest

property markets, but prices have more than doubled in recent years.

CHÂTELLERAULT

3 Founded in the 10th century, Châtellerault soon became a favoured stopover for travellers and pilgrims while the Henri IV bridge, constructed on the orders of Catherine de Médici, opened the way to development as a major river port. Visit the limestone underground caves at nearby Availles-en-Châtellerault – legend has it that they were inhabited by gnomes in the 12th century. The Discovery Farm at Thuré provides an introduction to local farming methods with insights into such things as the production of honey and goat's cheese.

A beautiful, busy spa town founded by the Romans in the 15th century, La Roche-Posay is frequently visited for its healing waters, and has an old town encircled by defensive walls

towering above the valley, with donjon and fortified church. There are nine- and 18-hole golf courses, a casino and horse racing, while the Tardes river is a favourite for kayaking. The nearby Parc Naturel Régional de la Brenne is one of the largest wildlife sanctuaries in Europe, popular with birdwatchers.

Cheap properties are available in the area, and although there is not a huge amount of foreign interest, demand still outstrips supply. French buyers are the biggest group, and this is a good location in which to invest.

A typical country house with three bedrooms costs from around €183,000.

As it is not primarily a tourist area, short-term rentals are not common in Châtellerault. The average rent for a two-bedroom property is €527 per week, while a three-bedroom property costs €633 per week. La Roche-Posay is a popular tourist destination in the summer, with an active short-term rental market.

Key facts

■ **POPULATION** 36,026

■ **TAXES** Taxe d'habitation 6.08%,taxe foncière 7.10%

■ **AIRPORT** Poitiers-Biard Aéroport, Biard, 86000 Poitiers, Tel: +33 5 49 30 04 40

■ **SCHOOLS** Cité Scolaire Internationale Grand Air, Lycée et Collège de Grand Air, 77 avenue du Bois d'Amour, 44500 La Baule Escoublac, Nantes, Tel: +33 2 40 11 58 00

■ **MEDICAL** Hôpital Camille Guérin, Rocade Est, 86106 Châtellerault, Tel: +33 5 49 02 90 90

■ **PROS** Cheap properties are available ■ Steeped in history, this area played a crucial role in the Hundred Years' War ■ There is still demand for farm complexes, and demand for all property outstrips supply ■ This remains a good property investment area ■ Most cheaper properties will require renovation.

■ **CONS** Châtellerault is not really a tourist area so rental returns will be weak and unstable ■ There are few foreign buyers, and the market is primarily French ■ There are limited employment opportunities and almost non for non-French speakers. ●

Property guide

The housing market in the Poitou-Charentes region is very buoyant at present, spurred on by the introduction of budget flights to La Rochelle which have generated a surge in the holiday rental market

MAISON DE LA FRANCE

La Rochelle, one of the most unspoilt towns in France, whose historic centre is a pedestrian's delight

THE INFLUX OF HOUSE HUNTERS INTO Poitou-Charentes has driven up prices, with properties within an hour's drive of the airport experiencing the steepest rises. Renovation properties dominate the market throughout Charente and you can expect to pay upwards of €100,000 for a decent derelict barn or village house – cheaper properties can be found but are likely to be tiny or need rebuilding from scratch. House values at the lower end of the market have at least doubled in the last few years. Urban property prices remain low, but are less popular with many foreign buyers who also seek gardens.

La Rochelle is popular with Parisian holiday-home buyers and although more expensive than other areas represents a solid investment. The average price of a three-bedroom home here is around €421,000. Properties in the southeast of Charente (Châtellerault) are excellent value.

Charente-Maritime (Île de Ré and Île d'Oléron) is considered a real alternative to the Dordogne and is good value for buy-to-lets. Although Île de Ré properties are expensive, pushed up by Parisian second-home owners, rental returns are good, with up to €531 per week for a two-bedroom property during high season. Tourism is big business in Charente-Maritime, and gîtes abound in and around La Rochelle and Île de Ré.

Buyers get less value for money in Cognac and Saintes because of the area's popularity with French and foreign visitors alike. Prices are rising steadily with increases of around 10 per cent in 2006. Modern pavillons (bungalows) are becoming more popular with British buyers due to the generous plot sizes. A three-bedroom pavillon with large gardens and a pool costs from €180,000. Large traditional farmhouses with land and a swimming pool needing little work start around €300,000.

Slightly nearer to Dordogne, Angoulême's prices are higher than elsewhere in the region. Between €150,000 and €300,000 will get you a modern pavillon or a modernised traditional-style house with large garden. ●

CHARENTAISE FARMHOUSE

FRENCH PROPERTY SHOP

- The typical Charentaise farmhouse is long and low, and is constructed using locally quarried stone and timber materials
- The roof is traditionally clad with ochre-coloured roof tiles and gently slopes to reduce the risk of tiles sliding off
- The building's outer walls are typically a creamy limestone colour
- The upper windows are small and the larger lower windows are framed with trademark shutters, often painted pale green, which block out the sun's rays and keep the interior of the house cool
- The interior walls of the house often feature exposed timber beams
- Other interior features include wood-burning stoves and tiled floors

WHAT CAN YOU GET FOR YOUR MONEY?

HAMLET HOME

Situated in a hamlet in the countryside of the Charente, this renovated barn enjoys a slightly elevated position, and has an unusual but attractive layout. The land – over a ¼ of an acre – surrounds the house, which is well-positioned to take advantage of the views with a sunny terrace at the rear. With a spacious living room with French doors and a modern kitchen, the property has three bedrooms.

€162,207 CODE FRA

RENOVATED PROPERTY

A beautifully renovated six bedroom maison de maître comes complete with a detached two storey barn with stabling block and is set within grounds of around 6.2 acres including woodland. Situated between two pretty villages and only 12kms from Saintes, this property has a total living area of 340 square metres and has been renovated to a very high standard by the present owners.

€625,000 CODE FRA

RENOVATION PROJECT

Located in Saulgond, this old stone property requires complete renovation.Set in 200 square metres of land, this ruin is situated in a small, characterful village and is close to all required amenities and facilities. Offering 80 square metres of living space and three main rooms, there is also a large attic and bread oven that comes with the property. This is a great opportunity to create you ideal home.

€33,500 CODE FPS

TRADITIONAL HOUSE

Located in a hamlet in the valley of the Clain River, this carefully restored traditional property is situated in a beautiful area. Boasting large, airy rooms and 190 square metres of living space, this country property offers a large reception room of 35 square metres with a cut stone floor and character fireplace, a fitted kitchen three bedrooms, recently installed central heating, a barn and stables.

€318,000 CODE FPS

MODERN BUNGALOW

With three-bedrooms and a large garden, this comfortable property is situated in a village which is located close to the N10 route giving it excellent transport links to the surrounding area. There is also a separate, partially completed outbuilding which was intended to be additional independent guest accommodation and once finalised this would be ideal for family, friends or rentals.

€172,385 CODE VEF

STONE-BUILT HOME

Fully habitable and offering five bedrooms and extensive gardens, this characterful stone property built in 1643 from the remnants of a local château – and subsequently sympathetically extended in the 1960s – is a rarity. All the original features have been preserved and the property just oozes style and history. It also boasts a terrace, separate 'hangar' garage and a gravel driveway.

€428,905 CODE VEF

PROPERTY GUIDE

AVERAGE HOUSE PRICES POITOU-CHARENTES

	2-bed	3-bed	4-bed	5/6-bed
Île de Ré & La Rochelle	€293,797 (£198,512)	€421,413 (£284,739)	€423,894 (£286,415)	€486,484 (£328,706)
Charente	€164,746 (£111,315)	€199,222 (£134,610)	€252,283 (£170,462)	€354,480 (£239,514)
Poitiers	€161,960 (£109,433)	€244,901 (£165,474)	€353,148 (£238,614)	€389,161 (£262,947)
Châtellerault	€152,204 (£102,841)	€183,485 (£123,977)	€205,278 (£138,702)	€351,412 (£237,441)

Limousin & Auvergne

Beautiful medieval towns and unspoilt countryside

JACQUES MAFAITY

FACT BOX

- ■ **POPULATION** 2,019,817
- ■ **UNEMPLOYMENT RATE** 8.7%
- ■ **AVERAGE 4-BED HOUSE PRICE** €224,000
- ■ **REGIONAL CAPITAL** Limousin: Limoges;
Auvergne: Clermont-Ferrand
- ■ **REGION SIZE** 42,920km²

Contents

Area profile

The rarely explored regions of Auvergne and Limousin offer delightful scenery and some terrific property bargains

GETTING THERE

AIR Ryanair (0871 246 0000; www.ryanair.com) flies to Limoges from Liverpool and Stansted. **Air France** (0845 084 5111; www.airfrance.co.uk) flies via Paris Orly to Clermont-Ferrand and Limoges from London City, Heathrow, Bristol, Glasgow, Manchester, Southampton, Newcastle, Edinburgh, and Aberdeen.

ROAD Take the A10 from Paris, continuing on the A10-E5 and then the A71-E9 at the junction with the A71 for Limoges. At the junction for the A85, take the A20-E09 into Limousin and Limoges. For Clermont-Ferrand and the rest of Auvergne, follow the A10 from Paris to Orléans, taking the A71-E9 and then Junction 5 on to the A71-E11, then the N9 into Clermont-Ferrand.

RAIL A TGV service operates between Gare d'Austerlitz in Paris and Limoges. Gare de Lyon is linked with Clermont-Ferrand by an efficient, quick link. Contact **Rail Europe** (0870 584 8848; www.raileurope.co.uk) for further details.

THE REGIONS OF LIMOUSIN AND AUVERGNE LIE roughly in the centre of France. Limousin is one of the least explored areas of the country and it remains relatively unspoilt compared with the coast. The landscape is blessed with lakes, river valleys and rolling, tree-covered hills, and there are many well preserved medieval towns and villages.

The capital of Limousin is Limoges, where fine porcelain and enamel have been produced since the 1770s – the city's museum houses an outstanding ceramics collection with exhibits dating back to the 12th century. Elsewhere, there's a beautiful old medieval quarter and a huge Gothic cathedral. East of Limoges, in the Creuse valley, lies Aubusson, a small town renowned for tapestry and carpet-weaving for over 500 years.

Further east is the Auvergne region, which is in the heart of the Massif Central, a vast mountain range with spectacular gorges and more than 80 dormant volcanos. Allier département in the north has the most gentle landscape and the impressive medieval town of Montluçon is its economic heart. Further south, the mountainous landscape is dotted with spa towns, which are built around the region's natural thermal springs. Le Puy-en-Velay, the capital of Haute-Loire, clings on to some rocky outcrops, but most amazing is the Chapelle St-Michel d'Aiguilhe, which sits on the peak of a rocky spur.

Churches and châteaux

Red sandstone houses are the norm in Collonges-la-

Historically, the area has a rich cultural legacy seen principally in the hundreds of Romanesque buildings that dot the countryside. The so-called Auvergne Romanesque school, which originated around Clermont-Ferrand, is widely considered to have produced the purest Romanesque architecture. Examples include St-Julien at Brioude, clad in basalt and marble and boasting magnificent capitals and murals; Notre-Dame-du-Port in Clermont-Ferrand, a UNESCO world heritage building; and the church of Notre-Dame at Orcival with its Romanesque Madonna dressed in gold.

The area has its fair share of beautiful châteaux. There are six châteaux routes in Auvergne that take in the best examples, such as the elegant rose-coloured St-Saturnin, the Château de Val in its

CLIMATE

	AVERAGE TEMPERATURE (Celsius)			AVERAGE RAINFALL (millimetres)	
9	Dec	7	106	Dec	81
13	Nov	10	107	Nov	78
16	Oct	14	104	Oct	70
21	Sep	19	92	Sep	65
24	Aug	21	88	Aug	62
25	Jul	22	81	Jul	59
22	Jun	20	94	Jun	58
15	May	17	104	May	57
16	Apr	13	91	Apr	56
10	Mar	10	95	Mar	64
6	Feb	7	89	Feb	72
6	Jan	6	94	Jan	77

FOOD AND DRINK

The food of this dominantly agricultural region is unsurprisingly very rustic in style. Traditional dishes include wholesome, warming soups, stews and casseroles. Organic meat and foie gras are regular players on the menu and are often accompanied by juicy berries from Corrèze. Favourite regional dishes are: potée Auvergnate (a stew of bacon, pork, potato and cabbage); truffade (fried sliced potatoes with Cantal cheese); and aligot (puréed potatoes mixed with cheese). Less appealing for some, perhaps, is tripoux – commonly a stuffing of sheep's feet or calf's innards, cooked in a casing of sheep's stomach lining. Fricandeau, a pork pâté, is also wrapped in sheep's stomach. Among Auvergne's superb cheese selection are: Cantal, Bleu d'Auvergne and St-Nectaire. Limousin's favourite hearty dessert is cherry clafoutis, a baked batter pudding.

Neither Limousin nor Auvergne are noted for their wines but this region does make some delicious liqueurs, including the hazelnut and walnut liqueurs of Limousin and those from Auvergne made from mountain herbs and gentian.

MAISON DE LA FRANCE

The basis for a tasty Limousin entrée

ALL PHOTOS MAISON DE LA FRANCE

ATTRACTIONS

■ **The city of Limoges**

■ **Walking or biking in the Parc des Volcans d'Auvergne**

■ **Lake Allier**

■ **The region's excellent ski resorts and network of cross-country pistes**

■ **The spectacular views from the Puy de Dôme mountain – walk or drive up early in the morning or late in the evening if you want to avoid the crowds**

■ **The medieval town of Riom**

■ **The Chapelle St-Michel perched on a volcanic chimney at Aiguilhe**

■ **The villages of Collonges-la-Rouge and Saler**

The economy

Both Limousin and Auvergne are popular with outdoor enthusiasts, including hikers, fishermen and windsurfers, and there are plenty of decent golf courses where you can enjoy the pleasant climate. As such, tourism dominates the Limoges economy, along with the technological industry, including the production of electrical fittings. Clermont-Ferrand, near Vichy, is home to the Michelin tyre factory and Limagrain, one of the world's largest seed providers. Auvergne has a thriving blend of industry and commerce. The relocation of part of the French civil service to Limoges, and the positive attitude given to new business development by the regional capital's Chamber of Commerce, illustrate the developing economy.

Social groups

Increased accessibility will bring in more foreign buyers, raising prices. An airport is planned for Brive in the next few years and a tram service is due for completion in Clermont-Ferrand in the next few years. More British buyers are moving here as prices rise even higher elsewhere. ●

fairytale location on the shores of Lake Bort, and Château de Billy, a bold and imposing 12th-century fortress.

Both regions boast a number of the officially designated most beautiful villages in France. The extraordinary red-sandstone Collonges-la-Rouge, St-Robert with its stunning medieval quarter, and Segur-le-Château perched beneath a rocky outcrop are in Limousin. Auvergne is home to Blesle with fine half-timbered houses, Montpeyreux and its 13th-century keep dominating the small village, and Salers with its dark lava stone buildings.

PROFILE

Property hotspots

MAP KEY

- **⑤** Hotspot
- Major town/city
- ✈ Airport
- ⛴ Ferry

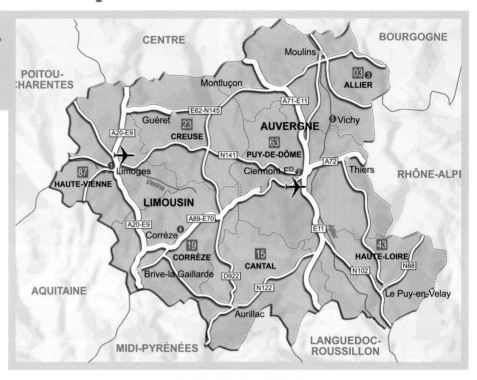

LIMOGES

1 Located in northern Limousin, a region criss-crossed by rivers and lakes, Limoges offers good value for money and attractive surroundings. Initially built by the Romans, Limoges is not only at the heart of France's lake district, but also provides all the shopping, gastronomic and cultural attractions of a historic regional capital. Lying between the Bordeaux and Loire regions, the area is blessed with a fertile soil ideal for vineyards; wines are aged in Limoges oak from nearby forests.

The city boasts 19 kilometres of tunnels, originally created by the Romans to supply the city with water from springs six kilometres away. By the Middle Ages, Limoges was known for its high-quality enamel work and in the 18th century the city became the world capital for ceramics and glass. On 28 December each year, Limoges hosts the St Innocent Fair, a winter extravaganza of produits du terroir in a tradition dating back to the 16th century.

The property market in Limoges is dominated by local French buyers, with little interest shown as yet by foreign buyers. Prices are affordable, with a three-bedroom property costing an average of €258,000.

Limoges offers the investor good rental potential. The market is driven by long-term lets to locals, with approximately 16 weeks of summer rentals for short-term visitors. As the surrounding area is relatively unknown from a tourism point of view, rental income may be hard to come by in out-of-the-way places, and there are very few established agents. A two-bedroom house can be let from an average of €517 a week.

Key facts

■ **POPULATION** 137,502
■ **TAXES** Taxe d'habitation 6.08%, taxe foncière 6.40%
■ **AIRPORT** Limoges/Bellegarde Airport, 87100 Limoges, Tel: +33 5 55 43 30 30
■ **SCHOOLS** Bordeaux International School, 53 rue de Laseppe, 33000 Bordeaux, Tel: +33 5 57 87 02 11
■ **MEDICAL** CHU de Limoges, 2 avenue Martin-Luther-King, 87042 Limoges, Tel: +33 5 55 05 61 23
■ **PROS** Limoges is the ideal place for a traditional French lifestyle ■ The city is packed with amenities and culture ■ The area has good transport links and employment opportunities
■ **CONS** A cooler than in the more southern regions ■ The relocation of part of the Parisian civil service has driven up property prices ■ Small English-speaking community.

CLERMONT-FERRAND

2 At the heart of Auvergne in the Massif Central, Clermont-Ferrand is one of France's oldest and most culturally dynamic cities, created when rival cities Clermont and Montferrand were merged under Louis XIV. Today's Clermont-Ferrand thrives as both a university city and the capital of the Puy-de-Dôme département. It is just half an hour's drive from Parc des Volcans, a geological exhibition sculpted by volcanic eruptions and glaciers. Many museums are dotted around this historic city. The yearly Court Métrage film festival has become an international affair, showing cinema shorts from around the world, and every Christmas an open-air ice rink is magically illuminated. To the south lies the Monts-Dore massif, known for spa towns like La Bourbole and the Super Besse ski resort.

Clermont-Ferrand is little known to the British and has been overlooked by buyers in favour of Provence and Côte d'Azur, despite property here costing half the price. The best value is in the suburbs, although as the city is being redeveloped, city centre property is likely to become expensive. Property prices are competitive, with a three-bedroom house costing around €190,000.

There is year-round interest in rentals in Clermont-Ferrand due to the town's proximity to the Mont-Dore ski station.

A five-bedroom house in Clermont-Ferrand starts at an average of €835 a week. Lets are usually long term.

Key facts

■ **POPULATION** 141,004
■ **TAXES** Taxe d'habitation 7.47%, taxe foncière 10.76%
■ **AIRPORT** Clermont-Ferrand Auvergne Airport, rue Youri Gagarine, 63510 Aulnat, Tel: +33 4 73 62 71 00
■ **SCHOOLS** École Internationale Michelin, 5 rue Bansac, 63000 Clermont-Ferrand, Tel: +33 4 73 98 09 70

HOTSPOTS

■ **MEDICAL** Centre Hospitalier Universitaire de Clermont-Ferrand, 58 rue Montalembert, 6300 Clermont-Ferrand, Tel: +33 4 73 75 07 50

■ **PROS** There are excellent transport links and budget flights to the area ■ The city has a large foreign population and a well-established and well-resourced international school ■ It is a place of cultural importance and national interest, with good job prospects

■ **CONS** Clermont-Ferrand is a university city and is lively and cosmopolitan ■ The city is very heavily industrialised in parts.

VOLCANIC MOUNTAINS & LAKES OF AUVERGNE

3 One of the cheapest places to buy property, the Allier département in the north of Auvergne is the birthplace of the Bourbon dukes, with 15th-century manor houses and châteaux available. With plenty of lakes and home to the Forest of Tronçais, this "land of 1,001 châteaux" is a historic treasure.

The capital of the region, the agricultural town of Moulins, is located on the Allier river, north of Lyon. Lake Allier is an activities haven, a 120-hectare expanse of water lined with open-air cafés, while to the centre of the département, the Bocage Bourbonnais is a cattle-rearing area known for its monuments, castles and fine Romanesque churches. South of Moulins, the volcanic Montagne Bourbonnaise is popular with hikers, mountain bikers, horse riders and skiers in winter.

This is a rural, undeveloped area that will not suit buyers after the active city life. But with so many outdoor pursuits available, it's perfect for tourism-based businesses. The foreign buyer is starting to take notice of this, so now is a good time to invest. Property is cheap, with a two-bedroom home from €117,000.

The short-term rental market is good, with tourists

quadrupling the population in peak season, creating high demand for 20 weeks a year.

Key facts
■ **POPULATION** Moulins 21,100
■ **TAXES** Taxe d'habitation 8.11%, taxe foncière 9.05%
■ **AIRPORT** Clermont-Ferrand Auvergne International Airport, rue Youri Gagarine, 63510 Aulnat, Tel: +33 4 73 62 71 00
■ **SCHOOLS** École Internationale Michelin, 5 rue Bansac, 63000 Clermont-Ferrand, Tel: +33 4 73 98 09 70
■ **MEDICAL** Centre Hospitalier Universitaire de Clermont-Ferrand, 58 rue Montalembert, 6300 Clermont-Ferrand, Tel: +33 4 73 75 07 50
■ **PROS** The Massif du Sancy offers plenty of outdoor activities including watersports ■ Culturally rich Clermont-Ferrand is easily accessible, and there is a comprehensive transport network serving the area ■ The Massif du Sancy is a well established tourist destination, with many foreign buyers rapidly coming to recognise the area's merits
■ **CONS** A car is essential to avoid isolation ■ The area is quiet and underpopulated in the off season

CORRÈZE

4 The Corrèze département, in the southern part of Limousin, has been very popular for some time with holiday-makers and buyers looking for a quality destination without the cost of the Dordogne. As a result of this, there's already a short-term lets market driven by tourists attracted by the region's beauty, culture and gastronomy.

Areas of interest in this region include Uzerche and Arnac-Pompadour, with their beautiful châteaux and fine Romanesque churches, plus the picturesque villages of Turenne and Collonges-la-Rouge, with their spectacular views over ridges and valleys to the mountains of Cantal and Gimel-les-Cascades.

Besse-en-Chandesse has had a 30 per cent growth in property prices in recent years. Property is

more affordable in northwestern Corrèze, where an average two-bedroom property costs €95,000 and a four-bed home €256,000.

Demand for properties to let is above supply, so rental potential is good. High season is predominantly June to August when the market is dominated by demand for short-term lets. A good-quality four-bedroom house in Corrèze could fetch about €629 per week. Around 80 to 90 per cent of people relocating to this area wish to establish a tourist-based business.

Key facts
■ **POPULATION** 84,927
■ **TAXES** Taxe d'habitation 5.68%, taxe foncière 11.61%
■ **AIRPORT** Limoges/Bellegarde Airport, 87100 Limoges, +33 5 55 43 30 30
■ **SCHOOLS** École Internationale Michelin, 5 rue Bansac, 63000 Clermont-Ferrand, Tel: +33 4 73 98 09 70
■ **MEDICAL** Centre Hospitalier de Tulle, 3 place du Dr Machat, 19000 Tulle, Tel: +33 5 55 29 79 68
■ **PROS** Brive-la-Gaillarde is easily accessible, with good transport links ■ Brive and Tulle, capital of Corrèze, have good facilities ■ There's a growing international community
■ **CONS** The weather is similar to the Dordogne but milder in the north ■ Property is hard to find in the popular areas of Corrèze.

VICHY

5 Renowned for its cuisine and thermal spas, Vichy is a spa town and the birthplace of the Bourbon dynasty, as well as Pétain's 'Vichy France'. Thanks to a decade-long revamp intended to give the town international appeal, the new-look town centre offers a relaxed cosmopolitan atmosphere and a certain belle époque charm.

Tourism is by far the biggest industry in the area, especially given that Vichy is centrally located, easily accessible from Clermont-Ferrand and its

airport, and within easy reach of motorways north and south. The town has begun to attract an increasing number of Dutch and French buyers, and demand for property is on the increase. With the property market becoming increasingly buoyant, property prices have risen accordingly, by about 30 per cent since 2003.

This blooming international market is split between those who are buying to retire and those who are permanently relocating to the area, and although there is an ever-increasing number of British buyers, 90 per cent of those who buy in Vichy are French; most Britons currently buy in the Ébreuil area, 28 kilometres away. Property is affordable, with an average two-bedroom house costing just over €120,000 and four-bedroom homes from around €202,000.

There's a good rental season from May to September, when a one-bedroom house earns about €289 per week and a two-bedroom property €363 a week. The season for thermal spas is April to October, when demand is high for rental property.

Key facts
■ **POPULATION** 25,500
■ **TAXES** Taxe d'habitation 8.11%, taxe foncière 9.05%
■ **AIRPORT** Clermont-Ferrand Auvergne International Airport, rue Youri Gagarine, 63510 Aulnat, Tel: +33 4 73 62 71 00
■ **SCHOOLS** École Internationale Michelin, 5 rue Bansac, 63000 Clermont-Ferrand, Tel: +33 4 73 98 09 70
■ **MEDICAL** Hôpital de Vichy, bd Denière, 03201 Vichy, Tel: +33 4 73 98 09 70, www.ch-vichy.fr
■ **PROS** An established centre of tourism, Vichy has been relaunched as a European health, beauty and fitness centre ■ An increase in Dutch and French tourists has created a short-term rental market ■ Near to Clermont-Ferrand, it is has good transport links
■ **CONS** Properties are more expensive than elsewhere in the Auvergne. ●

HOTSPOTS

Property guide

Property prices across the regions of Limousin and Auvergne increased by around 15 per cent during 2005, but the area still affords some very reasonably priced housing

MAISON DE LA FRANCE

The village of Turenne, with its mellow stone houses, is close to Brive yet in the heart of the countryside

LIMOUSIN IS THE MORE BUOYANT OF THE TWO regions, with the high demand from British and Dutch buyers continuing to drive prices upwards. Here, it's possible to find a farmhouse in need of renovation for as little as €150,000, but the average cost of a decent-sized, habitable farmhouse with, say, an acre of land is around €220,000. Demand is not so high in Auvergne. The region's proximity to the mountains makes it less accessible, and a farmhouse here will cost around €135,000.

Some of the best bargains are to be found in Limousin's rural département of Haute-Vienne – a four-bedroom house with garden on the outskirts of Limoges is currently selling for €156,400. There are also fantastic bargains to be had in the up-and-coming area of Bellac where a four-bedroom house goes for as little as €130,000. Creuse also offers some

of France's cheapest prices, with many of the bargain properties requiring little work. Property costs in Corrèze might be the most expensive in Limousin but they still offer excellent value for money. Renovation properties are harder to find here though, and a large house requiring work will generally cost you over €150,000.

Although rental properties command lower returns than in other parts of France because of the poorer climate, these regions still offer good buy-to-let opportunities. Corrèze's rental market is very healthy, particularly in the west where there is high demand. Its proximity to Brive and planned improvements to the transport links give this area great long-term investment potential. A gîte for up to five persons in Creuse offers a weekly income potential of up to €1,060. In Auvergne, the villages around the Puy-de Sancy mountain have a healthy year-round rental season. Clermont-Ferrand is competitively priced and the rental market provides good returns for short- and long-term lets. Parisians favour it for second homes and its strong winter rental market is fuelled by the Mont-Dore ski station. The Massif Central has growing tourist popularity and good investment potential.

The regions offer a diverse choice of properties, the most popular with foreign buyers being the traditional maison-ferme. Prices vary considerably from area to area, costing up to €400,000 in Besse-en-Chandesse for a habitable property. ●

CHARENTAISE FARMHOUSE

- The Clermont-Ferrand area features houses built from local black lava rocks
- In Limousin a small single-storey farmhouse (maison basse monocellulaire) has one room and rustic paving slabs. A maison pluricellulaire is similar in style, but also has a cellar, which was often used as a workshop or housed an oven
- The traditional farmhouse (maison-ferme) of Limousin consists of many single-storey, multi-functional buildings used as living quarters, stables, barns and garage
- The maison-ferme is most prevalent in the Haute-Vienne region
- Building materials used in the construction of these farmhouses were sourced from the region, using locally quarried stone

WHAT CAN YOU GET FOR YOUR MONEY?

TRADITIONAL COTTAGE

Character stone house with outbuildings, set in over half an acre enclosed grounds. Built in 1900, interior in need of some decorating & comprising: living room with fireplace, fitted kitchen (in need of decorating), 4 bedrooms, 2 bathrooms, convertible attic, basement. Oil central heating. In a village with shop & primary school, 17kms from La Souterraine with amenities.

€203,300 CODE LAT

LAKESIDE FARM

With one hectare of land, this habitable property comes with two bedrooms. This attractive-looking stone property dates back to around the 1800s and is situated on the edge of a peaceful and pretty hamlet – one of the buildings is currently being used as a 'creperie' (pancake restaurant). The property overlooks a lake and also comes with an attached barn, the restaurant and 1.5 hectares of land.

€323,285 CODE VEF

IMPOSING CHÂTEAU

This 18th-century chateau is situated near a village on the border between Allier and the Puy de Dome . With five reception rooms, seven bedrooms and two bathrooms this is an imposing property that resides in 2.5 hectares of grounds. The Chateau, which is in good condition with beautiful original features, occupies a commanding position with a magnificent view overlooking the valley of the Sioule.

€1,290,323 CODE SIF

ORIGINAL HOME

18th century detached stone house with over quarter acre (1352m2) garden & pool. The property was restored in 1995 & offers 120m2 living space comprising: Ground floor: open-plan living/dining room/kitchen, bedroom, shower room/wc. First floor: 2 bedrooms, shower room, wc. Electric heating, double-glazing, heated pool with terrace. Situated not far from the Gorges de Truyere.

€244,000 CODE LAT

COUNTRY MANOR

This eight bedroom, three bathroom chateau dates back to the 17th century and comes complete with a swimming pool. Located close to Argentat with all shops and facilities and only 50 minutes from Brive, this wonderful stone château has been fully restored and now offers 900 sqaure metres of habitable space over two floors. This is a charming property, situated in peaceful countryside.

€1,275,000 CODE SIF

RENOVATED LONGÈRE

This charming, renovated property was once a fortified tower house. Offering outbuildings and one acre of land, this property boasts stunning views and has loads of potential. With a cluster of buildings, this could be ideal as a holiday home or as a gîte complex. The main building offers two bedrooms, as does the medieval tower, although this does require some internal renovation work.

€400,000 CODE FRA

AVERAGE HOUSE PRICES LIMOUSIN & AUVERGNE

	2-bed		3-bed		4-bed		5/6-bed	
Limoges	€181,461	(£122,609)	€257,657	(£174,093)	€277,251	(£187,332)	€423,877	(£286,404)
Clermont-Ferrand	€139,580	(£94,311)	€190,356	(£128,619)	€197,516	(£133,457)	€299,926	(£202,653)
Rural Auvergne	€116,820	(£8,933)	€187,089	(£126,412)	€188,408	(£127,303)	€211,123	(£142,651)
Corrèze	€94,609	(£63,925)	€173,299	(£117,094)	€255,508	(£172,641)	€299,509	(£202,371)
Vichy	€120,583	(£81,475)	€190,193	(£128,509)	€201,891	(£136,413)	€X293,424	(£198,260)

Rhône-Alpes

Beaujolais, gastronomic Lyon and the stunning Alps

MAISON DE LA FRANCE

FACT BOX

- **POPULATION** 2,908,359
- **UNEMPLOYMENT RATE** 9%
- **AVERAGE 4-BED HOUSE PRICE** €895,000
- **REGIONAL CAPITAL** Lyon
- **REGION SIZE** 43,694km²

Contents

Area profile

Four magnificent World Heritage sites, a generous helping of Michelin-starred restaurants and wonderful Alpine resorts

GETTING THERE

AIR AirFrance (0845 0845 111; www.airfrance.co.uk) flies to Lyon from Heathrow. **British Airways** (0870 240 0747; www.britishairways.co.uk) flies to Lyon from Birmingham, Heathrow and Manchester. **easyJet** (0870 600 0000; www.easyjet.com) flies to Lyon from Stansted and Grenoble from Luton and Gatwick. **Ryanair** (0871 246 0000; www.ryanair.com) flies to St Étienne and Grenoble from Stansted.

ROAD From Calais the A26 leads you down to Reims and on to Troyes, from where the A5 takes you into Burgundy. The A6 from Paris will take you straight to the heart of Burgundy, passing through Sens, Chablis, Beaune, and finally Mâcon. The A43 also runs south from Lyon through Burgundy and on into the Rhône-Alpes, leading into Lyon. From Lyon, the A43 runs into the A48 and on into Grenoble. From there, the A41 runs north into Annecy, and the N75 runs south into Provence. The A43 runs east from Lyon to Chambéry.

RAIL From Paris there is a direct **TGV** (www.tgv.co.uk) link to Dijon. Contact Rail Europe (0870 584 8848; www.raileurope.co.uk) for details.

T HE RHÔNE-ALPES REGION ENCOMPASSES SOME of Europe's most spectacular scenery, fabulous ski resorts, France's second city Lyon, and the rolling vineyards of Beaujolais. In the east of the region, the Alps serve as a natural border with Switzerland in the north and Italy in the south.

The Rhône-Alpes region definitely has a split personality. The Rhône valley has a decidedly Mediterranean feel with its sultry climate, its rocky plateaus, its spicy wines and its relaxed air. However, the eastern half, towards the Alps, feels much more Swiss, where menus feature melted cheese dishes and the countryside becomes gradually more mountainous.

The Rhône valley

The Rhône valley cuts through the mid-western section of the region and it's here you discover the lush, fertile hills and vineyards of Beaujolais. A short drive south is Lyon – capital of the region, the nation's gastronomic capital and a city that has prospered for many hundreds of years. France's second city, famed for its student and immigrant population, has a lively, cosmopolitan air, with friendly bars and countless restaurants featuring specialities from around the world. Its wealth was originally built on printing and weaving, and today it has four UNESCO World Heritage sites as well as many of the country's finest Michelin-starred restaurants. Overlooking the river Saône, Lyon's Old Town features narrow streets and 17th-century townhouses, and elsewhere in the city you'll find the

amazingly well preserved Roman amphitheatres.

To the south of Lyon there are more Roman sites at Vienne, Valence and St-Romain-en-Gal. Between Vienne and Valence are some of the most celebrated vineyards in France, including those of the Côte Rôtie and Hermitage appellations.

The French Alps

Southeast of Lyon is Grenoble, the capital of the French Alps and home to more than 40,000 students and numerous high-tech research companies. With lots of museums and yearly festivals, the city is a great cultural centre and a good location from which to explore the nearby mountain ranges.

Further east, along the border with Switzerland and Italy in the départements of Savoie and Haute-Savoie, are some of Europe's finest winter resorts including Chamonix, Morzine, Megève, Albertville, Méribel, Courchevel and Val d'Isère. Many of these towns are exclusive and hugely expensive, particularly during the skiing season when they are crammed with visitors, who come to stay in the typical Alpine chalets and indulge in skiing, snowboarding and, of course, the après-ski.

In the summer months – when it's generally dry and very warm – the Alps are quieter, but they still attract hikers, mountaineers, paragliders, pony trekkers, and those who just want to relax and enjoy the breathtaking mountain scenery. And in the northeast département of Haute-Savoie, the lakes of Annecy and Léman (better known as Lake Geneva) offer the chance to do some rowing, sailing, windsurfing or swimming.

CLIMATE

RHÔNE-ALPES		LONDON		RHÔNE-ALPES		LONDON	
5	Dec	7		52	Dec	81	
6	Nov	10		68	Nov	78	
13	Oct	14		80	Oct	70	
15	Sep	19		68	Sep	65	
22	Aug	21		70	Aug	62	
22	Jul	22		68	Jul	59	
21	Jun	20		74	Jun	58	
16	May	17		68	May	57	
13	Apr	13		58	Apr	56	
11	Mar	10		50	Mar	64	
5	Feb	7		47	Feb	72	
4	Jan	6		48	Jan	77	

AVERAGE **TEMPERATURE** (Celsius)

AVERAGE **RAINFALL** (millimetres)

FOOD AND DRINK

Lyon, the nation's gastronomic capital, is home to many of France's top-notch restaurants, but there are also plenty of low-budget bistros (bouchons) serving hearty fare. Regional specialities include: quenelle de brochet (poached pike mousse), boudin noir (black pudding sausage often served with potatoes in butter) and cervelle de canut (cream cheese mixed with garlic and chives). Favourite desserts are gâteau de Savoie, made with potato flour, and Grenoble's walnut cake, sometimes soaked with the locally produced Chartreuse liqueur. From Lyon there are bugnes (lemon fritters) and almond-filled pastries, while Montélimar is famous for its nougat.

The region's wines include powerful, full-bodied reds dominated by the Shiraz grape, such as Côtes de Rhône and Châteauneuf-du-Pape; world-famous Beaujolais, based on the fruitier Gamay grape; fantastic whites, such as the exclusive Condrieu and Château-Grillet; and Clairette-de-Die, an extremely delicate sparkling wine.

MAISON DE LA FRANCE

■ The best skiing in France if not Europe is found in Savoie département at resorts like Val d'Isère and Courchevel

■ Wander through the narrow streets of Annecy's Old Town, taking in its tranquil canals and brightly coloured houses

■ For the thrill of a lifetime, come to the Alpine foothills and go paragliding off the hillsides

■ The region's capital, Lyon, is known for its Roman remains, its restored Old Town and its huge number of restaurants

■ The vineyards of the Rhône valley produce top quality red wines that shouldn't be missed

■ Visit the refurbished spa of Évian-les-Bains and taste the delicious spring water… for nothing!

■ Visit the Olympic Village in Albertville, constructed for the 1992 Winter Games

■ If you prefer watersports, take yourself to Lake Annecy or Lake Geneva, where you can sail, windsurf, row, canoe, swim or just relax on a pedalo

The Rhône-Alpes region is certainly a region of contrasts and it attracts visitors throughout the year. If you choose to live here, there's never a dull moment.

The economy

Not surprisingly, significant income in Rhône-Alpes is generated from winter tourism – the Alpine ski resorts of Val d'Isère and Megève, in particular, are among the most expensive in the world. The resorts around Mont Blanc have tourism-based economies, as do the Lake Annecy villages and the popular resorts of Annecy, Talloires and Thonon-les-Bains.

Apart from tourism, which brings in money throughout the year, the area has a thriving industrial heritage, particularly around Grenoble where many of the country's biggest high-tech companies are based. Lyon, the major commercial centre in the region, is big on banking and commerce. Wine production and wine tourism drive the Beaujolais economy; southwest of Villefranche is one of France's premier wine routes.

Social groups

Grenoble and Chambéry are both home to small British communities, while the exclusive skiing resorts attract the glitterati from all over the continent. Talloires and Annecy boast some excellent all-year-round amenities, and many British buyers make use of the pistes around La Clusaz and Grand Bornard. ●

Property hotspots

MAP KEY

- **5** Hotspot
- ● Major town/city
- ✈ Airport
- ⛴ Ferry

LAKE ANNECY

1 Annecy is a charming Alpine town with a medieval quarter, canals, flower-covered bridges and narrow streets. In the 19th century, European nobility rediscovered it and built lavish palaces on the lake, reputedly Europe's cleanest. Outdoor pursuits such as swimming, sailing, and cycling give it a standing on a par with the Côte d'Azur, and there are many ski resorts within a 90-minute drive.

Villas with swimming pools, chalets and apartments are much cheaper in and around the lakeside villages than in the mountain resorts. Some villages can be reached by steamer, and many have their own beaches. Talloires, 13 kilometres south, houses the Michelin-starred Auberge du Père-Bise restaurant and the luxurious Hôtel de l'Abbaye (Cézanne and Churchill were famous residents). In August, French families come to hike and camp. A two-bedroom property will set you back roughly €352,000, with four-bedroom properties priced from around €530,000. Properties with lake views are especially pricey – a three-bedroom, renovated chalet will set you back around €517,000. A shortage of building land has also pushed up prices.

Many foreign buyers choose Talloires for year-round stays, and the average rental for a two-bedroom house in Talloires is €573 a week. Winter is peak season in this popular tourist resort, when Annecy's average rental fees are from €395 to

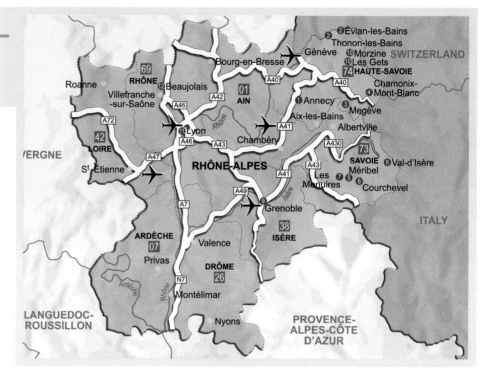

€1,700 per week for a two-bedroom villa. For maximum income, pick a property close to the ski slopes.

Key facts

■ **POPULATION** 53,571
■ **AIRPORT** Annecy Metz Airport, 8 route de Côte Merle, 74370 Metz-Tessy, Tel +33 4 50 27 30 06, www.annecy.aeroport.fr
■ **SCHOOLS** Nearest: Albertville, Megève and Ferney Voltaire
■ **MEDICAL** Centre Hospitalier, av Trésum 1, 74000 Annecy, Tel: +33 4 50 88 33 33
■ **PROS** Plenty of tourist attractions ■ Excellent transport links ■ On a par with the Côte d'Azur for French retirees ■ Annecy Old Town is very attractive ■ Golfing facilities are nearby
■ **CONS** Annecy is very crowded in summer ■ Limited winter rentals; skiers prefer to be closer to the slopes.

LAKE GENEVA

2 Popular with aristocrats during the belle époque, Thonon-les-Bains spa lies in the lower Chablais region, north of Haute-Savoie on Lake Geneva. Constructed on three levels between lake and mountains in a naturally arched bay, it offers magnificent views of Lake Geneva from the upper part of town, while the spa centre of Les Thermes overlooks the waterfront.

The Versoie spring was first discovered by the Romans and opened to the public in the 19th century. Thonon-les-Bains is also the first stage on the Route-des-Alpes, covering the main Alpine passes and several nature reserves from Lake Geneva to the Mediterranean. Thonon's fishing port, tucked behind Rives castle, is active throughout the year, and a large market sells produce every Monday and Thursday.

The average cost of a two-bedroom home in the region is €409,000, rising to €497,000 if you want four bedrooms. For a five/six-bedroom property you are looking at around €556,000.

This is a prime rental location,

well positioned for tourists drawn to the French Alps and Annecy. Thonon-les-Bains is good for rentals for four to six months of the year, and the price for a one-bedroom apartment averages €525 per week. Short-term average rental for a two-bedroom apartment is €675.

Key facts

■ **POPULATION** 37,480
■ **AIRPORT** Geneva Airport, PO BOX 100, CH-1215 Geneva 15, Switzerland, Tel: + 41 227 177 111
■ **SCHOOLS** Nearest: Albertville, Megève and Ferney Voltaire
■ **MEDICAL** Annecy Centre Hospitalier, av Trésum 1, 74000 Annecy, Tel: +33 4 50 88 33 33 ■ Hôpitaux du Léman, avenue de la Dame 3, 74 200 Thonon-les-Bains, Tel: +33 4 50 83 20 00, www.ch-leman.fr
■ **PROS** Amenities include golf and skiing in La Clusaz and Grand Bornand ■ Excellent transport links to the area
■ **CONS** Not really a winter spot, Thonon is a 40-minute journey from the ski resorts ■ Nearby Évian-les-Bains attracts hordes of visitors.

MEGÈVE

3 West of Mont Blanc, the medieval Savoyard town of Megève is ultra-chic. 'Discovered' by the Baroness de Rothschild in 1921, it still attracts the rich out of season from the French Riviera, and most of its visitors are French. The 290 kilometres of ski-runs are a skier's paradise. Chamonix is less than 30 minutes away and is included on the Mont Blanc ski pass, which accesses 13 other resorts. This World Cup ski venue is a good choice for non-skiers too, who can easily access Michelin-starred mountain restaurants and enjoy a first-class spa or lively, varied après-ski.

Property is expensive, with a choice of large luxury chalets rather than new apartments. The main hotspots of Mont d'Arbois (on a golf course, set above the resort) and villages such as Ormaret, with views of Mont Blanc, attract premium prices.

Centrally located chalets start from around €560,000 for two bedrooms, while four-bedroom properties cost over €1,146,000. Properties in the nearby villages of Combloux and St-Gervais are more reasonably priced.

The rental season lasts longer than 15 weeks, from December to April, and the average price per week is €438 for a two-bedroom chalet.

Key facts
■ **POPULATION** 4,509
■ **AIRPORT** Chambéry/Aix-les-Bains Airport, Chambre de Commerce, 73420 Viviers du Lac, Tel +33 4 79 54 49 54
■ **SCHOOLS** Nearest: Megève
■ **MEDICAL** Centre Hospitalier, route Pèlerins 509, 74400 Chamonix Mont Blanc, Tel: +33 4 50 53 84 00
■ **PROS** Hailed as the most beautiful of the French ski resorts, it combines the modern jet-set feel with an old-world charm ■ Top international resort with winter and summer appeal ■ Good golf course, restaurants and hotels ■ Excellent transport links

■ **CONS** Roads can become very congested during the winter months; chains for your wheels are mandatory ■ The snow record is relatively poor as Megève lies at a low altitude ■ The area is besieged by tourists for the winter sports.

CHAMONIX

4 Situated at the foot of Mont Blanc and at the crossroads of France, Italy and Switzerland, with easy access to Italy via the Mont Blanc tunnel, Chamonix is much sought after for both its sporting and scenic qualities. Although developed as a summertime mountaineering centre, the resort is renowned as a top destination for expert skiers, so there's a demand for quality property.

Throughout the year the town is busy, but it has retained its charm, with narrow streets lining the car-free centre and a river flowing through the valley floor. Most visitors choose to ski at high altitude, taking in a circuit from the main town to the valley across Le Brévent, La Flégère, Les Grand Montets, and Le Tour, including seven glaciers and a lift-served vertical drop of 2,807 metres.

New, traditionally constructed apartments are good buys and often have superior mountain views and a concierge. Two-bedroom properties average around €842,000. With precious little building land available and a strong demand from wealthy buyers across the world – despite the already high prices – Chamonix remains one of the region's most exclusive resorts.

With excellent rental potential, the season lasts for more than 15 weeks (December to April) in this fashionable, cosmopolitan resort. The average rental price per week is €629 for a two-bedroom property, although during peak season, you can expect far higher returns.

Key facts
■ **POPULATION** 9,830
■ **AIRPORT** Chambéry/Aix-les-Bains Airport, Chambre de Commerce, 73420 Viviers du Lac, Tel: +33 4 79 54 4954
■ **SCHOOLS** Nearest: Megève
■ **MEDICAL** Centre Hospitalier, route Pèlerins 509, 74400 Chamonix Mont Blanc, Tel: +33 4 50 53 84 00
■ **PROS** Budget easyJet flights into Geneva airport have made travelling to a second home here cheap ■ Best in the region for advanced skiers ■ Dog sledding, mountain biking, paragliding, helicopter trips, an ice-rink, and a climbing centre are available here
■ **CONS** Lots of traffic and people ■ Difficult access; skiers rely on shuttle buses or cars to reach the slopes ■ A seven-hour car journey from Paris.

MÉRIBEL

5 High up in the Alps at 1,450 metres, in the centre of the Trois Vallées, Méribel has access to 720 kilometres of pistes, both nursery slopes and off-piste for the more experienced skier. Méribel's night life revolves largely around British-run bars with live music. Restaurants specialise in Savoyard dishes like raclette, tartiflette and pizza savoyarde, made with Beaufort, Comté and Emmental cheese over dried meats. Méribel-les-Allues is 10 minutes from the lift station at Chaudanne, and is a quieter base from which to explore the Trois Vallées.

La Chaudanne Olympic Park has a swimming pool, sauna, ice rink, parapenting, snowbiking, ice karting and dog sledding. Almost everything built since development started in 1931 has been traditional in style, making Méribel one of the most tasteful French purpose-built resorts. Chalets are rarely available and average €1,478,000 for four bedrooms, though some of the region's cheapest prices can be found here as well. Buyers prefer newer propertics, particularly apartments, as they have larger rooms and are of better quality,

but the dearth of such properties in

Val d'Isère and Méribel sends buyers to cheaper areas like Ste-Foy, half an hour away, where high-quality, detached, new chalets are built to blend with the old.

This resort is a popular international location with lots of potential for permanent and second homes, and an excellent rental season from December to April. A standard, two-bedroom apartment fetches from €678 per week and a four-bedroom apartment from €1,554.

Key facts
■ **POPULATION** 1,850
■ **AIRPORT** Chambéry/Aix-les-Bains Airport, Chambre de Commerce, 73420 Viviers du Lac, Tel: +33 4 79 54 49 54
■ **SCHOOLS** Nearest: Albertville
■ **MEDICAL** Nearest: Hôpital de Moutiers, rue École des Mines, 73600 Moutiers Toulentaise, Tel: +33 4 79 09 60 60
■ **PROS** Budget easyJet flights and excellent transport networks ■ Méribel is the most British-dominated resort in the Alps ■ Plenty of après-ski amenities ■ **CONS** Busy tourist location and slightly less sophisticated than other resorts in the region ■ Almost seven hours from Paris by road.

COURCHEVEL

6 Courchevel is located in the Trois Vallées ski area, along with Méribel, Les Menuires and Val Thorens. With 640 kilometres of piste and superb skiing, this area is the largest interconnected ski resort in France. Here, the world's largest cable car and numerous ski lifts carry 52,000 skiers per hour.

Four hours from Geneva, the resort is built on four levels, named according to their elevation in metres: 1300, 1550, 1650, and 1850. All have luxury private villas or chalets that are ski-in, ski-out, but Courchevel 1850 is the most upmarket, drawing royalty and celebrities. Extensive and varied terrain suits everyone from beginners to experts, though some slopes get very crowded. Courchevel 1650 has an extra hour's sunlight per day. The two lower areas are Le Praz (1,300m), a traditional Savoie hamlet; and family-friendly La Tania (also at 1,300m).

Chalets are built in the traditional Savoyard style of architecture, featuring exposed stone, large roof beams and handcrafted wooden doors. A decreasing amount of land to build on has led to a strong market, with ski companies chasing chalets to run as winter rentals. A three-bedroom property in Courchevel costs an average of €895,000.

The high-season rental potential is excellent, with a 15-week plus season. The average rent per week is around an average of €896 for a three-bedroom chalet.

Key facts
■ **POPULATION** 1,850
■ **AIRPORT** Annecy Metz Airport, route de Côte Merle 8, 74370 Metz-Tessy, Tel: +33 4 50 27 30 06, www.annecy.aeroport.fr
■ **SCHOOLS** Nearest: Albertville
■ **MEDICAL** Hôpital de Moutier, rue Ecole des Mines, 73600 Moûtiers Tarentaise, Tel: +33 4 79 09 60 60
■ **PROS** easyJet flies into Geneva Airport and has made travelling quick, easy and cheap ■ Courchevel exudes luxury and glamour, both on and off the piste ■ Luxury shops, gourmet restaurants, an active après-ski life and an illuminated sledge run make this a popular region
■ **CONS** The town gets taken over by tourists in the winter ■ Slightly off the beaten track, the resort does not offer easy access ■ The top resort hotels only open in winter.

LES MENUIRES

7 Many consider Les Menuires the least

attractive resort in the Alps, with few woodland slopes. Located in the Belleville valley at the head of the Trois Vallées ski area, it remains in demand as a purpose-built resort, offering immediate access to the challenging pistes of La Masse, and is rarely used by visitors from the other valleys.

The main intermediate and beginner slopes benefit from a lot of sun while Allemands, the red run twisting from the top of Roc des Trois Marches into Les Menuires, is one of the finest. Split into three levels, the resort consists of Reberty (the highest and most appealing section); the main resort of Croisette; and low-lying Preyerand.

Reberty is made up of two parts – 1850 and 2000; the latter is slightly higher up. In 1850, you can acquire a north-facing, furnished property with two-bedrooms from €316,000 or a three-bedroom property facing southwest for around €338,000.

A shortage of land for new-builds has fuelled the rental market, which is excellent from December to April. The average rent for this area per week is €725 for a two-bedroom property.

Key facts
■ **POPULATION** 2,532
■ **AIRPORT** Annecy Metz Airport, route de Côte Merle 8, 74370 Metz-Tessy, Tel: +33 4 50 27 30 06
■ **SCHOOLS** Nearest: Albertville
■ **MEDICAL** Hôpital de Moûtiers, rue École des Mines, 73600 Moûtiers Tarentaise, Tel: +33 4 79 09 60 60
■ **PROS** Nearly 650km of pistes and three snow-makers, ensuring snow ■ A family-orientated resort with some cheap hotels ■ Convenient link to Val Thorens, Europe's highest ski resort
■ **CONS** Many unattractive apartments ■ An unsightly resort ■ More than seven hours by road from Paris.

VAL D'ISÈRE

8 Located at high altitude, with the peaks of La

Grande Motte and La Grande Casse in the background, Val d'Isère enjoys frequent snowfalls and is one of France's finest skiing resorts. It is not a picturesque resort, with unattractive high-rise apartment blocks at La Daille, but the town centre has a more upmarket feel and over the years the resort has proved popular with the British.

Val d'Isère's slopes are divided into three sectors: Bellevarde, reached from the centre; La Daille, Solaise, also reached from the centre; and Col de L'Iséran, which is reached from Le Fornet. The Pissaillas glacier is open from late June to mid-August.

In summer, there are few facilities for the non-skier, so the Trois Vallées is a better choice for buyers sourcing a property for both summer and winter seasons, while still having access to a large ski area. Apartments sell very quickly, especially those recently built. Prices start at a hefty average of €1,481,000 for a three-bedroom chalet. Smaller houses start at a shade under €877,000, but if you have a more modest budget, consider the nearby resort of Ste-Foy, which has retained its original charm, yet is only 30 minutes by car from Val d'Isère. Here, new chalets blend in with existing homes, some of which are more than a century old.

An excellent winter resort, Val d'Isère has international, year-round appeal with a five-month-long winter season. The average rental price for a two-bedroom property is €1,752 a week, while prices for three bedrooms rise substantially, to over €3,000 a week.

Key facts
■ **POPULATION** 45,000
■ **AIRPORT** Annecy Metz Airport, route de Côte Merle 8, 74370 Metz-Tessy, Tel: +33 4 50 27 30 06
■ **SCHOOLS** Nearest: Albertville
■ **MEDICAL** Nearest is Hôpital, rue

Nantet 139, 73700 Bourg St-Maurice, Tel: +33 4 79 41 79 79
■ **PROS** One of the best resorts in the region and a favourite with skiers ■ Covers a massive area and has more than 100 lifts with numerous ski runs ■ Après-ski for serious party-goers, with lots of bars and more than 70 restaurants ■ Long ski season and good snow record ■ Masses of winter sports
■ **CONS** Lack of available property ■ A high demand for larger apartments and chalets.

GRENOBLE

9 Grenoble, the capital of the French Alps, is a beautiful, university city with some wonderful heritage sites, such as the Dauphinois museum and the Fort de la Bastille, accessible by cable car over the river.

Capital of the Dauphiné – a former province – Grenoble has an exceptional geographic setting, with the skiing season beginning from mid-November. Close to Switzerland, Italy, and the Mediterranean, it offers a fast gateway to Les Deux Alpes and Alpes d'Huez, which are just half an hour away. It is not generally considered to be a hotspot, but the lack of new-builds in the ski resorts makes property here a good investment and prices are climbing.

For superb rural views, try St-Pierre-de-Chartreuse, a peaceful, medieval mountain village in the heart of the Chartreuse Regional Park. Two-bedroom apartments can be picked up for under €270,000, while five/six-bedroom homes average just over €537,000.

Grenoble's rental potential is good, given its international appeal and its 50,000 university students who fuel the long-term rentals market. Average rental prices are €373 per week for a one-bedroom apartment and €517 for a two-bedroom apartment.

Key facts

◼ **POPULATION** 156,203
◼ **AIRPORT** Grenoble St-Geois Airport, 38590 St-étienne-de-St-Geois, Tel: +33 4 76 65 48 48
◼ **SCHOOLS** Cité Scolaire International Europole, 4 place de Sfax, Grenoble, Tel: +33 4 38 12 25 00
◼ **MEDICAL** Mutuelle Générale de l'Éducation Nationale, rue Félix Poulat 38000 3, Grenoble, Tel: +33 4 76 86 63 63
◼ **PROS** Perfectly placed for Italy, Switzerland and the Mediterranean ◼ Excellent range of adventure sports available ◼ The city is surrounded by three French Alpine ranges
◼ **CONS** Grenoble gets very crowded between December and January.

LES PORTES DU SOLEIL (LES GETS & MORZINE)

10 Set on a sunny mountain pass, just over the border from Switzerland in Haute-Savoie, family-friendly Les Gets is a traditional Alpine village that is also one of the most popular smaller ski resorts. Part of the Portes du Soleil network that links 12 resorts on either side of the French/Swiss border, Les Gets appeals to the many families who want to sample the great outdoors rather than après-ski. The skiing area spreads to both sides of Les Gets with the smaller, but less crowded, Mont Chéry offering more challenging skiing, while Les Chavannes is a much more suitable area for families and beginners or intermediates.

In Les Gets, brand new locations near the Chavannes ski slope, close to the village centre, are highly desirable. Prices are rising and stringent property laws apply to new-builds. Planning permission is now only given for 'filling in' existing hamlets, or if a property fronts a main road. Further building in Les Gets is banned for two years. Chalet builders are snapping up blocks of land to ensure their businesses keep running, so recent builds have been bought 'off-plan'. In the area as a whole, two-bedroom properties average under €388,000, but you can pay much more in exclusive blocks. Four-bedroom homes average €584,000.

With a winter rental season stretching from December to April, the average property will generate between €416 and €1,400 per week.

Key facts

◼ **POPULATION** 1,369
◼ **AIRPORT** Annecy Metz Airport, route de Côte Merle 8, 74370 Metz-Tessy, Tel: +33 4 50 27 30 06, www.annecy.aeroport.fr
◼ **SCHOOLS** Nearest: Morzine and Thonon les Bains
◼ **MEDICAL** Hôpitaux du Léman, avenue de la Dame 3, 74200 Thonon-Les-Bains, Tel: +33 4 50 83 20 00, www.ch-leman.fr
◼ **PROS** Budget flights into Geneva airport ◼ Lots of family-friendly outdoor activities are available ◼ A Mecca for the sporty, with 19 mountain walks and cross-country cycle routes
◼ **CONS** Les Gets is quite low (1,175m), the top reaching 2,350m with access to high-level skiing areas ◼ It is unknown to many British as a summer resort.

LYON

11 With more restaurants per square metre than any other city in the world, Lyon is justifiably the gastronomic capital of France, with a lively night scene and cultural life.

Top Michelin restaurants sit alongside bouchons (bistros) serving Lyonnais specialities in a picturesque setting.

The city is graced by Roman amphitheatres, Renaissance architecture and a silk-weaving tradition, found in the district of Le Croix-Rousse. The traboules, or secret passageways, link streets and houses and were used by the Resistance during the Second World War. The Old Town's landmark is the Basilique Notre-Dame de Fourvière, whose interior is adorned with ornate stone carvings and gilded mosaics. The Le Croix-Rousse, Fourvière, Presqu'ile and Vieux-Lyon neighbourhoods are listed World Heritage sites.

A two-bedroom property costs an average of €366,000, a four-bedroom house €503,000. This is a working city with a long-term rental market. The average rental per week is €732 for a two-bedroom property and €1,077 for three bedrooms.

Key facts

◼ **POPULATION** 453,187
◼ **AIRPORT** Lyon-Exupéry Aéroport, BP113, 69125 Lyon, Tel: +33 7 72 22 72 21, www.lyon.aeroport.fr
◼ **SCHOOLS** Cité Scolaire Internationale, place de Montréal 2, 69361 Lyon Cedex, Tel: +33 4 78 69 60 06
◼ **MEDICAL** Hôpital de l'Hôtel Dieu, place de l'Hôpital, 69288 Lyon Cedex, Tel: +33 4 72 41 30 24, www.chu-lyon.fr
◼ **PROS** A commercial centre with great employment opportunities ◼ Well-served by TGV trains, it has a convenient link to Paris for commuters, and its own international airport ◼ A thriving array of amenities
◼ **CONS** You may need to be willing to learn French to relocate here.

BEAUJOLAIS

11 The Beaujolais is a region of lush, fertile hills peppered with a range of charmingly picturesque villages and sprinkled with a selection of rolling vineyards in the southeast of France. Perched above the valley of the river Saône and surrounding the town of Villefranche-sur-Saône, with numerous vineyards in which to sample the area's wines, the Beaujolais offers a glimpse of the traditional vineyard lifestyle and local life. The vineyard region stretches for nearly 100 square kilometres from Lyon in the south to Mâcon in the north, and properties are often former stone-built winegrowers' homes.

Eastern Beaujolais is the best known part, and Villefranche-sur-Saône has become the economic hub of this area of the Rhône, succeeding Beaujeu, the historic capital. Villefranche-sur-Saône's church dates back to the 12th century and there are fine Renaissance houses and a 17th-century hospital. Two-bedroom homes average just under €219,000, but it will cost around €551,000 for five or six bedrooms.

This area is rich in history and architecture, with many of the tiny, wine-producing villages containing some architectural gems. Properties are generally slightly cheaper from La Clayette to Tarare, an area dominated by mountains.

A one-bedroom apartment costs €550 per week, while a four-bedroom place will set you back €1,300. The market is fairly busy during the wine festival, as you'd expect, season, but it can be difficult to secure rentals at other times when demand is not quite so high.

Key facts

◼ **POPULATION** 31,213
◼ **AIRPORT** Lyon-Exupéry Aéroport, BP113, 69125 Lyon, Tel: +33 772 22 72 21, www.lyon.aeroport.fr
◼ **SCHOOLS** Cité Scolaire Internationale, place de Montréal 2, 69361 Lyon Cedex 07, Tel: +33 4 78 69 60 06
◼ **MEDICAL** Centre Hospitalier de Villefranche-sur-Saône, Quilly Gleizé BP 436, 69655 Villefranche-sur-Saône Cedex, Tel: +33 4 74 09 29 29, www.ch-villefranche.fr
◼ **PROS** An area full of rivers, tributaries, granite peaks, farms and forests ◼ Full of gastronomic delights, olive oil and fine wines ◼ Villefranche has excellent restaurants and shops
◼ **CONS** Properties in the Lyon to Mâcon area are expensive. ●

HOTSPOTS

Property guide

With many low-cost airlines now providing services to the lively cities of Lyon, St-Étienne and Chambéry, interest in the region must surely grow

The village of Turenne, with its mellow stone houses, is close to Brive yet in the heart of the countryside

SURPRISINGLY FOR ONE OF FRANCE'S LARGEST regions, the demand from second-home owners and relocators is small across the Rhône-Alpes as a whole. This is true both of foreign buyers and local French investors, and is due mainly to the region's perceived inaccessibility, but with many low-cost airlines now providing services to the lively cities of Lyon, St-Étienne and Chambéry, and a slow but growing realisation that the regions is actually rather easy to get to, interest is bound to grow.

The Rhône-Alpes is home to the world's largest ski area, and property prices in the famous resorts, such as Courchevel, Morzine and Chamonix, command premium rates. While you'll have no trouble maintaining a rental income here, you can expect to pay top dollar for your property. A two- to three-bedroom chalet with pool and mountain views in one of these ski centres will cost you upwards of €440,000. However, the high demand for holiday accommodation in these popular resorts coupled with the year-round rental potential should ensure a good return on your investment, with weekly yields of up to €4,000 per property.

Megève's lower position on the slopes and poor snow record would seem to make this international resort an insecure investment, but thanks to its golf course, hotels and restaurants, it's a year-round rental proposition. Val d'Isère's ski season and good snow record make it a safe buy-to-let option.

A rising star for relocators is the area in Beaujolais between La Clayette in the north and Tarare in the south. Its remoteness makes its properties cheaper to buy than the former wine-growers' homes around Mâcon overlooking the Saône valley.

Village houses around Chamonix, Annecy, and Chambéry are sound investments, as the long-term rental potential is good. A shortage of building land and increasing land prices in the winter ski resorts of Chamonix, Morzine, Val d'Isere and Chambéry plus a current ban on building permits in Les Gets point to demand outstripping supply.

The most prevalent property type in the Rhône-Alpes region is the traditional chalet. Away from the mountains, properties include luxury city loft apartments, farmhouses requiring restoration, modern villas and maisons de maître with land.

ALPINE CHALETS

- Chalets were traditionally built high up on the sunny side of mountains to provide shelter for the owners and their livestock during the harsh winter months
- Most chalets were two or three storeys high. The ground level was used for storing cheese and housed the cowshed. The first floor was used as living quarters, and the top floor was where hay was stored.
- Chalets were built either of wood (chalet en bois) or of wood, slates and stone
- In a chalet en bois the floor is made of stone slabs and the walls are built of logs. Small wooden tiles (tavaillons) sometimes cover the walls to provide insulation
- Chalets in the Savoie have covered balconies for drying hemp, corn and firewood

WHAT CAN YOU GET FOR YOUR EUROS?

SKI HOUSE

Newly-built chalet with over quarter of an acre garden, in ideal location close to ski-slopes. The property offers 217m2 living space on two floors, with basement: games room, 2 cellars, guest wc, living room leading onto balcony, dining area, open-plan kitchen, bedroom with shower room & balcony, garage, 4 bedrooms, 2 shower rooms, bathroom. Situated in the resort of Le Grand Bornand.

€1,150,000 CODE LAT

CHALET IN SIXT

This picturesque south-facing chalet is set on a plot of 2,284 square metres in the pretty village of Sixt. It sleeps eight people in all, and has a traditional warm and welcoming Savoyarde interior. The spacious living area has a magnificent fireplace, a fully equipped kitchen, utility room, cellar, and a bathroom with shower. There's also parking, plus a regular ski service just 50 metres from the chalet!

€438,000 CODE FPS

FARMHOUSE WITH POOL

This incredible 18th-century farmhouse has been lovingly restored. Along with six bedrooms and five bathrooms, it also boasts a large outdoor swimming pool, along with a separate pool house, plus sprinklers, double glazing, electric gates with an intercom, and an alarm system. The farmhouse is located in a pretty and picturesque valley and is set in 2,000 square metres of grounds.

€600,000 CODE SIF

18TH-CENTURY CHÂTEAU

This magnificent 18th-century château lies in 30 hectares of AOC vineyards in the heart of the Beaujolais region. There's plenty of space, with two towers, a wing, and three hectares of landscaped grounds, which include a pool, a lake and a tennis court. Inside, 15 of the château's 26 main rooms are bedrooms, while the outbuildings include an orangerie, a caretaker's house and vaulted cellars.

€4,239,200 CODE SIF

RENOVATION OPPORTUNITY

This is a fantastic renovation project. Made up of three stone buildings set on the roadside in Drôme Ardèche, the property was once a café. Today it's a little run down, although recent refurbishments include a new roof. The main house has five bedrooms, and there's a small one-bedroom studio property attached to the garden. Cellars, some of which are vaulted, run underneath the main house.

€167,585 CODE VEF

WELL-LOCATED PROPERTY

This four-bedroom property is actually on an island, although it doesn't feel like it – the village of Roche-de-Glun is set on a substantial amount of land between the Rhône River and the Rhône Canal. It's perfect for those who want luxurious touches, such as an outdoor pool and landscaped gardens, and who can't decide whether they prefer the Drôme or the Ardeche!

€483,525 CODE VEF

AVERAGE HOUSE PRICES RHÔNE-ALPES

	2-bed		3-bed		4-bed		5/6-bed	
Lake Annecy	€351,667	(£237,613)	€516,665	(£349,098)	€529,561	(£357,812)	€606,643	(£409,894)
Lake Geneva	€408,633	(£276,104)	€428,317	(£289,404)	€497,322	(£336,029)	€556,009	(£375,682)
Megève	€559,700	(£378,176)	€860,365	(£581,328)	€1,146,261	(£774,501)	€1,324,104	(£894,665)
Chamonix	€842,441	(£569,217)	€965,837	(£652,593)	€1,258,196	(£850,133)	€1,276,328	(£862,384)
Méribel	–		€802,297	(£542,093)	€1,477,928	(£998,600)	€2,049,360	(£1,384,703)
Courchevel	–		€895,411	(£605,008)	€1,144,174	(£773,091)	€1,424,801	(£962,704)
Les Menuires	€315,916	(£213,457)	€338,379	(£228,635)	€590,084	(£398,706)	€930,592	(£628,779)
Val d'Isère	€876,608	(£592,303)	€1,480,904	(£1,000,611)	€2,187,738	(£1,478,202)	€2,645,230	(£1,787,318)
Grenoble	€270,353	(£182,671)	€354,331	(£239,413)	€445,585	(£301,071)	€537,136	(£362,930)

Aquitaine

Vineyards, world-renowned wine and culture

MAISON DE LA FRANCE

FACT BOX

- **POPULATION** 2,908,359
- **UNEMPLOYMENT RATE** 10.2%
- **AVERAGE 4-BED HOUSE PRICE** €451,000
- **REGIONAL CAPITAL** Bordeaux
- **REGION SIZE** 41,407km²

Contents

Area profile

This corner of France is renowned for its quality Bordeaux wines, fine foods, Basque culture, and France's best surfing

GETTING THERE

AIR British Airways (0870 850 9850; www.britishairways.co.uk) flies to Bordeaux from Gatwick. **Flybe** (0871 700 0535; www.flybe.com) flies to Bordeaux from Belfast, Bristol, Edinburgh, Glasgow, Jersey and Southampton and to Bergerac from Belfast, Birmingham, Bristol and Southampton. **BMI Baby** (0870 264 2229; www.bmibaby.com) flies to Bordeaux from Birmingham and Manchester. **Ryanair** (0871 246 0000) flies to Bergerac from Liverpool and Stansted.

ROAD The region's main motorway is the A10, which connects Paris and Poitiers with Bordeaux and Toulouse. For Biarritz, take the A63. As the A10 is often highly congested, you may prefer to travel on smaller roads. From Paris the A71/A20 leads to Limoges, from where the N20 takes you to Toulouse. For Pau, take the A64. The A20 for Limoges provides access to Dordogne and Quercy, while the Autoroute des Deux Mers (A62-A61) links Bordeaux, the Atlantic coast and the Mediterranean.

RAIL The TGV offers services from Paris Gare Montparnasse to Bordeaux, and from Gare d'Austerlitz to Toulouse and Biarritz. Contact **Rail Europe** (0870 584 8848; www.raileurope.co.uk) for details.

AQUITAINE STRETCHES ALONG THE SOUTH-WEST of France from Poitou-Charentes down to the Pyrenees and the border with Spain. Home to the world's largest wine-growing region and 200 kilometres of unspoilt Atlantic coast, it's a very popular area with British holiday-makers and homebuyers.

This water-blessed region was named 'Aquitania' by the Romans after the many rivers criss-crossing the land, but thousands of years before the Romans arrived the area was inhabited by prehistoric tribes. Their unique cave paintings, some over 30,000 years old, are found in caves in the Dordogne. In the Middle Ages, Aquitaine had a chequered history and was ruled by the French, English and Basques. Eleanor of Aquitaine is the region's most famous historical figure, one of history's greatest female rulers. Wife first of Louis VII of France, then of Henry II of England, Eleanor fought in the Crusades and was Richard the Lionheart's mother.

Fine wine and Atlantic rollers

The capital of the region is Bordeaux, France's fifth largest city, a bustling, cosmopolitan port with a population approaching 750,000. Its 18th-century classical architecture is a testament to its past as a major centre for trade with Europe and the Americas. The Bordeaux region is most renowned for its fine wines, which are ranked under a highly complex system going back centuries and include top châteaux such as Margaux, Lafitte, Latour, Haut-Brion and Mouton-Rothschild.

Northwest of Bordeaux, the Dordogne

département, with its rolling landscapes, is one of the most popular areas for British homebuyers and holiday-makers. Boasting some 10 per cent of France's châteaux and offering everything from protected parks and fortified towns to protected cave paintings, the Dordogne embraces much of what the French know as Périgord. This land of plenty is split into four colour-defined territories: Périgord Vert (green), named after the lush valleys in the north; Périgord Blanc (white), so called because of the limestone in the centre; Périgord Pourpre (purple), in honour of the vineyards in the southwest; and Périgord Noir (black), named after the ancient oak trees in the southeast.

Lot-et-Garonne département is the agricultural heartland of Aquitaine, with vast areas dedicated to orchards of fruit trees, while on the coast is 'Les Landes', a vast sandy plain dotted with thousands of pine trees and boasting Europe's longest beaches and highest dunes. The Atlantic winds buffet the beaches and offer some of continental Europe's best surfing, windsailing and kite-surfing.

In the far southwest of the region is the seaside resort of Biarritz. In the 19th century it became a fashionable place for rich Europeans to congregate, and the grand architecture from that period is still very much in evidence. A few miles east is the capital of French Basque country, Bayonne, where the majestic Cathédrale Ste-Marie dominates the skyline. The local speciality served in the centre's many cafés is frothy hot chocolate.

Further south are the magnificent Pyrenees whose high mountains are often snow-capped in winter.

CLIMATE

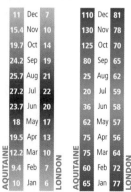

AQUITAINE		LONDON	
11	Dec	7	
15.4	Nov	10	
19.7	Oct	14	
24.2	Sep	19	
25.7	Aug	21	
27.2	Jul	22	
23.7	Jun	20	
18	May	17	
19.5	Apr	13	
12.2	Mar	10	
9.4	Feb	7	
10	Jan	6	

AVERAGE TEMPERATURE
(Celsius)

AQUITAINE		LONDON	
110	Dec	81	
130	Nov	78	
125	Oct	70	
80	Sep	65	
25	Aug	62	
20	Jul	59	
36	Jun	58	
62	May	57	
75	Apr	56	
75	Mar	64	
60	Feb	72	
65	Jan	77	

AVERAGE RAINFALL
(millimetres)

FOOD AND DRINK

Known for quality and diversity, the culinary specialities of Aquitaine range from black truffles, foie gras, confit of duck, and boar stew in the north to oysters and seafood paellas in the southern Basque area. Bayonne is home to jambon de Bayonne (prime ham) and exquisite chocolates. Frothy hot chocolate is a Bayonne speciality much loved by visitors and locals alike. Other well known produce from Aquitaine includes cream, cheese, still and sparkling white wines from the north, and rich beef stew in wine (usually red) from the south.

The Bordeaux wine region is the largest vineyard in the world, accounting for some 500 million bottles each year, ranging from the finest 'clarets' of the Médoc and St-Émilion, to dry whites from the Graves region, sweet dessert wines from Sauternes, and everyday table wines from Entre-Deux-Mers. Many other wines from Aquitaine are internationally acclaimed, including Bergerac, a delicate red with a violet aroma.

MAISON DE LA FRANCE

ATTRACTIONS

■ A leisurely stroll round the old quarter of Bergerac

■ Surfing on the Atlantic beaches

■ Biarritz – see and be seen along the promenade at dusk

■ A river cruise on the Garonne, including panoramic views of Agen

■ The Bordeaux vineyards and wine cellars

■ Les Landes Regional Park

■ The lovely harbour town of St-Jean-de-Luz, south of Biarritz on the Basque coast

■ The reproductions of the cave paintings in Lascaux

This area forms part of Pays Basque, whose territory once also included the Basque country in northeast Spain. French Basques are an independent people (though not so militant as their Spanish counterparts), with their own unique language (Euskera) and culture, clearly visible in the local architecture and fairs and festivals.

The economy

Renowned for producing some of France's finest food and wines, the region owes its immense wealth to its vineyards and pine forests. The area has diversified into the aerospace industry, agri-foodstuffs and the wood pulp industry, while the strikingly beautiful coastline has helped to contribute to the development of the tourist industry. Lot-et-Garonne, one of France's largest fruit producers, is known as the 'granary of France' and is particularly famous for its truffles.

Social groups

Dordogne is popular with many British buyers, as well as with Dutch and Germans. Some of the area's towns and villages are dominated by people who have moved here from abroad and there are pockets of expat communities. Cosmopolitan Bordeaux has large North African and student populations.. ●

Welcome to the Atlantic Coast

PROPERTIES & LAND, CLOSE TO NATURE, FROM JUST €25,000

JUST A SMALL EXAMPLE OF PROPERTIES AVAILABLE AT TIME OF GOING TO PRESS TO SEE OUR FULL CURRENT PORTFOLIO PLEASE VISIT OUR WEBSITE, OR CALL US TO DISCUSS YOUR REQUIREMENTS

» WT186 *Village Viticoles*

Large 4 bedroom stone house with small garden - perfect as a family holiday home. Large 30m² living room, traditional features (wood flooring, fireplaces etc) & garage. Some renovation needed.

€126,000 (approx £87,500)

» WT182 *Le Littoral*

Recently renovated 3 bedroom stone house (87m²) in an excellent area just 13km from the best beaches of the Medoc. New boiler and rewired. Gas central heating.

€134,000 (approx £93,050)

» WT122 *Ports de la Gironde*

Very well renovated stone town house in charming port of the Gironde. Very calm. Living area of 180m², in good clean condition. Offering 3 bedrooms. Beautiful interior and external stonework, wood flooring. Attractive garden of 450m².

€154,000 (approx £106,945)

» WT188 *Villages Viticoles*

A rare opportunity to buy a lovely stone house and a wonderful price. Charming setting, close to the village, this property offers a generous 180m² living area, on a plot of 600m². Five bedrooms, two garages.

€159,000 (approx £110,415)

» WT035 *Villages Viticoles*

100 year old countryside house with large 3,600m² private garden in a quiet hamlet 20km from the sea. Large property of 170m² offering 3 bedrooms, 2 bathrooms, garage, outbuilding.

€194,000 (approx £134,725)

» WT114 *Village Viticoles*

Five bedroom detached house with 2 bathrooms, garage & swimming pool. Beautiful large garden of 3,000². Nicely finished in good, clean condition.

€295,000 (approx £204,850)

www.webterre.com

Email: contact@webterre.com   Tel. 0033 (0)5 56 59 11 97

OUR OFFICE IS BASED IN THE FAMOUS 'MEDOC' WINE REGION OF FRANCE,
OFFERING EASY ACCESS VIA BORDEAUX INTERNATIONAL AIRPORT

WHY CHOOSE THE MEDOC?

The Médoc is one of the most prestigious wine growing regions in Bordeaux. 'Médoc', in local dialect, means 'the middle land', bordered by the Atlantic Ocean to the west from which it is protected by a huge forest, and the Gironde Estuary on the east. The geographical location of the region, as a peninsula set between two large bodies of water, helps to create a micro climate extremely favourable to the growing quality wines. The Aquitaine has a long history, which is waiting to be discovered hidden away under the blanket of pine trees covering this part of the Medoc. Calm is the word that springs to mind as you step out of your car. The speed of city life is a distant memory as you head for a relaxing day on the beach. You will find activities for all age groups and tastes. If its sport which leads you; the sea and the freshwater lakes on your doorstep will be your playground for fishing, canoeing, kite surfing, sailing and surfing. Alternatively try out the archery, bike tours, horse riding, go-karts, motor-cross, speed sailing and tennis which are all on offer. The market (open every day during summer months) with its colourful mix of over 200 stalls and stands is world famous for its produce (particulary oysters and wine) and atmosphere.

Focus on Dordogne

Known as 'Dordogneshire', France's most stunning *département* is home to many expats who are living the dream of relocating to France…

SITUATED IN THE HISTORIC DORDOGNE, which boasts more than a thousand castles, Bergerac and Périgueux are within easy reach of superb châteaux, fortified towns crowning precipitous hills, and gently rolling countryside. The Dordogne is one of the oldest inhabited regions of France, with some of the world's greatest prehistoric cave settlements.

Devastated during the Wars of Religion, Bergerac is the main market centre for the surrounding maize and tobacco farms and vineyards. Its prosperity is founded on the success of the tobacco trade and the Musée du Tabac pays homage to this. The old quarter has lots of charm, with numerous late-medieval houses, and in the square there's a statue of Cyrano de Bergerac, the town's literary hero. Try sampling the local sweet wine from Château Monbazillac, or enjoy a coffee in the timeless Café des Tilleuls.

To the east is Sarlat, the capital of Périgord Noir, which avoids the traditional image of a 'home away from home' for the British buyer. Boasting an alluring medieval quarter, packed with houses of historical interest, Sarlat has been protected from the overdevelopment that has plagued parts of the Dordogne since the 1960s, and as such remains a traditional and attractive town. Périgueux, the old

"Cheap flights into Bergerac have helped to sustain the continued appreciation in prices that the region has seen"

capital city of Dordogne, boasts one of the largest clusters of ancient Roman ruins outside Rome itself, a medieval Old Town, and a colourful Wednesday market. It is famous for its cuisine, which often features foie gras and truffles.

Cheap flights into Bergerac have helped to sustain the continued appreciation in prices that the region has seen over the past few years. Prices have risen annually by around 10 – 15 per cent over the last five years, and this trend looks all set to continue. The Dordogne is popular with the international and French buyer so demand has soared, and this has had the obvious affect of increasing prices.

Owing to the vast numbers of British people who move to the area, prices are high for this particular part of rural France. The average cost of a four-bedroom home is around €360,000, but you can easily pay a lot more. ●

DORDOGNE FACTS

■ **Outside Paris, the Dordogne boasts more monuments and historic artefacts than anywhere else in France**

■ **The Dordogne is famous for the Lascaux caves and their prehistoric art**

■ **The Dordogne is known as Périgord by the French, and is divided into four regions: Périgord Vert (green), Blanc (white), Pourpre (purple), and Noir (black)**

■ **One of the Dordogne's most bizarre inhabitants was the lawyer Antoine de Thounens who became King of Araucania in 1860 until the Chilean authorities forcefully ejected him**

The Dordogne's scenery is irresistible to relocators

MAISON DE LA FRANCE

ESSENTIALS

■ **POPULATION** 212,494
■ **TAXES** Taxe d'habitation 5.96%, taxe foncière 15.73%
■ **AIRPORT** Bergerac-Rouman Aéroport, route d'Agen, 24100 Bergerac, Tel: +33 5 53 22 25 25   Limoges Airport, 87100 Limoges, Tel: +33 5 55 43 30 30

KEY FACTS

■ **SCHOOLS** Bordeaux's international school is the only one in the area and is 95km from Bergerac   Bordeaux International School, 53 rue de Laseppe, 33000 Bordeaux, Tel: +33 5 57 87 02 11, www.bordeaux-school.com
■ **MEDICAL** Centre Hospitalier, 80 av Georges Pompidou, 24000 Périgueux, Tel: +33 5 53 45 25 25
■ **RENTALS** One of the most popular holiday areas in France southwest Dordogne, the most popular part, is scattered with holiday rental properties   The area generates a huge amount of rental income and guarantees a rental season from June to September   Rentals become long-term in winter
■ **PROS** The climate in southwest Dordogne is warmer than it is in the north   Low-cost flights to the region have developed the foreign market
■ **CONS** The area is becoming overcrowded and risks becoming spoiled and overrun by tourists   Massive price rises have forced many buyers to seek property in damper north Dordogne   The area is heavily colonised by British buyers.

Property hotspots

MAP KEY

- **5** Hotspot
- ● Major town/city
- ✈ Airport
- ⛴ Ferry

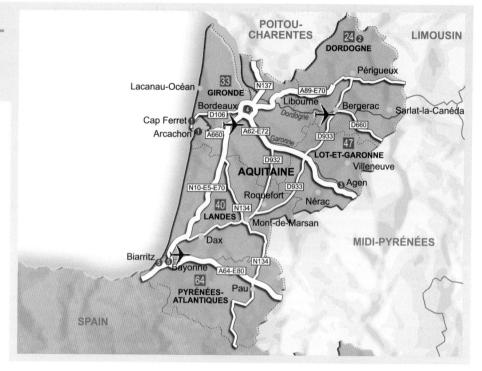

CAP FERRET & BAY OF ARCACHON

1 Cap Ferret and the Bay of Arcachon are situated on the Aquitaine peninsula, where sand dunes stretch west, flanking miles of breathtaking bays coves and inlets. The peninsula is covered with 7,000 hectares of forest, and there are many oyster-farming villages.

Arcachon, on the southern side of the Bassin d'Arcachon (Bay of Arcachon), was built during the 19th century, a combination of Swiss chalets, villas and grand mansions. Enjoying a mild climate, the town has long had a reputation as an exclusive holiday resort. The town is divided into the Ville d'Été (summer town) and the more upmarket Ville d'Hiver (winter town), perched on high dunes and constructed like a labyrinth to help to protect it from the more blustery winter weather.

One of Arcachon's most appealing attractions is its lively Saturday market, where you will find a tempting range of local produce, including fresh oysters and Bayonne ham. This makes local restaurants well worth indulging in. The oyster-farming harbours of Gujan-Mestras and Biganos are both worth a visit, or you could take a trip to the natural salt marshes of Arès. Nearby, the Dune de Pyla has the distinction of being the highest sand dune in the whole of Europe.

This is a popular place with both French and international buyers, especially the Dutch, British and German, and there is a great demand for holiday homes in the area. The average cost of a two-bedroom property on the Aquitaine peninsula is roughly €323,000, rising to €685,000 for a similar five or six bedroomed property.

The area is also very popular for rentals, particularly with the local French market, and Arcachon's location makes the holiday rental market a lucrative one. Guaranteeing a good rental income, the season generally lasts from June to September. A two-bedroom property will generate on average €585 per week, and a similar four-bedroom property around €768.

Key facts

- **POPULATION** Arcachon: 1,800; Cap Ferret: 6,307
- **TAXES** Taxe d'habitation 6.49%, taxe foncière 8.33%
- **AIRPORT** Bordeaux/Mérignac airport, Cedex 40, 33700 Merignac; Tel: +33 5 56 34 50 00
- **SCHOOLS** The nearest international school is in Bordeaux, which is 70km (50 minutes) from Arcachon: Bordeaux International School, 53 rue de Laseppe, 33000 Bordeaux, Tel: +33 5 57 87 02 11, www.bordeaux-school.com
- **MEDICAL** Medical Centre de Secteur, 68 boulevard Deganne, 33120 Arcachon, Tel: +33 5 57 52 55 90 ■ Hôpital St-André, 1 rue Jean Burguet, Centre Ville, Bordeaux, Tel: +33 5 56 79 56 79
- **PROS** Arcachon is the preserve of the wealthy and a highly exclusive resort ■ Located on the northern headland of the Bassin d'Arcachon, Cap Ferret is a protected area with miles of stunning beaches and coves
- **CONS** During the high season, Arcachon tends to become extremely overcrowded ■ Certain bay areas, particularly Lacanau-Océan, can be overpriced ■ Outside the tourist season, a lack of tourist attractions can give the area a deserted feel.

DORDOGNE

2 For information on Hotspot 2, the Dordogne region, see the special feature on page 143.

AGEN

3 Lot-et-Garonne département, rich with orchards, vines and picturesque villages, is the agricultural heartland of Aquitaine. Its prosperous capital, Agen, has earned culinary praise for its famous prunes and plums.

Rue Beauville, with its beautifully restored medieval houses, leads through to rue Voltaire, which has many ethnic restaurants. The Musée Municipal des Beaux-Arts, housed in four 16th- and 17th-century mansions, displays archaeological finds, medieval furniture and paintings, including five by Goya.

The town is built along the banks of the Garonne, prone to periodic flooding but one of France's most attractive rivers. You can cross the river by footbridge close to the gardens at Le Gravier. This former island became the site of one of the area's most important medieval fairs, which is now protected by a flood-proof esplanade. Agen's canal bridge is the second longest in France, offering panoramic views of the town; or you may prefer to gaze upwards at it from a river boat.

Lot-et-Garonne département has always been expensive, even in the days before the Dordogne became popular. A large, stone farmhouse with a pool and terrace will cost around €530,000; a two-bedroom home in Agen around €161,000.

Agen itself is not noted for its rental market, but there is a guaranteed rental season around Agen and throughout the Lot-et-Garonne countryside during June to September.

Key facts

■ **POPULATION** 32,180
■ **TAXES** Taxe d'habitation 7.55%, taxe foncière 14.61%
■ **AIRPORT** Bergerac-Roumanière Aéroport, route d'Agen, 24100 Bergerac, Tel: +33 5 53 22 25 25
■ **SCHOOLS** Bordeaux's international school is the only one in the area and is 94km from Bergerac-Bordeaux International School, 53 rue de Laseppe, 33000 Bordeaux, Tel: +33 5 57 87 02 11; www.bordeaux-school.com
■ **MEDICAL** Medical Centre Hospitalier d'Agen, RN 21/route de Villeneuve, 47000 Agen, Tel: +33 (0) 5 53 69 70 71
■ **PROS** This is the capital of the Garonne, a 'rural unhurried town' ■ It is well located, halfway between Bordeaux and Toulouse ■ Reliant upon agriculture, Agen is known for its production of prunes and plums ■ Place Goya is the centre of Agen's most interesting area
■ **CONS** Lot-et-Garonne département was always very expensive, even before the Dordogne became popular.

BORDEAUX

4 Bordeaux has been a wealthy city since Roman times and recently received millions of euros for urban regeneration. Yet apart from its elegant 18th-century centre,

graced by buildings constructed from limestone and adorned by ornate cast-iron balconies, this urban sprawl of more than half a million people is, in parts, decidedly shabby.

The city centre is easily explored on foot and its attractions include restaurants selling the region's world-renowned wines. The Palais de la Douane et de la Bourse, and the residences of well-to-do merchants, display window arches adorned with bunches of grapes and sculptures of Bacchus. The opulent 18th-century Grand Théâtre is surrounded by Corinthian-style columns and is said to possess perfect acoustics to match a near-perfect interior.

This is primarily an area in which the French live and work. It has encouraged long-term property lets and generated interest from the local, rather than international property market. International interest is centred on Bordeaux's surrounding countryside which attracts many Britons, and property prices have soared in recent years as a result. The most seductive landscape is the vast pine-covered expanse of Les Landes, to the south, or the expansive Atlantic beaches. Prices are lower around the city, where four-bedroom properties cost around €476,000.

Rentals are targeted at the long-term French market, rather than the foreign holiday market. Most Britons tend to focus on the areas outside Bordeaux.

Key facts

■ **POPULATION** 735,000
■ **TAXES** Taxe d'habitation 6.49%, taxe foncière 8.33%
■ **AIRPORT** Bordeaux-Mérignac Airport, Cedex 40, 33700 Mérignac, Tel: +33 5 56 34 50 00
■ **SCHOOLS** Bordeaux International School, 53 rue de Laseppe, 33000 Bordeaux, Tel: +33 5 57 87 02 11, www.bordeaux-school.com
■ **MEDICAL** Medical Hôpital St-

André, 1 rue Jean Burguet, Centre Ville, Bordeaux, Tel: +33 5 56 79 56 79
■ **PROS** As a city of wealth, Bordeaux is an expensive place in which to live and stay ■ Home to the Bordeaux wine trade and one of the oldest trading ports in France, Bordeaux produces more than 44 million cases of wine each year ■ Bordeaux is a dynamic city with a university that boasts 60,000 students ■ Easily accessible and the transport hub for the region
■ **CONS** Apart from its small 18th-century city centre, Bordeaux is a relatively shabby city with some less attractive areas ■ As Bordeaux is primarily a city in which the French live and work, it is not geared towards foreign buyers and most activity takes place in areas outside the city.

BIARRITZ & BAYONNE

5 Once christened 'the Monte Carlo of the Atlantic coast' after being complewtely transformed by Napoléon III in the 19th century into a playground for the important and affluent socialites of the world, Biarritz was overshadowed by the rise of the Côte d'Azur. Now rediscovered by Parisians, surfers and celebrities, the town is a showcase of impressive Victorian buildings alongside traditional Basque homes and modern apartments. Blessed with a long sandy beach, a casino, a promenade and numerous restaurants, Biarritz also has a quieter side, with sheltered beaches next to the Plage du Vieux Port. Place Clémenceau is the main shopping area and there is a good selection of museums; the Bonnat Museum displays works by Rubens, Titian and Raphaël.

A short distance inland from Biarritz at the Adour-Nives river junction lies Bayonne, the region's capital. Although it is more commercial than Biarritz, Bayonne celebrates its Basque identity – something reflected in its tall, half-timbered houses

with their woodwork painted in the traditional Basque colours of green and red. The Basque people are fiercely proud of their distinct, lively culture - and rightly so. They are passionate abotu their language, their reputation and their fast and furious wall game, pelota.

Bayonne is very popular with the affluent French market. Don't expect very many bargains in this area. A south-facing three-bedroom maison de ville starts at €456,000, while a five-bedroom propety will be preiced at around €705,000.

Situated in a well-known resort area, the towns of Biarritz and Bayonne have always been popular with the international rentals market. The area's exclusivity is guaranteed to produce rental income in a season that generally lasts from June to September. Appealing mainly to the French market, the two resorts are expensive. A two-bedroom property can generate an income of around €565 per week.

Key facts

■ **POPULATION** 72,000
■ **TAXES** Taxe d'habitation 7.30%, taxe foncière 8.38%
■ **AIRPORT** Biarritz-Bayonne-Anglet Airport, 7 esplanade de l'Europe, 64600 Anglet, Tel: +33 5 59 43 83 83
■ **SCHOOLS** Bordeaux International School, 53 rue de Laseppe, 33000 Bordeaux, Tel: +33 5 57 87 02 11, www.bordeaux-school.com
■ **MEDICAL** Medical Centre Hospitalier de la Côte Basque, 13 avenue de l'Interne J Loëb, 64100 Bayonne, Tel +33 (0) 5 59 44 35 35
■ **PROS** Located very close to the Spanish border, an area popular for relocation ■ Enjoying a warm winter climate, this is an attractive, coastal area ■ It's easily accessible and close to major roads and airports.
■ **CONS** This popular area can become very busy and overrun ■ Biarritz is almost exclusively a French resort ■ Property bargains are difficult to find, and renovations are almost non-existent. ●

Property guide

Across the region as a whole, house prices have begun to stabilise, although increases are still being recorded in some areas, such as Lot-et-Garonne, and the lesser-known but equally pretty northern part of the Dordogne

MAISON DE LA FRANCE

Dordogne département has the highest concentration of British expats in France

ACCOMMODATION IN AQUITAINE IS PRICIER than in most regions, but the area's growing accessibility is drawing increasing numbers of foreign investors. So saying, most of the region, apart from the Dordogne, is still fairly unknown.

In the last few years, the ever-popular Dordogne has seen annual rises of approximately 15 per cent, while in the southern Dordogne, demand from French and international buyers has caused prices to skyrocket. Few good-value areas remain, and there is little chance of finding a renovation property. Owing to the vast influx of Britons, prices are high for rural France, and a family home costs upwards of €360,000. Cheap flights to Bergerac have attracted British buyers (mainly families and retirees) and sent prices soaring.

Lot-et-Garonne has always been expensive due to its position between Bordeaux and Toulouse, and prices continue to rise. Properties on the southwest coast, from Arcachon to Biarritz and Bayonne, are very pricey, with demand from both French and foreign markets. Both Biarritz and Arcachon are very popular, particularly with French and British buyers. The Pyrénées-Atlantiques area is popular with the French and is forecast to be the next up-and-coming foreign market; even though prices are rising, it's still the cheapest part of the region. Cheap flights to Pau have driven up prices quite substantially, particularly for coastal homes and those with sea views. Move inland however, and you'll find cheaper properties and renovation projects.

The rental potential in Aquitaine is very good, particularly in the Dordogne and Lot-et-Garonne, although the market in southern Dordogne is pretty well saturated. The estimated yield from a five-bedroom gîte is €1,239 per week, but these properties are not cheap to buy.

The most popular choice of property in Aquitaine is the traditional farmhouse. An ancient but modernised three-bedroom Périgordian farmhouse outside Bergerac sells for around €470,000. Châteaux abound in southern Dordogne, and on average, they will cost you upwards of €1,000,000. ●

TYPICAL PROPERTIES

■ In the south, half-timbered Basque farmhouses are painted a distinctive dark red
■ The north features high-roofed Périgordian-style houses
■ Characteristic properties of the Dordogne include quaint dovecotes (pigeonniers) and traditional stone farmhouses (bastides) with outbuildings

DORDOGNE DOVECOTES (*PIGEONNIERS*)

■ These pretty buildings were status symbols during the 17th and 18th centuries
■ The pigeons, often as many as 2,000 pairs at a time, were kept for their excrement which was used as fertiliser for the vineyards
■ Small holes allowed the pigeons access, and interior shelves were built for nesting
■ It was quite common for a dovecote to be as ostentatious as the main house

WHAT CAN YOU GET FOR YOUR EUROS?

TRADITIONAL LONGÈRE

Set in 15 acres of spectacular wooded land, this is an exceptional example of a traditional Colombages-style rural property. Located in the beautiful and peaceful countryside around Laluque, this is ideal if you want to get away from it all, or if you love the outdoors. The house boasts a huge living room of 108 square metres, three bedrooms, a mezzanine and a bathroom.

€200,000 CODE FPS

RURAL CAMPSITE

This modern house near Monsegur in Gironde offers a great business opportunity as it features a rural campsite on its five acres of land, along with a lake. The house itself has four bedrooms, a bathroom and converted basement. There's permission for a six-place campsite, and a sanitary block with two showers and two toilets is on site, along with a workshop.

€314,400 CODE FPS

STONE-BUILT HOUSE

This awesome property near Montpon-Menesterol is a restored stone house 30 minutes from Bordeaux airport. It's set in 21 acres, with a gorgeous garden, meadow and infinity pool. Inside, the house offers everything from a dark room and wine cellar to a library and a study. The terracotta floors have underfloor heating, there are four bedrooms, a vast kitchen, pantry, fireplace and more.

€1,484,000 CODE FRA

17TH-CENTURY PROPERTY

This pretty Dordogne home has five bedroom and three bathrooms, along with a charming enclosed garden and pool. Period features include original beams, panelling, wooden doors and exposed stonework. Modern touches include a large, airy gym with cross trainer, sauna and shower, all included in the price. The property is in a quiet village with a restaurant and lovely valley views.

€530,000 CODE SIF

CHARMING VILLAGE HOME

This pretty, recently renovated property is set in a fabulous location. It's on a quiet road away from the village centre, with easy access to the road linking Pau to Oloron Sainte Marie and the ski resorts. The three-bedroom home has original fireplaces, exposed beams and stone walls. The renovation has been done tastefully, and includes a new roof made of locally manufactured tiles.

€311,500 CODE VEF

AUTHENTIC HOUSE

This four bedroom house is located in Aquitaine and it's a beautiful, traditional and completely authentic property. Originally a small cottage built in the 17th century, it has been gradually extended to create a collection of buildings, all set around a central courtyard. Even the entrance gates and courtyard walls have been retained, making this an exceptional and unique property.

€622,800 CODE VEF

AVERAGE HOUSE PRICES AQUITAINE

	2-bed		3-bed		4-bed		5/6-bed	
Cap Ferret & Bay of Arachon	€321,543	(£217,259)	€406,449	(£274,628)	€543,948	(£367,533)	€684,701	(£462,636)
Dordogne	€180,275	(£121,808)	€211,814	(£143,118)	€359,515	(£242,916)	€392,632	(£265,292)
Agen	€160,849	(£108,682)	€172,306	(£116,423)	€312,956	(£211,457)	€471,628	(£318,668)
Bordeaux	€283,433	(£191,509)	€368,041	(£248,677)	€475,948	(£321,587)	€632,716	(£427,511)
Biarritz	€338,356	(£228,619)	€454,866	(£307,342)	€563,954	(£381,050)	€704,818	(£476,229)

Midi-Pyrénées

Gascony, the mountains and the lure of Lourdes

MAISON DE LA FRANCE

FACT BOX

- **POPULATION** 2,552,687
- **UNEMPLOYMENT RATE** 10%
- **AVERAGE 4-BED HOUSE PRICE** €350,000
- **REGIONAL CAPITAL** Toulouse
- **REGION SIZE** 45,382km²

Contents

Area profile

In this southwestern region you'll find everything from skiing resorts and hearty local dishes to peaceful religious retreats

GETTING THERE

AIR British Airways (0870 850 9850; www.britishairways.com) flies to Toulouse from Gatwick. **Air France** (0845 084 5111; www.airfrance.co.uk) flies from Heathrow to Toulouse via Paris. **Ryanair** (0871 246 0000; www.ryanair.com) flies from London Stansted into Rodez and from London Stansted, Dublin and Liverpool into Carcassonne, **BMI Baby** (0870 264 2229; www.bmibaby.com) flies from Manchester into Toulouse, **easyJet** (0871 750 0100, www.easyjet.com) flies to Toulouse from Gatwick, while **Flybe** (0871 700 0535; www.flybe.com) flies to Toulouse from Bristol and Birmingham.

ROAD The A71/A20 runs from Paris through Limoges and from there the N20 continues on to Toulouse. The D938/7 runs to Lourdes and the N21 continues from there to Cauterets. From the Channel ports, travel to Le Mans and then follow the N138 and N143, then the A20 at Châteauroux, to get to Toulouse.

RAIL The TGV service runs from the Gare d'Austerlitz in Paris through to Toulouse. Contact **Rail Europe** (0870 584 8848; www.raileurope.co.uk) for all the details of local services. There is a comprehensive network of local services from Toulouse that operates throughout the Midi-Pyrénées region.

THE LARGE REGION OF MIDI-PYRÉNÉES HAS something for everyone – lush valleys to rival those of neighbouring Dordogne, sun-soaked plains that equal those in Languedoc, and mountain resorts much quieter than those in the Alps. The region is made up of eight large départements, six of which are named after the major rivers which flow through the region (Lot, Aveyron, Gers, Tarn, Tarn-et-Garonne, and Haute-Garonne), plus Hautes-Pyrénées and Ariège. Between them they encompass the towering peaks of the Pyrenees, bustling ski resorts, breathtaking valleys, national parks, and beautiful fortified towns.

Rocamadour to Lourdes

The lush valley of the river Lot, which lies in the most northerly département of the region, might be less well known than the Dordogne but its ancient villages and towns, such as its capital Cahors, and the spectacular pilgrimage site of Rocamadour, are hugely popular with tourists, and rightly so. Capital of Midi-Pyrénées, and of the Haute-Garonne département, is Toulouse, known as 'la cité rose' (the pink city) thanks to its red sandstone churches and buildings which reflect the bright sunlight and give off a rosy glow at dusk. It has a large university and is home to the second largest student population in France – more than 100,000 live here. Even outside term-time, the city has a lively air, boasting good value restaurants, friendly cafés, bustling markets, and lively clubs. Toulouse, the fourth largest metropolis in the country, houses a number of high-tech

MAISON DE LA FRANCE

Fortified medieval villages characterise the area

industries together with a large aerospace concern.

To the north of Toulouse, the countryside's hilltops are surmounted by bastide, or walled, towns, most of which were constructed in the 13th century just before the Hundred Years' War. Cordes-sur-Ciel, with its medieval alleyways and buildings, is one of the most beautiful of these former strongholds.

Northeast of Toulouse lies Albi, capital of the Tarn département, a stunning city dominated by its imposing 13th-century Cathédrale Ste-Cécile. Albi is home to the largest collection of the work of artist Henri de Toulouse-Lautrec, the town's most famous son.

South of Toulouse the countryside becomes steeper and more rugged. The mountains are scattered with hiking trails that lead you through the beautiful scenery between pretty spa towns and ski

CLIMATE

MIDI-PYRÉNÉES	LONDON		MIDI-PYRÉNÉES	LONDON	
9.8	Dec	7	110	Dec	81
15.5	Nov	10	130	Nov	78
19.3	Oct	14	125	Oct	70
25	Sep	19	80	Sep	65
27.2	Aug	21	25	Aug	62
27.6	Jul	22	20	Jul	59
26.4	Jun	20	36	Jun	58
19.1	May	17	62	May	57
18.3	Apr	13	75	Apr	56
12.3	Mar	10	75	Mar	64
9	Feb	7	60	Feb	72
10	Jan	6	65	Jan	77

AVERAGE **TEMPERATURE** (Celsius)

AVERAGE **RAINFALL** (millimetres)

FOOD AND DRINK

The cuisine of the Midi-Pyrénées is rich in poultry and game. Duck and goose foie gras are delicacies of Gers and Lot. Garbure, a filling Pyrenean speciality, is a tasty soup packed with potatoes, cabbage, beans and pork. Cassoulet de Toulouse, another favourite, is a stew of white beans, kidney beans and confit of duck sausage, cooked in goose fat. Other mainstays are lamb and Lacaune's cooked pork meats. For dessert lovers there's gâteau à la broche (a spit-roasted, cone-shaped cake) and pastis gascon, with its delicate layers of puff pastry. Local fruit is eaten in abundance, while the prestigious, cave-matured Roquefort cheese is world famous.

There are numerous wineries producing dry, fruity whites and full-bodied reds, with over 15 AOC wines, including Cahors and Gaillac. Gers is home to Armagnac, France's oldest brandy.

MAISON DE LA FRANCE

resorts, which become more lively in winter, but never overcrowded.

One of the world's most famous pilgrimage sites lies in the far southwest of the Midi-Pyrénées. Lourdes attracts more than five million visitors from across the globe every year. The nearby town of Tarbes is one of the region's largest commercial centres and it provides a lot of accommodation for visiting pilgrims. North of Tarbes, in Gers département (formed from the area known historically and more romantically as Gascony), is Auch, a small city with a UNESCO-listed cathedral.

The economy

Toulouse is home of the French aerospace industry, and it is here that the new SuperJumbo A380 – the world's largest passenger plane – has been developed by Airbus. The aerospace and related companies, as well as other high-tech industries, employ hundreds of thousands of workers. However, tourism is gradually growing in the area, thanks to flights into Rodez and, in neighbouring Languedoc, Carcassonne. Traditionally an agricultural area, the region has seen its ecomony expand in recent years, despite depopulation, and agriculture remains one of the region's economic drivers.

Social groups

British buyers are discovering the mountainous beauty of the Midi-Pyrénées and the Gascon countryside in ever-increasing numbers. They also tend to proliferate in and around Toulouse. Part of the Midi-Pyrénées is Basque, which has its own language and customs. The French Basques are generally less separatist in nature than their Spanish counterparts, though only about 10 per cent of the Basque region is situated in France. ●

ATTRACTIONS

■ Enjoy an early evening drink at one of Toulouse's city squares and watch the buildings give off a pink glow in the sunset

■ Millions of visitors make the pilgrimage to the religious site of Lourdes every year

■ Seek out Albi, the birthplace of Henri Toulouse-Lautrec, where there's a museum devoted to his life and work

■ Discover Auch, with its landmark Tour d'Armagnac

■ Go skiing in the French Pyrenees , at resorts such as Gavarnie, Barèges La Mongie and Somport

■ Follow the GR10 walking route through the Parc National des Pyrénées

■ Visit some of the many spa towns in the mountains, such as Cauterets and Argelès-Gazost

■ Try to catch a game of rugby in 'le rugby' capital of Toulouse, or in high-altitude Tarbes

■ Don't leave Toulouse without tasting the famous Toulouse sausages

■ Tour the delightful hilltop towns, such as Cordes-sur-Ciel in Tarn

PROFILE

Focus on Gascony

With a wealth of fortified towns, pretty villages and a spectacular rolling landscape, Gascony has long been a favourite with homebuyers from the UK

TRADITIONALLY AN AGRICULTURAL AND WINE-producing area blessed with fertile soils, Gascony – now known as Gers – is the most rural département in France, famed for its preserves, pâtés and particularly foie gras. During the Middle Ages, the area was in the firing line between British forces based in Bordeaux and the French at Toulouse, giving rise to the many fortified hillside towns and villages. One of France's most 'French' areas – despite an invasion by British buyers – Gascony remains unspoilt and retains much of its rural charm.

The capital Auch is an outstanding Gallo-Roman city on the St James of Compostela pilgrims' route. The city retains its medieval style, with ochre stone and rose-coloured tiles gracing many of the old houses around its centre. The late Gothic Cathédrale Ste-Marie has beautifully carved choir stalls and stained-glass windows created by a Gascon artist, Arnaud de Moles. South of the cathedral, in place Salinis, stands the Tour d'Armagnac, an ecclesiastical court and prison in the 14th century from where a monumental stairway of 234 steps heads down to the river.

On the way down, there's a statue of d'Artagnan, of The Three Musketeers fame. Outside Auch there are a handful of peaceful towns, offering a genuine taste of French rural life. Condom in the north has an

"One of France's most 'French' areas – despite an invasion of British buyers – Gascony remains unspoilt and retains much of its rural charm"

impressive cathedral, the Armagnac museum and some attractive winding streets, while Fleurance and Lectoure are both attractive hillside towns with medieval houses, town halls and central squares.

Auch is the main focal point of the Gascony property market and is regarded as the gateway into the region. As such, prices here are higher than in other areas. Gascony is very popular with the foreign buyer, the majority of whom are British, and a standard property is a spacious stone-built farmhouse. While there is little cheap property available in Gascony, better value homes can be found away from Auch in the surrounding rural areas, and a two-bedroom property can be picked up for around €170,000; this will probably be a property in need of some renovation - you can find cheaper and more expensive properties depending on the level of renovation you want to carry out. ●

GASCONY FACTS

■ Brave and skilled Gascon soldiers were the inspiration for Alexander Dumas's d'Artagnan and Edmond Rostand's Cyrano de Bergerac

■ Gers is France's biggest producer of foie gras, which has been a Gascon speciality since the 16th century

■ Armagnac originates from Gascony, where it was first produced in 1411

■ Marciac is world famous for its two–week summer Jazz Festival which is held in August and is one of the biggest in Europe

Gascony is famous for its agriculture and fertile soil

ESSENTIALS

■ **POPULATION** 172,300
■ **TAXES** Taxe d'habitation 25.36%, taxe foncière 62.13%
■ **AIRPORT** Toulouse-Blagnac, BP 103, 31703 Blagnac Cedex, Tel: +33 5 61 42 44 00, Fax: +33 5 61 42 45 55

KEY FACTS

■ **SCHOOLS** Contact the Rectorat de l'Académie de Toulouse, Place St-Jacques, 31073 Toulouse, Cedex, Tel: +33 5 61 36 40 00, Fax: +33 5 61 52 80 27 for advice on education
■ **MEDICAL** Centre Hospitalier, route Tarbes, 32000 Auch, Tel: +33 5 62 61 32 32
■ **RENTALS** Gascony has always been popular with the British market, and is a popular tourist area ■ The rental season is guaranteed to last from June to September, with 10 weeks of rentals being the least you can expect ■ More people are moving to the area, seeking to set up a holiday rentals business
■ **PROS** Easily accessible from Toulouse, the major airport in the region ■ Property in Gascony is spacious and includes a lot of land, with homes often being extremely luxurious ■ Prices average just under €200,000 for a three-bedroom property
■ **CONS** Renovation properties do exist, but take longer and more organisation to complete, due to a shortage of artisans ■ For those seeking immersion in French culture and to distance themselves from British life, there are a lot of British buyers in the area.

Property hotspots

MAP KEY

- **5** Hotspot
- Major town/city
- ✈ Airport
- ⛴ Ferry

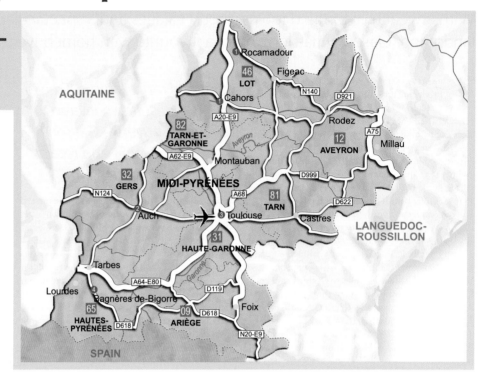

CAHORS & ROCAMADOUR

1 Capital of the Lot département and built on a rocky peninsula, Cahors dates back to 1 BC and was an important centre during the Middle Ages. Pope John XXII, who was born here, founded the University of Cahors in the early 14th century, an institution which later became the University of Toulouse. Interesting sites include the 12th-century cathedral of St-Étienne, the Roman aqueduct ruins and the Pont Valentré, a formidably fortified stone bridge with three magnificent towers.

Also known globally for its deep ruby-red wines (the vineyard trail can be followed west of town), Cahors has the biggest property market in the Lot and draws a huge amount of international interest. Prices in the Midi-Pyrénées have been increasing by around 13 per cent annually, and Cahors experiences a high turnover of properties. Nevertheless, the more luxurious properties have not been as popular in recent years – if you are looking for a substantial château, you can pick one up for upwards of €500,000.

Prices in the Lot are slightly above the national average but it is possible to find a range of homes with land in and around Cahors. Prices start at €185,000 for a renovated two-bedroom property, although there are still one or two ruins available to renovate that will cost substantially less. A typical four-bedroom house will cost €369,000.

Hugely popular with tourists, the areas surrounding Cahors and Rocamadour have great rental potential. The rental season is guaranteed to last from June to September, with longer-term lettings becoming popular in the winter months.

A two-bedroom property rents for €576 per week, a three-bedroom property for €832.

Key facts

- **POPULATION** Cahors 23,128, Rocamadour 46,500
- **AIRPORT** Toulouse-Blagnac, BP 103, 31703 Blagnac Cedex, Tel: +33 5 61 42 44 00, Fax: +33 5 61 42 45 55
- **SCHOOLS** International School of Toulouse SA, Route de Pibrax, 31770 Colomiers, Tel: +33 5 62 74 26 74, www.intst.net
- **MEDICAL** Centre Hospitalier Cahors 335 rue Président Wilson, 46000 Cahors, Tel: +33 5 65 20 50 50, Fax: +33 5 65 20 50 51
- **PROS** The Lot area has a mild climate during the winter months and has stunning rural surroundings ■ This is an ideal area for a family home and those

seeking rental income ■ The area has a strong market where property is continuing to appreciate
- **CONS** Rocamadour is inundated with coach tours and tourists, which are damaging the beauty of the area ■ Industry here is almost non-existent so most jobs are in the service sector.

GASCONY

2 For information on Hotspot 2, the Gascony region, see the special feature on page 153.

TOULOUSE

3 One of the most vibrant and metropolitan provincial cities in France, Toulouse is dubbed La Ville Rose thanks to the pink-brick buildings constructed from local clay. Transformed since the Second World War into a centre for high-tech industry, the city leads the way in aeronautics, being home to Aérospatiale, the dynamics behind Concorde,

Airbus, and the Ariane space rocket. The National Space Centre and European Shuttle programme are also based here and Toulouse has France's biggest university outside Paris.

Old Toulouse is split by two 19th-century streets: the long north-south rue d'Alsace-Lorraine/rue du Languedoc and the east-west rue de Metz. The Dominican church of Les Jacobins, which inspired Dali's painting, and the resplendent Renaissance town houses, known as hôtels particuliers, are worth a look. Parks include the formal gardens of the Grand-Rond and Jardin des Plantes.

Being a large city dominated by French buyers, Toulouse is expensive, although cheaper properties are available in the surrounding area. A traditional, fully renovated five-bedroom house within 30 minutes of Toulouse costs from €527,000, while in the city the average price for a three-bedroom property is €292,000.

HOTSPOTS

Toulouse's rental market is dominated by long-term rentals for the local French market. Typically, a one-bedroom property will rent for an average of around €377 per week, while a similar property with three bedrooms will fetch around €971 per week.

Key facts

■ **POPULATION** 390,350
■ **AIRPORT** Toulouse-Blagnac, BP 103, 31703 Blagnac Cedex, Tel: +33 5 61 42 44 00, Fax: +33 5 61 42 45 55
■ **SCHOOLS** International School of Toulouse SA, route de Pibrax, 31770 Colomiers, Tel: +33 5 62 74 26 74, www.intst.net
■ **MEDICAL** Centre Hospitalier Universitaire de Toulouse, place du Dr Baylac, 31059 Toulouse, Cedex 3, Tel: +33 5 61 77 82 03, www.chu-oulouse.fr
■ **PROS** Toulouse is a dynamic and vibrant city, ideal for those who are seeking a metropolitan lifestyle and lots of distractions ■ Toulouse enjoys good road and rail connections to most major urban centres
■ **CONS** Primarily an area dominated by the local French market ■ Most foreign buyers live in the suburbs around Toulouse, especially along the many autoroutes ■ Property prices have increased dramatically throughout the Toulouse area ■ Not a big English language community.

BAGNÈRES-DE-BIGORRE

3 At an altitude of 2,877 metres, this elegant spa town in the heart of the Pyrenees owes its wealth to the local grey marble which was used to construct both the Paris Opera House and the National Assembly. Today, Bagnères-de-Bigorre produces high-tech railway equipment and has recently seen a boost in slate quarrying.

While enjoying a mild climate, Bagnères-de-Bigorre draws homebuyers with an interest in the nearby intermediate ski resort of Barèges La Mongie, which offers access to 64 pistes at much lower prices than higher-profile resorts in the Alps.

To the south, the Pic du Midi has splendid panoramas and hiking opportunities over the Pyrenees. Every June, the Fête de la Transhumance is celebrated with folk singing, films and pageantry while in July, dedicated amateur cyclists try their luck on the legendary Tour de France passes of Col de Tourmalet and Col d'Aspin. Outdoor activities include an 18-hole golf course, fly fishing in the Adour river and visits to the Grottes de Medous.

It is much cheaper to buy in Bagnères-de-Bigorre than in the surrounding ski resorts, with a five-bedroomed chalet at the base of the Pyrenees costing an average of €457,000. Although the market tends to be mainly French, it is also an area that's up and coming with the foreign buyer. A traditional villa with three double bedrooms is priced from €210,000 while a smaller house with two bedrooms can be found from €176,000.

The close proximity of the town to the expensive ski areas guarantees good rental potential, with the season lasting from at least December through to April; in the summer, activity holidays generate income. A two-bedroom property here will rent for €583 per week, while a property with three bedrooms will usually attract around €866 per week.

Key facts

■ **POPULATION** 8,423
■ **AIRPORT** Pau-Pyrénées, 64230 Lescar, Tel: +33 5 59 33 33 00
■ **SCHOOLS** International School of Toulouse SA, route de Pibrax, 31770 Colomiers, Tel: +33 5 62 74 26 74, www.intst.net
■ **MEDICAL** Hôpital de Bagnères-de-Bigorre, 15 rue Gambetta, 65200 Bagnères-de-Bigorre, Tel: +33 5 62 91 41 11
■ **PROS** Bagnères-de-Bigorre is an excellent location, only 20 minutes away from the ski resorts ■ Barèges La Mongie, the main ski resort in the Pyrenees, is easily accessible ■ Residents benefit from a more peaceful lifestyle by living outside the main resorts ■ The town is unspoiled by modern development
■ **CONS** The area itself is fairly remote with poor road and rail links ■ French language skills are necessary ●

It is much cheaper to buy in Bagnères-de-Bigorre than it is in the nearby ski resorts

JUSTIN POSTLETHWAITE

Property guide

Prices have been on the up throughout the region over the last few years but properties are still sensibly priced

A 19th-century manoir in a Haut-Garonne village

HUGE DEMAND IN NEIGHBOURING Languedoc-Roussillon has driven property seekers inland, boosting foreign interest in the Midi-Pyrénées, which offers easy access to the coast as well as the ski resorts. This factor, combined with improved transport links and budget flights to Toulouse, has increased interest from international purchasers upping prices, particularly in Haute-Garonne and its environs, though there are still several départements providing good investment opportunities.

Gers is the priciest and most popular département, a source of well-priced period homes, offering spacious stone properties with a lot of land. Gers attracts foreign buyers, mostly British. Better value homes are to be had further away from the capital, Auch, in the surrounding rural areas, where a two-bedroom property costs around €170,000.

The Hautes-Pyrénées département still has plenty of renovation properties. If hunting for property near the Pyrenean ski resorts, Cauterets, La Mongie and the northern Hautes-Pyrénées regions are the areas to focus on. The up-and-coming département of Aveyron, opened up to the foreign buyer by budget flights to Rodez and the new A20 motorway, has fairly cheap properties and Tarn is also worth considering. Ariège offers some of the best bargains in the southwest of France, with a plentiful supply of barns, farmhouses and pigeonniers suitable for conversion. Cheap flights to nearby Carcassonne and Perpignan make it highly accessible.

The rental market in this region is strong, and you can expect a good return on your investment. In Toulouse rentals are generally long-term and aimed at the French. With its large student population, prospects are good with rents for a two-bedroom apartment starting at around €635 per week. Prices range from around €170,000 for an unrenovated farmhouse to €527,000 for a manor house. At the high end of the market, a small château costs upwards of €550,000, while a fully renovated, exclusive property has a price tag of €800,000-plus. ●

TYPICAL GERS ARCHITECTURE

- Architectural styles in Gers vary according to the locally available materials
- In northern Gers, homes are mainly built from sandstone
- In the south, buildings are mainly constructed from river stone (flint) and clay
- In the east the architecture is of a lower standard, with many farmhouses being built of mud bricks
- To the west, one finds more colombage (half-timbered) houses, their exposed oak framework packed with straw and mud
- Homes are often characterised by terre-cuite (tiled) floors, wide stone fireplaces, carved oak staircases, and built-in, fruit-wood cupboards
- There are three characteristic types of roof tile used in the area. Flat, baked clay tiles are typically used for steeper roofs. Gersois roofs usually have a flatter pitch and feature a bevelled clay tile –these roofs need more maintenance as the tiles tend to slip. Closer to the mountains, slate tiles are used.
- Auch has retained much of its medieval style which is reflected in the ochre-stone houses and rose-coloured tiles

WHAT CAN YOU GET FOR YOUR EUROS?

RENOVATED STONE HOUSE

This four-bedroom stone-built prooperty is in a wonderful country setting with panoramic views. It's near to Villefranche-de-Rouergue, and it's 10 kilometres from shops and amenities. The house includes a living area of 125 square metres, including a large fitted kitchen, bathroom and four bedrooms. Outside, there's a small garden of 800 square metres, along with a terrace.

€230,000 CODE FRA

QUIET CHÂTEAU

This small 14th-19th-century stone château is located at the end of a gorgeous, long, tree-lined drive. It's set within four hectares of mature, tranquil parkland in Gers, and it features ancient trees, a guesthouse and a pool. Many of the original features of the château have been beautifully restored, while it has seven bedrooms, four bathrooms and four reception rooms to enjoy.

€875,000 CODE SIF

SUPERB MOUNTAIN CHÂTEAU

Just one hour from Toulouse and its airport, this 14-bedroom, nine-bathroom château is set in fantastic grounds of 1.7 hectares, on the edge of a peaceful hamlet. This includes mature trees and lovely views of the foothills of the Pyrénées. The 17th-19th-century property also offers a four-bedroom caretaker's apartment, wine cellar, swimming pool, pool house and 19th-century chapel.

€1,470,000 CODE SIF

GORGEOUS MAISON DE MAITRE

This elegant 18-century maison de maitre is set in pleasant, mature grounds in a quiet location only five kilometres from the nearest shops in Tarn-et-Garonne. It has been carefully restored and retains original features, such as fireplaces and floors. Along with the seven-bedroom, five-bathroom main property, there are over 1,000 square metres of outbuildings, with plenty of renovation opportunities.

€1,100,000 CODE SIF

RURAL STONE GÎTE

If you want to get away from it all and live an idyllic French lifestyle, this is the ideal property for you. This modest four-bedroom old stone house is ideally located in the countryside, with the fields and hills of Tarn and Garonne surrounding it. It's currently let out as a gîte, so this could be a fantastic business opportunity, or just a perfect holiday home. It's in a secluded location, but isn't isolated.

€256,605 CODE VEF

TRADITIONAL GÎTE

This is a fantastic four-bedroom old stone property, set in the rolling Aveyron countryside. The house has been renovated to a modern standard and offers a spacious living area. There's a separate house to the side which is equally large and has been divided into two separate gîtes, one newly constructed and one newly finished, making this a good business opportunity.

€483,955 CODE VEF

AVERAGE HOUSE PRICES MIDI-PYRÉNÉES

	2-bed	3-bed	4-bed	5/6-bed
Cahors & Rocamadour	€184,504 (£124,665)	€312,703 (£211,286)	€368,759 (£249,162)	€423,735 (£286,308)
Gascony/Gers	€170,063 (£114,908)	€1,130,851 (£764,089)	€331,200 (£223,784)	€430,358 (£290,783)
Toulouse	€211,466 (£142,883)	€292,043 (£197,327)	€430,444 (£290,841)	€527,186 (£356,207)
Bagnères-de-Bigorre	€175,776 (£118,768)	€210,294 (£142,091)	€271,545 (£183,477)	€457,179 (£308,905)

www.kaydreamhomes.com.fr

Dream homes in the southern Charente-Maritime

Christopher Kay at Immobiliere Internationale

Telephone: 0033 681 749 846

53 rue Général Leclerc, 17260 Gémozac, France

(At the traffic lights, across from the Post Office)

Where is the South Charente-Maritime?

Look at the map and locate the Gironde Estuary in the South West of France
and the area to the east of the Gironde Estuary is the south Charente-Maritime

Why the south Charente-Maritime?

- It is the second sunniest part of France with 2250 hours of sunshine each year.
- Even at the 'coldest' time of year the climate is mild and we do not have 'winter', going straight from autumn to spring.
- Royan has 40 km of continuous sandy beaches and down the Estuary we have charming fishing villages such as Port Maubert, Mortagne, St Seurin d'Uzet, Meschers and Talmont.
- The A10 motorway comes from the north to the area so that it is within one day's drive of the Channel.
- The countryside is breathtaking, made up of gently rolling hills and pretty forests.
- Property is attractive and prices are still reasonable.
- The area is one of the last undiscovered parts of France.
- The area is easily accessed by cheap flights from the UK

. . . to La Rochelle, Bergerac, Poitiers or Limoges from Stansted, or Limoges from Liverpool by Ryan (www.ryanair.com, 0871.246.0000),

to Bordeaux via Birmingham and Gatwick from many points in the UK, by BA (www.britishairways.com, 0870.850.9850),

to La Rochelle, Bergerac or Bordeaux from Southampton or to Bordeaux or Bergerac from Bristol
or to Bergerac and La Rochelle from Birmingham by British European (www.flybe.com, 0871.700.0535),

to Bordeaux from Dublin or London by Air France, (www.airfrance.co.uk, 0870.142.4343),

to Bordeaux from either Nottingham (East Midlands) or from Manchester by BMIBABY, (www.bmibaby.com, 0870.720.0156)

- and all of my properties are within 1 hour of one of these airports.

Why 'kaydreamhomes.com.fr'?

- Our office has been in the same location for 63 years, is fluently bilingual and everything we do is in English, including the contract to buy your home.
- Our website www.kaydreamhomes.com.fr is always current.
- We can offer help with excellent accommodation for your visit.

'We make your dreams come true'

Languedoc-Roussillon

MAISON DE LA FRANCE

FACT BOX

- ■ **POPULATION** 2,295,648
- ■ **UNEMPLOYMENT RATE** 9%
- ■ **AVERAGE 4-BED HOUSE PRICE** €359,000
- ■ **REGIONAL CAPITAL** Montpellier
- ■ **REGION SIZE** 27,448km²

Contents

Area profile

Diverse and spectacular, Languedoc-Roussillon encompasses French Catalonia, Montpellier and the Mediterranean coast

GETTING THERE

AIR Languedoc-Roussillon has an international airport in Montpellier, and three smaller but extremely active airports in Nîmes, Perpignan and Carcassonne. **Ryanair** (0871 246 0000; www.ryanair.com) flies directly into Montpellier from Stansted, Carcassonne from Dublin, Liverpool and Stansted, Nîmes from Liverpool, Luton and Stansted, and Perpignan from Stansted. **GB Airways** (0870 551 1155; www.gbairways.com) flies into Montpellier from Gatwick. **Flybe** (0870 700 0535; www.flybe.co.uk) flies to Perpignan from Birmingham, Edinburgh and Southampton.

ROAD The A9 runs along the coastline of Languedoc-Roussillon from Nîmes through Montpellier and down to Perpignan. From Paris the A10 leads on to the A20 from Orléans to Toulouse, while the A61 motorway provides access from the west, and the A75 enters from the north. The smaller road networks are well-maintained, making for easy access throughout the whole of the region.

RAIL TGV (www.tgv.co.uk) runs a service between Paris Gare de Lyon and Nîmes, Montpellier and Perpignan, while Motorail operates from Calais to Narbonne. For more details on local services, contact **Rail Europe** (0870 830 2008; www.raileurope.co.uk).

THE LANGUEDOC-ROUSSILLON REGION arches between the Midi-Pyrénées and Provence, and then along the Mediterranean coast through the heart of French Catalonia to the border with Spain. The coast offers great beaches and, inland, spectacular scenery encompassing mountains and lakes, much of which is protected within national and regional parks. As well as hiking, cycling and fishing, the Pyrenees offers great skiing in the winter months.

This Mediterranean region combines the fiercely proud Languedoc, formerly an independent province with its own language, and Roussillon, a Catalan region. Traditionally less popular than Provence, Languedoc-Roussillon offers all that its neighbour can offer and more.

The Languedoc coast

The Languedoc coast is characterised by sandy beaches and family-friendly resorts such as Agde and La Grande Motte. Inland you'll find the university city of Narbonne, the beautiful hilltop city of Béziers, and the lively Languedoc capital, Montpellier, whose medical school is the oldest in Europe. Much of Montpellier's city centre is pedestrianised and its wide boulevards, open squares and fountains make this a pleasant place in which to stroll, perhaps after a day at the beach. Throughout the region you'll find evidence of the Romans, from ruined baths to the straight roads, and nowhere is this better exemplified than in Nîmes, with its almost intact amphitheatre, Les Arènes, its city walls and the Maison Carrée, a former Roman

temple which still stands in its entirety. Bullfights and concerts are held regularly at Les Arènes, which was modelled on the Colosseum in Rome. Just outside the city is the Pont du Gard, a three-tiered Roman aqueduct built to provide the city with water. This UNESCO World Heritage site is one of the most visited places in the region.

Rising out of the plains southwest of Montpellier, Carcassonne is, quite simply, one of France's most visually stunning cities – its medieval hilltop citadel, fortified by double walls and turrets, looks positively Disneyesque from a distance. Originally established as a Roman fort, the streets, buildings and basilica of the Cité, by which the walled fortress is known, mostly date back to the 12th and 13th centuries. The Cité was rebuilt in the latter part of the 19th century, and today attracts several million visitors each year.

The Canal du Midi, a miracle of 17th-century engineering that connects the Garonne – and hence the Atlantic – to the Mediterranean, reaches its highest point near Carcassonne. Travelling by boat along it, or walking or cycling along the canal's tree-lined towpath, is one of the most rewarding ways of experiencing this region of France.

Catalan connections

Southeast of Carcassonne and only 20 kilometres from the border with Spain, Perpignan, capital of Roussillon, has a marked Catalan feel, not just because of the beating sun. Its signs are written in both French and Catalan, and it is actually Catalonia's third largest city. The distinctive cathedral is built from pebbles and brick, while touches of its Spanish

CLIMATE

13.5	Dec	7	61	Dec	81
16	Nov	10	50	Nov	78
21	Oct	14	68	Oct	70
26	Sep	19	48	Sep	65
28	Aug	21	31	Aug	62
28.5	Jul	22	12	Jul	59
26.5	Jun	20	33	Jun	58
20	May	17	50	May	57
17.5	Apr	13	50	Apr	56
12.5	Mar	10	40	Mar	64
12.5	Feb	7	40	Feb	72
12.5	Jan	6	61	Jan	77

LANGUEDOC-ROUSSILLON — LONDON

AVERAGE TEMPERATURE (Celsius)

LANGUEDOC-ROUSSILLON — LONDON

AVERAGE RAINFALL (millimetres)

FOOD AND DRINK

Given its varied landscape, Mediterranean coastline and shared border with Spain, it's little wonder that the cuisine of Languedoc-Roussillon is so diverse. Rich in ingredients such as seafood, olive oil, tomatoes, garlic, onions, peppers and fresh herbs, strong southern Mediterranean influences abound. Languedoc's chief dish is cassoulet, a meat and bean casserole. Roussillon has a similar beef stew called ouillade. Other regional specialities include: oysters from Bouzigues, Gardiane (bull stew with rice), aligot (mashed potato and goat's cheese), morue Catalane (cod with tomatoes and pepper), boles de picolat, a Catalan favourite of meat balls in tomato sauce with ham and olives. To finish off, there's crème Catalane (crème brûlée with lemon, vanilla and fennel seed) and a first-rate selection of cheeses, such as pélardon, bleu des causses, and tomme (goat's cheese). Wine producers in Languedoc-Roussillon have been working hard to improve quality. Red wines predominate and tend to be fruity, spicy and full-bodied. Corbières, Coteaux du Languedoc and St Chinian wines offer good value for money.

MAISON DE LA FRANCE

ALL PHOTOS MAISON DE LA FRANCE

ATTRACTIONS

∎ Visit the harbour towns of the Vermilion Coast south of Perpignan, inspiration for many an artist

∎ Head to the pretty town of Sète for the water jousting tournaments in August

∎ Marvel at the Pont du Gard aqueduct, the highest the Romans ever built

∎ Take a coffee break at one of the cafés lining Montpellier's main square, in the shadow of the grand opera house

∎ Time your visit to coincide with one of the concerts held in Nîmes's splendid amphitheatre, Les Arènes

∎ Go skiing at Font-Romeu, one of the largest resorts in the French Pyrenees

∎ Soak up the Catalan atmosphere in Perpignan, especially during Easter week when processions fill the street on Good Friday

∎ Seek out the medieval Cathar castles of Quéribus and Peyrepertuse, in Corbières country

∎ Walk or cycle along the tree-lined Canal du Midi – even better, take a boat

∎ Don't miss Carcassonne, one of Europe's finest medieval citadels

past can be seen in the Palais des Rois de Majorque, built in the 13th century when Roussillon was ruled by Mallorcan kings.

South of Perpignan are colourful harbour towns such as Collioure and Amélie-les-Bains, which have inspired artists from Matisse to Rennie Mackintosh. Northwest of Perpignan are swathes of vineyards that make up the winemaking area of Corbières.

The economy

Languedoc-Roussillon is the largest wine-producing area in France, with the highest concentration of vineyards – many of its vineyards are turning to New World vintners to improve their output. The region is also a leading centre for the scientific and medical industries, as well as for biotechnology. Tourists flock to the sun-soaked beaches here and tourism is a major contributor to the region's economy.

Social groups

In the last six years, there has been a huge growth in the property market, with prices doubling in many parts of the region. Major interest has been shown by the British, German and Swiss markets, and Uzès, on the outskirts of Nîmes, is now effectively a British suburb. ●

Property hotspots

MAP KEY

5 Hotspot
○ Major town/city
✈ Airport
⛴ Ferry

HOTSPOTS

PERPIGNAN

1 Lying just 20 kilometres from the Spanish border, Perpignan is the capital of the Pyrénées-Orientales département (in effect the old province of Roussillon) and Catalonia's third largest city. It offers an intriguing blend of French and Spanish lifestyles, with a significant part of the population claiming Spanish ancestry, many from refugees of the Spanish Civil War. Catalan culture and cuisine is dominant, with road signs and street names displayed in Catalan and French.

The place de la Loge, in the renovated and pedestrianised Old Town, is dominated by the late Gothic Loge de Mer, built to house the stock exchange and boasting Venetian arches, Catalan archways and gargoyles. To the south, the two-storey Palais des Rois de Majorque with its 13th-century Moorish courtyard offers the best views of Perpignan. Enjoy a leisurely glass of locally produced muscat at one of the many cafés laid out along the banks of the Basse.

The Languedoc-Roussillon region is not as expensive as the Côte d'Azur and demand for property here rose a sharp 28.4 per cent last year – more than in any other region. So saying, Perpignan is primarily a working city with a housing market driven by local rather than international buyers. A five-bedroom villa in Perpignan costs anything from €445,000 while a traditional three-bedroom villa sells for around €301,000. Apartments are becoming increasingly popular here, a two-

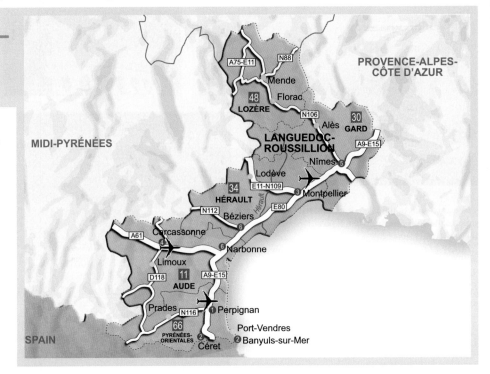

bedroom flat costing an average of €205,000.

Perpignan is not a major resort and has little to offer tourists, so the short-term rental market is small. The main market is for long-term rentals to French workers. A one-bedroom property will generate an average of €475 per week in high season.

Key facts

■ **POPULATION** 108,000

■ **TAXES** Taxe d'habitation 7.36%, taxe foncière 9.91%

■ **AIRPORT** Aéroport Perpignan, avenue Maurice Bellonte, 66000 Perpignan, Tel: +33 4 68 52 60 70, Fax: +33 4 68 51 31 03

■ **SCHOOLS** Rectorat de l'Académie de Montpellier, 31 rue de l'Université, 34064 Montpellier, Cedex 02, Tel: +33 4 67 91 47 00

■ **MEDICAL** Hôpital Maréchal Joffre, 20 avenue du Languedoc, BP 4052, 66046 Perpignan, Tel: +33 4 68 61 66 33

■ **PROS** The city is conveniently located for both the coast and the mountains, with excellent walking in summer and skiing in winter ■ Located only 15

minutes from the Spanish border ■ The area experiences good weather and very warm winters ■ Property here is cheaper than on the nearby Côte d'Azur

■ **CONS** Perpignan's coastal position makes it vulnerable to bombardment by winds from Tunisia, on a similar scale to the Marseille mistral ■ Since it is primarily an industrial city, parts of Perpignan are fairly unattractive.

SOUTHERN ROUSSILLON

2 To the southwest of Perpignan, towards the Spanish border, the Roussillon settlements of Céret and Banyuls both enjoy a Mediterranean climate. Céret, an ancient town on the river Aude with a Catalan flavour, is known for its cherry harvest, the earliest in France. The trees sometimes blossom in January and, traditionally, cherries are sent to the French president each spring. The pink and russet houses of the old town are grouped around the small, colourful bay. Said to be the

birthplace of Cubism, Céret was a favourite with Picasso, whose works are on display at the local museum of modern art alongside paintings by Chagall, Dali, Dufy and Matisse.

Banyuls, a fishing village on the Côte Vermeille, is set amid vine-clad hills, palms and eucalyptus. A quiet place with no through traffic, Banyuls is noted for its sweet, port-like red wine. Inhabitants claim that Banyuls is the sunniest village in Roussillon.

Properties in the area are stone-built and prices have leapt in the last few years. Céret is dominated by the English market. A modern villa with three bedrooms close to Céret starts at €382,000, while a traditional property with five bedrooms will sell for around €657,000. Cheaper properties are still available in rural areas, although these are becoming scarce.

Buying to rent in this area should be a sound investment. It's a well-known area, there's a steady influx of British holiday-makers, and the rental season lasts from June to September as the weather is mild and the surroundings attractive. A property with three bedrooms will generate an average of €846 per week.

Key facts
■ **POPULATION** 13,000
■ **TAXES** Taxe d'habitation 7.36%, taxe foncière 9.91%
■ **AIRPORT** Aéroport Perpignan, avenue Maurice Bellonte, 66000 Perpignan, Tel: +33 4 68 52 60 70, Fax: +33 4 68 51 31 03
■ **SCHOOLS** Rectorat de l'Académie de Montpellier, 31 rue de l'Université, 34064 Montpellier, Cedex 02, Tel: +33 4 67 91 47 00
■ **MEDICAL** Centre Hospitalier Spécialisé Léon Jean Grégory, Centre de jour La Tuilerie, 7 chem Vivès, 66400 Céret, Tel: +33 4 68 87 38 87
■ **PROS** Typical properties in the area are built of stone and generally come with a good deal of land ■ Since it's a border area, Spain is easily accessible ■ There are good road connections to the rest of France
■ **CONS** An expensive area, with renovation properties costing from E200,000, while a habitable four-bedroom property starts at E400,000 ■ Banyuls can be very isolated in winter, being some 40 minutes from Perpignan.

MONTPELLIER

3 The capital of the Languedoc-Roussillon region and the département of Hérault is a stunning city, sparkling with modern stylish buildings, open squares and fountains. Dating back to the 13th century, Montpellier University is internationally acclaimed for its faculty of medicine, which was France's first teaching hospital, counting Nostradamus among its students. The city is a must-see location, its attractions including 17th-century mansions with inner courtyards, the new and controversial Antigone quarter, neo-classical developments of futuristic flats and offices, and an Olympic swimming pool.

The vast 18th-century marble place de la Comédie – known as 'L'Oeuf', or the Egg, due to its curved central roundabout – is the most lively part of town. The ornately sculpted Fontaine des Trois-Graces forms the centrepiece, while cafés and the well-known statue, Les Trois-Graces, face the Opéra, a copy of the Paris Opera House.

Demand for property in and around Montpellier is ever-increasing. A three-bedroom property will cost upwards of €346,000, while a townhouse with four bedrooms will cost around €412,410. Villas to renovate are rare in Montpellier, and if you do find one, expect to pay more than €120,000. Try looking in one of the villages just outside the city, where a traditional house with three bedrooms can be found for around €220,000.

Montpellier's coastal location, and the fact that Parisians are increasingly drawn to the area, guarantees a good rental income during the peak rental season between June and September, when a four-bedroom property will secure an average rental of €667 per week.

Key facts
■ **POPULATION** 250,000
■ **TAXES** Taxe d'habitation 8.24%, taxe foncière 11.69%
■ **AIRPORT** Aéroport Montpellier Méditerranée, Chambre de Commerce et Industrie de Montpellier, 34035 Montpellier Cedex 4, Tel: +33 4 67 20 85 00
■ **SCHOOLS** Rectorat de l'Académie de Montpellier, 31 rue de l'Université, 34064 Montpellier, Cedex 02, Tel: +33 4 67 91 47 00
■ **MEDICAL** Centre Hospitalier Universitaire, 39 avenue Charles Flahault, 34000 Montpellier, Tel: +33 4 67 33 58 17
■ **PROS** This is a lively and forward-thinking city, with a quarter of the population under the age of 25 ■ Montpellier is an international city, which draws a large number of foreign buyers and students ■ Properties are rising in value and are expected to continue to do so
■ **CONS** It is estimated that the population of Montpellier will have doubled by 2015, due to its continuing popularity ■ The area has seen a lot of modern new developments.

CARCASSONNE

4 Medieval Carcassonne, one of the most dramatic UNESCO World Heritage cities in France, is divided into two quite distinct areas by the river Aude. The Ville Basse, or lower town, on the left bank, founded in the 13th century, carries on its daily life as the busy, administrative capital of the Aude département. But it's the Cité – a castle within a castle, with huge ramparts, straddling the hill on the right bank – that attracts over three million visitors each year.

First fortified by the Romans in the sixth century, and much improved over the centuries, the fortress was the site of the Cathar uprising, which was put down in 1209 by the crusading Simon de Montfort, who then extended the fortifications. The Cité took on major strategic significance as a border citadel during the Hundred Years' War, but by the 17th century its military importance had waned and it fell into disrepair.

Under the 19th-century architect Viollet-le-Duc, the city's 52 towers and two immense walls were restored to their former glory. Nowadays the Cité houses the inevitable souvenir shops, museums, restaurants and cafés, but there is no denying the atmosphere of both the inner fortress and the beautiful church of St-Nazaire, and despite the hordes of fellow tourists this is a place not to be missed. Carcassonne celebrates its rich heritage with a month-long festival in July, crowned with spectacular fireworks on Bastille Day.

Carcassonne has a vibrant foreign property market, with prices dictated by the city's excellent location, good weather, and proximity to Toulouse. A three-bedroom townhouse costs around €217,000, while a five-bedroom villa will cost over €351,000. Good-value properties can be found to the north of Carcassonne, where a three-bedroom house might cost around €220,000

This is an extremely popular tourist area, with a rental season lasting from June to September. Demand for holiday rentals is high, and long-term winter lets are an option. A three-bedroom property in Carcassonne can be rented for an average of €851 per week.

Key facts
■ **POPULATION** 44,400
■ **TAXES** Taxe d'habitation 8.64%, taxe foncière 19.39%
■ **AIRPORT** Aéroport de Salvaza, route de Montréal, 11000 Carcassonne Cedex, Tel: +33 4 68 71 96 46
■ **SCHOOLS** Rectorat de l'Académie de Montpellier, 31 rue de l'Université, 34064 Montpellier, Cedex 02, Tel: +33 4 67 91 47 00
■ **MEDICAL** Hôpital de Carcassonne, route St-Hilaire, 11000 Carcassonne, Tel: +33 4 68 24 24 24
■ **PROS** Carcassonne's fortress is one of the most visited attractions in France ■ The city has many good hotels and restaurants n In addition to its own airport, Carcassonne is close to Toulouse, which is easily accessed by flights from the UK
■ **CONS** The climate in Carcassonne is slightly chillier than in other parts of Languedoc because of its proximity to the Black Mountains ■ During the winter months there is little activity.

NÎMES

5 On the border between Provence and Languedoc,

Nîmes is capital of the Gard département and is best known as the home of denim (serges de Nîmes) and for the influence of ancient Rome. The latter's impact is visible in some of the most spectacular ancient remains in Europe. Recently given a hi-tech look by various architects and designers, including Philippe Starck and Norman Foster, Nîmes is bidding to be the foremost city of innovation in today's southern France.

There are many prized ancient landmarks, such as Diana's Temple in the Jardin de la Fontaine and the Arènes amphitheatre, now covered with a retractable roof and used to stage bullfights. The Rhône valley's gently rolling hills surround Nîmes, and the Pont du Gard aqueduct is within 20 minutes of the city.

Nîmes's proximity to Avignon draws many buyers as well as those seeking rental property in the area. International demand is great, with the British being particularly drawn to Uzès on the outskirts of Nîmes. Recent price hikes have pushed prices close to Côte d'Azur levels. A villa with three bedrooms costs €348,000, while a house with two bedrooms will sell for €203,000. Out of town you can purchase a mas, a traditional house or farm, in an acre of land with a pool for €705,000, or a large modern property with all mod-cons for €475,000.

Nîmes offers easy access to the coast and Montpellier, making it good for rental income. This is a popular area for holiday-makers and families, and the most in-demand properties are three-bedroom houses, which command rent averaging €1,100 per week.

Key facts
■ **POPULATION** 133,424
■ **TAXES** Taxe d'habitation 8.89%, taxe foncière 13.18%

■ **AIRPORT** Nîmes-Garons Aéroport, 30800 St-Gilles, Tel: +33 4 66 70 49 49, Fax: +33 4 66 70 91 24
■ **SCHOOLS** Rectorat de l'Académie de Montpellier, 31 rue de l'Université, 34064 Montpellier, Cedex 02, Tel: +33 4 67 91 47 00
■ **HOSPITALS** Hôpital Caremeau, place du Professeur Robert Debré, 30029 Nîmes Cedex 9, Tel: +33 4 66 68 68 68
■ **PROS** Nîmes's proximity to Avignon draws a lot of buyers and tourists to the area ■ Nîmes is one of the biggest tourist attractions in the south of France ■ The city has recently undergone a facelift, with various high-profile architects and designers giving it a new vibrancy and modernity ■ There is a healthy demand for property, with many British buyers moving to the area
■ **CONS** There have been major price hikes due to high demand.

BÉZIERS & NARBONNE

6 Located in the Hérault département, Béziers was already a thriving city when the Romans arrived in 36 BC and it is still an important trade centre for wines and liqueurs. The 18th-century arena, known for its bullfights, was designed initially as an opera house, and in August now hosts the four-day, Spanish-style feria, a spectacular pageant of music, dancing and fine food. The Cathédrale St-Nazaire sits high above the city, whose focal point is Allées Paul-Riquet, a broad esplanade lined with cafés that leads into a delightful park planted with ponds, palm and lime trees.

Narbonne is a medium-sized university city which has benefited greatly from tourism, chiefly from the interest in canal holidays – the Canal de la Robine, a branch of the Canal du Midi, passes through the heart of the city. The city is dominated by its Gothic Cathédrale de St-Just-et-St-Pasteur. There are great views from its north tower.

Béziers is one of the cheapest

areas in the region, but with the completion of the A75 motorway, property prices have been rising steadily. The minimum price for a villa is now €200,000, and this rises steeply with the addition of land. A few renovation properties are available from €100,000 and the average two- or three-bedroom townhouse costs from €200,000 to around €220,000. Just outside Béziers, a renovated village house with two bedrooms will cost you €150,000, while a renovated mill close to a river and with a pool is available for €427,000.

Béziers is well located, close to the sea and in a popular part of Hérault. Béziers and Narbonne are important destinations for the French, and have started to attract the interest of international holiday-makers. Prices here can be cheaper than elsewhere in the Languedoc-Roussillon region; a property with two bedrooms will typically rent for €673 per week.

Key facts
■ **POPULATION** Béziers 77,996, Narbonne 46,510
■ **TAXES** Taxe d'habitation 8.24%, taxe foncière 11.69%
■ **AIRPORT** Aéroport Montpellier Méditerranée, Ch. de Commerce et Industrie de Montpellier, 34035 Cedex 4, Tel: +33 4 67 20 85 00
■ **SCHOOLS** Rectorat de l'Académie de Montpellier, 31 rue de l'Université, 34064 Montpellier, Cedex 02, Tel: +33 4 67 91 47 00
■ **MEDICAL** Centre Hospitalier, 2 rue Valentin Hauy, 34500 Béziers, Tel: +33 4 67 35 70 35
■ **PROS** Béziers is currently one of the cheapest areas in which to purchase property ■ It is increasingly popular with the foreign market, so expect prices to rise in the future ■ Narbonne is an attractive and peaceful area, close to Béziers and the coast
■ **CONS** The development of the new A75 motorway has inevitably pushed up local property prices ■ Most British buyers focus on the outskirts, such as St-Chinian, Roquebrun, Clermont-l'Hérault and Lamalou-les-Bains ■ Narbonne can be excessively windy. ●

The Languedoc is home to many picturesque villages such as Campagne Pont Rivièreski resorts

HOTSPOTS

Property guide

The property market here is extremely healthy and although house prices are expensive and rising, they are still much cheaper than in Provence and the Côte d'Azur

With much of the land covered in vineyards and demand for houses high, prices are rising fast in the region

THE GARD AND HÉRAULT ARE PARTICULARLY popular départements within Languedoc-Roussillon and command high prices. The larger cities, such as Nîmes and especially Carcassonne, are very pricy places to live, while Montpellier, the most expensive city in the Languedoc-Roussillon, has seen increases of 40 per cent in the last seven years. The French Catalan city of Perpignan is regarded as the most fashionable spot and is therefore expensive, although you can pick up a two-bedroom villa on the outskirts for an average of €200,000. Those who wish to relocate to the coast will find a wealth of coastal resorts to choose from, but you must be prepared to pay a premium.

Cheaper properties do exist further inland, particularly in the Pyrénées-Orientales département in the far south. Better value can also be found in Aude. Undiscovered Lozère also offers great value for money. Along the coast, renovation properties retail at over €380,000 for three bedrooms, and you'll need to head further inland to find the bargains, although these are a scarcity in this region. Throughout Languedoc-Roussillon, the property market is developing, making this a good time to invest.

Spiralling prices within the Côte d'Azur have forced investors to seek out alternative locations on the western coast. Frequent cheap flights make Languedoc much more accessible as a weekend destination, and it's predicted that the area will soon be as popular as the Côte d'Azur. The problem with the region is the scarcity of property. With much of the land covered in vineyards, there is little room for property development, which is driving prices up.

The rental market is stable and good returns are possible. A six-bedroom property in Carcassone has a weekly rental yield of between €1,160 and €1,300 per week. In Montpellier a two-bedroom property charges a weekly rate of €497, while a village house near Béziers averages weekly earnings of €364.

The most popular style of property in the region is the traditional village house, and prices start at around €110,000. For a decent plot with a small, garden, you are looking at around €165,000. At the luxury end of the market, substantial maisons de maitre and châteaux are quite widely available. ●

MAISONS DE MAÎTRE

- ■ These large, roomy manor houses are found in small towns and rural locations. Decent renovations can command hefty price tags, but there are still very cheap unrenovated properties around if you hunt hard enough
- ■ They typically have from three to five rows of windows and enclosed gardens
- ■ There are usually three storeys – the reception rooms on the ground floor, private rooms on the upper floors and servants' quarters in the attic
- ■ From the 1850s onwards, the bourgeoisie added ornate towers and went overboard with chintz decor, in an effort to emulate the nobles
- ■ The specific styles of the building vary from region to region and are determined largely by the locally available construction materials

WHAT CAN YOU GET FOR YOUR EUROS?

14TH-CENTURY CHÂTEAU

Dating from 1902, this beautiful château is set in a pretty village on the edge of the Canal du Midi. With 600 square metres of space arranged over three floors, the property boasts three elegant reception rooms and four bedrooms. Attractive period features include original floors, fireplaces and stained glass windows. A swimming pool and outbuildings are set in the 1,582 square metres of grounds.

€1,070,000 CODE SIF

MAISON DE MAITRE

Offering two reception rooms, 11 bedrooms and two bathrooms this stylish house is situated less than 40 minutes from Toulouse and dates back to the 14th century. An attractive old Lauragais farm, there is a habitable living area of 570m2 as well as a second smaller Maison de Maitre and three gites. The property is set in 12 hectares of peaceful countryside, complete with woods and meadowland.

€795,000 CODE SIF

WINE-GROWERS HOUSE

Located near Clermont l'Hérault, this former winegrower's house chas been converted into a beautiful characterful property and comes complete with a fully equipped kitchen, a spacious living room, a separate dining room, four bedrooms, three bathrooms and 1,800 square metres of Mediterranean gardens. Situated in a calm and peaceful environment this is a truly unique – and stunning – property.

€535,000 CODE SIF

DETACHED VILLA

Fully habitable this four-bedroom property is situated close to the town of Elne. A thriving Kiwi farm it's secluded and quiet but not far from civilisation. The property is surrounded by 2000 square metres of land that at the moment are planted with Kiwi trees. The property has been built to a modern design with 190 square metres of living space and comes with a large swimming pool and pretty gardens.

€599,417 CODE VEF

SECLUDED FARMHOUSE

This four-bedroom property is only 10 minutes drive from Perpignan. and was built at the end of the 19th century. It's still a working farm where grapes are harvested for the local wine co-operative and has 12,000 square metres of land, full of fruit trees and vines. Partially restored it has a living space of 250 square metres and a renovated kitchen. Ready to move this mas offers bags of rustic charm.

€821,491 CODE VEF

STUNNING VILLA

Located in Herault, close to Saint-Martin-de-Londres, this single-storey villa comes with a swimming pool and is situated on private land in the heart of an oak forest. Only walking distance to the nearest village and amenities, this south-facing property has 116 square metres of living space and is set in 4,015 square metres of land. A charming property with mountain views, and a stone's throw of Montpellier.

€446,000 CODE FRA

AVERAGE HOUSE PRICES LANGUEDOC-ROUSSILLON

	2-bed		3-bed		4-bed		5/6-bed	
Perpignan	€203,355	(£137,402)	€241,000	(£163,000)	€301,140	(£203,500)	€445,000	(£301,000)
Southern Roussillon	€243,000	(£164,000)	€382,000	(£258,100)	€462,000	(£312,000)	€657,000	(£444,000)
Montpelier	€224,500	(£152,000)	€346,240	(£234,000)	€412,410	(£279,000)	€633,000	(£428,000)
Carcassone	€166,321	(£112,400)	€217,000	(£146,300)	€285,000	(£192,400)	€351,420	(£237,450)
Nimes	€203,000	(£137,000)	€348,000	(£235,000)	€435,230	(£294,100)	€447,000	(£302,000)
Beziers & Narbonne	€200,425	(£135,422	€219,000	(£148,000)	€257,331	(£174,000)	€340,000	(£229,500)

Côte d'Azur, Provence & Corsica

FACT BOX

- ■ **POPULATION** 4,766,347
- ■ **UNEMPLOYMENT RATE** Côte d'Azur: 10.8%;
Provence: 12%; Corsica: 11.7%
- ■ **AVERAGE 4-BED HOUSE PRICE** €846,000
- ■ **REGIONAL CAPITAL** Côte d'Azur and Provence:
Marseille; Corsica: Ajaccio
- ■ **REGION SIZE** Côte d'Azur and Provence: 31,436km²;
Corsica: 8,680km²

Contents

Area profile

Enjoy sophisticated resorts on the French Riviera, the good life in rural Provence, or escape from it all on Corsica

GETTING THERE

AIR British Airways (0870 850 9850; www.britishairways.co.uk) flies to Marseille from Gatwick, and to Nice from Birmingham, Gatwick, Heathrow and Manchester. **easyJet** (0871 750 0100; www.easyjet.com) serves Nice from Bristol, Gatwick, Liverpool, Luton, Newcastle and Stansted and Marseille from Gatwick. **BMI** (0870 607 0555; www.flybmi.com) flies to Nice from East Midlands. **Jet2** (0870 737 8282; www.jet2.com) flies to Nice from Leeds-Bradford and Manchester. **Air France** (0845 359 1000; www.airfrance.co.uk) flies to Figari and Calvi via Orly airport.

.**ROAD** The A6 passes through Paris, Lyon, then the A7 to Orange and Avignon links to the A8 for Cannes and Nice. The A1 joins the A6, via the N412/A1 junction. At junction A9, the A6 joins the A6/E15 to Villefranche. Join the A46, then the A42/E611 at the A42 junction, linking back to the A46, via the A43. Take the A7/E15 to Aire de Mornas-Village from the A46. Take the junction with the A9 on to the A7/E714, then the A8/E80 into Nice.

RAIL TGV (www.tgv.co.uk) operates from Paris and Lille to Aix-en-Provence, Marseille and Nice, and **Rail Europe** (0870 584 8848; www.raileurope.co.uk) runs from London Waterloo to Aix-en-Provence, Antibes, Cannes, Marseille, Nice, Nîmes and Toulon.

CLIMATE

Côte d'Azur, Provence and Corsica (°C)	Month	London (°C)
14	Dec	7
18	Nov	10
21	Oct	14
24	Sep	19
28	Aug	21
28	Jul	22
24	Jun	20
21	May	17
17	Apr	13
14	Mar	10
11	Feb	7
13	Jan	6

AVERAGE **TEMPERATURE** (Celsius)

Côte d'Azur, Provence and Corsica (mm)	Month	London (mm)
78	Dec	81
120	Nov	78
100	Oct	70
60	Sep	65
20	Aug	62
10	Jul	59
30	Jun	58
80	May	57
86	Apr	56
90	Mar	64
80	Feb	72
100	Jan	77

AVERAGE **RAINFALL** (millimetres)

THE ASTONISHING NATURAL BEAUTY OF Provence and the Côte d'Azur has inspired numerous artists and writers, from Van Gogh and Cézanne to F. Scott Fitzgerald. This tremendously varied region – formally known as Provence-Alpes-Côte d'Azur – encompasses the sophisticated resorts of the French Riviera, the wildlife-rich wetlands of the Camargue, the Roman towns of inland Provence, and the Alpes-Maritimes, with their gorges, rivers, and unspoiled villages. The South of France is home to some of the most evocative images of France – winding mountain roads, fields of lavender, olive groves, sun-soaked beaches, yacht-filled marinas and Roman ruins – and it's where many people, in an ideal world, would love to live and work.

The Mediterranean coast

Stretching from the Italian border to the southern tip, the Côte d'Azur, or French Riviera, is one of the world's best known tourist areas, receiving more foreign visitors than any other region in France, most people arriving via Nice airport. Places such as Menton, Monte-Carlo, Nice, Antibes, Juan-les-Pins, Cannes, Fréjus, St-Tropez and Hyères have long had glittering international reputations as the summer playgrounds of the rich and famous.

Nice, capital of the Riviera, was founded by the Greeks (named by Nicosia) and has a venerable history. The Old Town is all narrow, winding streets, while the main part of the city is made up of wider avenues, lined with tall townhouses. It's a centre of culture, with its Matisse Museum, newly built modern art museum, opera house and galleries, but it's also a great place to relax, with its pebbly beach and wide seafront promenade.

The French Riviera is lined with lively beach resorts, golf courses and casinos – most famously in Monte-Carlo, in the tiny principality of Monaco. Places like Cannes – most famous for its annual film festival which attracts the cream of Hollywood – and St-Tropez exude an air of exclusivity, but inland from the coast, the countryside is rugged and hilly. This is one area of France where vineyards are outnumbered by orchards bearing olives, lemons and oranges and lavender fields. Stunning hilltop villages, such as Grasse, known as the perfume-making capital of the world, Tourrettes, La Turbie and Tourtour are definitely worth making a detour to for their cobbled alleyways and bougainvillea-clad stone houses.

The stretch of coast between Toulon and Marseille is the region's most underdeveloped coastline and has spectacular cliffs with views to match. Marseille, France's second biggest city, is a thriving port with a cosmopolitan atmosphere thanks to its large immigrant population. It has a renowned fish market, superb museums, there's a cacophony of street performers, and its restaurants provide a melting pot of world cuisine.

Along the coast from Marseilles, Arles trades on the magnificence of its Roman amphitheatre, and its connections with Van Gogh, to attract visitors. Inland from Marseilles, Aix-en-Provence, the medieval capital of Provence, is stunningly beautiful,

FOOD AND DRINK

Provençal cuisine revolves around fresh, simple ingredients such as tomatoes, aubergines, olives, olive oil, garlic, basil, rosemary, thyme, and seafood. A favourite starter eaten with bread is tapenade – a paste of black olives, anchovies, garlic and olive oil. Meat is seldom eaten in Provence, with locals preferring meals such as ratatouille and salade Niçoise. That said, boeuf en daube (beef stewed with red wine, onions, garlic, vegetables and herbs) is a winter mainstay. Provence's most well-known dish is arguably bouillabaisse, a filling soup of lobster, crab, mussels and clams.

Corsican cookery is steeped in Italian culinary tradition and dishes are far more meat orientated. While fish and shellfish dishes are served all over the island, many regularly opt for sausage, ham, goat or lamb. Island specialities are cheese and dishes made with sweet chestnut.

Popular local wines are the dry, fruity, rosé, notably Côtes de Provence, and reds such as Châteauneuf-du-Pape and Côtes de Rhône.

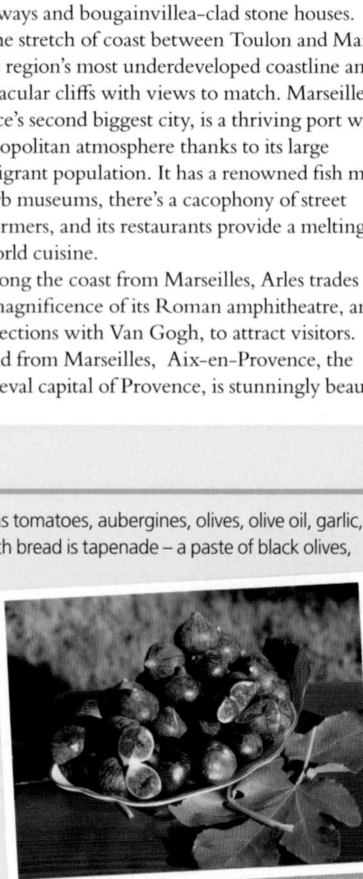

MAISON DE LA FRANCE

The quintessential fruit of the South of France

ALL PHOTOS MAISON DE LA FRANCE

with elegant avenues and fountains, and a wonderful place to just relax and wander. Avignon, further north, teeming with culture and history, is another of Provence's unmissable cities.

Corsica

In contrast to the glitz of the French Riviera, Corsica remains undiscovered by mass tourism, and is all the more enjoyable for that. Its remoteness is one of its main attractions. The birthplace of Napoléon, it's one of the Mediterranean's largest islands, and is an area of unspoiled beauty, with huge areas of uninhabited forest, snow-clad mountains and over 600 kilometres of beaches, coves and villages to explore. Half of the population is spread between the towns of Ajaccio and Bastia.

The economy

Tourism is definitely the major economy in the Provence-Alpes-Côte d'Azur region, and thanks to the great weather and the number of flights to Nice and Marseille airports, it receives visitors all year round. Agriculture is an important contributor to the economy, particularly in the coastal region, with the production and export of olives, olive oil, citrus fruit, lavender and other herbs, grapes and wine. Provence's coastal villages and vineyards provide a mix of tourism and industry, while Marseille is home to

France's largest port. Corsica, too, is reliant on its idyllic position and beaches for a tourist-based economy, while also engaging in some agricultural activity.

Social groups

Many British residents have been drawn to the area in the wake of Peter Mayle's bestselling book and subsequent TV series A Year in Provence. There's a genuine mix of people moving here, from those seeking second homes with a view to retiring, to younger, more career-driven people who take advantage of the fast train to Paris and the accessibility of Nice airport. However, the area is popular with buyers from all over Europe, as well as North America and the Middle and Far East. ●

ATTRACTIONS

■ See how the other half live by visiting St-Tropez, where the rich and famous moor their yachts in the harbour

■ Bask in the sunshine in the Hautes-Alpes region, where there are 300 days of sunshine each year – ideal for hiking in summer and skiing in winter

■ Relax on the promenade des Anglais on the Nice seafront

■ Admire the amazing Roman architecture of Arles's bullring

■ Soak up the hustle and bustle of Marseille, and don't leave without tasting the local speciality, bouillabaisse

■ The fragrant lavender fields of inland Provence are an evocative image of rural France

■ Check out one of Europe's most beautiful yet least discovered beaches: Palombaggia on the east coast of Corsica

■ Take a boat ride off the southern tip of Corsica to see the townhouses of Bonifacio clinging to the cliffs overhanging the sea

■ Visit the magificent papal palace at Avignon

Property hotspots

MAP KEY

- **5** Hotspot
- ○ Major town/city
- ✈ Airport
- ⛴ Ferry

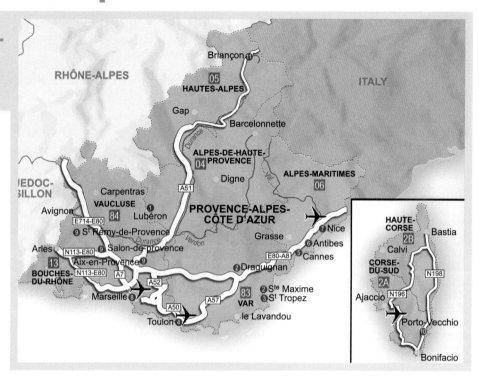

VAUCLUSE (LUBÉRON)

 This region has long been an escape for well-to-do Parisians, the Dutch and the British, with buyers drawn to traditional Provençal houses, or mas, with their exposed stone walls, arches, open fireplaces, spacious rooms, warm colours and terracotta. Those found on the edge of villages often have beguiling views, while village houses with balconies and small courtyards invite you to dine al fresco and enjoy the Mediterranean climate.

The best-value properties are to be found to the north of the Vaucluse at Bollène (a town famous for its troglodyte antecedents) and the Côtes du Rhône villages of Visan and Sault to the east. Although these areas are supposedly less chic, they are a gateway to the serene beauty of the high plateau.

The whole département is extremely expensive, but there are certainly cheaper properties in the north. Lubéron, with its mountain villages, offers spectacular views of the countryside and the average three-bedroom property costs from €321,000. Basic two-bedroom homes start from €216,000.

Rental income in Lubéron averages at around €531 per week for a two-bedroom property . A three-bedroom house costs €682 per week.

Key facts
■ **POPULATION** 499,685
■ **TAXES** Taxe d'habitation 6.08%, taxe foncière 7.85%

■ **AIRPORT** Avignon/Caumont Airport, RN7, route de Marseille, 84140 Montfavet, Tel: +33 (0) 4 90 81 51 51
■ **SCHOOLS** See Aix-en-Provence
■ **MEDICAL** Centre Hospitalier du Pays d'Apt, route de Marseille, 84400 Apt, Tel: +44 (0) 4 90 04 34 00; Centre Hospitalier de Cavaillon,119 avenue Georges Clémenceau, 84300 Cavaillon, Tel: +33 (0) 4 90 78 85 00
■ **PROS** The region is easily accessed by the A7 motorway ■ There's a growing foreign community, including British
■ **CONS** Houses are very expensive, at 11,500 per square metre.

INLAND VAR (DRAGUIGNAN, STE-MAXIME)

2 One of the areas first discovered by the British, the Var region remains a very popular area, offering prices under €330,000, although renovation properties are relatively rare. Inland Var is blessed with vineyards and olive groves, lavender plantations and swathes of beautiful sunflowers.

This département is well-situated between the mountains and the sea, with medieval hilltop villages offering a quieter lifestyle than St-Tropez. The superb climate, with more than 300 days of sunshine each year, is another bonus. Skiers are near to Les Arcs, with its TGV station providing a good connection to the rest of Europe.

Draguignan, the former capital, is a large town with many museums, while the towns of Lorgues and Brignoles have excellent markets. The village of Fayence is the hang-gliding capital of Europe, while Le Muy, a traditional Provençal town, has a huge selection of food shops and a wonderful market. Ste-Maxime is in a quiet location, right next to St-Tropez, and has a traditional harbour.

Prices have stabilised, with best-value buys found far north around Aups, a town on the edge of the Alps, which is famous for its truffle market. Another area to consider is Lac de St-Croix,

the largest man-made lake in Europe. The cost of a four-bedroom house is €408,000.

Rentals are very good in the summer, with the average weekly rental for a one-bedroom property being €579 and a three-bedroom house €961. Houses are generally more popular for lets, with a two-bedroom house generating €713 per week.

Key facts
■ **POPULATION** Draguignan 30,183, Ste-Maxime 12,000
■ **TAXES** Taxe d'habitation 5.29%, taxe foncière 6.40%
■ **AIRPORT** St-Tropez Aéroport du Golfe, Le Mole, Aerodrome de St Tropez, 83310 La Mole, Tel: +33 (0) 4 94 49 57 29
■ **SCHOOLS** See Aix-en-Provence, Cannes and Nice
■ **MEDICAL** Centre Hospitalier de Draguignan, route Montferrat, 83300 Draguignan, Tel: +33 (0) 4 94 60 50 00
■ **PROS** Many of the towns and villages in the region have retained their Provençal atmosphere
■ **CONS** Not directly on the coast.

ST-TROPEZ

3 Nestling at the foot of the Massif de Maures, St-Tropez still has its tiny squares and pastel-coloured houses that beguiled Guy de Maupassant in the 1880s and a succession of bohemians and artists. The film And God Created Woman (1956), starring Brigitte Bardot, established St-Tropez with the international jet-set, who each year take up residence in multi-million dollar yachts along the restaurant-lined waterfront.

Despite the traffic jams and the hordes of tourists in the height of summer, St-Tropez retains its charm. There is an excellent market at the place aux Herbes, and the famous brasseries Le Gorille and Sénéquier are unmissable. Just outside the town there are some magnificent beaches where you can escape the crowds and claim a section of beach a little bit bigger than your towel.

Because property in the town is phenomenally expensive, you need to be quite wealthy to buy here. Two-bedroom homes average around €730,000, while an extra bedroom costs almost double. Five-bedroom homes start at over €3,913,000 but, of course, it's not difficult to pay much, much more than this.

As St-Tropez is in such demand, buyers can make a tidy profit from renting out their properties, prices for short-term lets ranging from average to excellent according to location and furnishings. Average weekly rents are €484 for a one-bedroom apartment and €747 for a two-bedroom apartment.

Key facts
■ **POPULATION** 5,542
■ **TAXES** Taxe d'habitation 5.29%, taxe foncière 6.40%
■ **AIRPORT** St-Tropez Aéroport du Golfe, Le Mole, Aerodrome de St-Tropez, 83310 La Mole, Tel: +33 (0) 4 94 49 57 29

■ **SCHOOLS** See Cannes and Nice
■ **MEDICAL** Centre Hospitalier de St-Tropez, 12 avenue Foch 83990, St-Tropez, Tel: +33 (0) 4 94 47 58 08
■ **PROS** If you buy a property here it will hold its value
■ **CONS** As in Cannes, you need a huge bank balance ■ Some think St-Tropez has been overrun by tourists and become a little tawdry.

TOULON & HYÈRES

4 While Toulon centre is not considered a hotspot, the Mont Faron area offers impressive views of the city's port and bay. Expect to find houses painted in pastel shades, with the stone door and window frames integrated into the façades. Close by, the fortified town of Hyères is desirable thanks to its position at the foot of the Maures hills, bordered by the Mediterranean.

With 14,000 hectares of protected scenery and watersports facilities, Hyères is consistently awarded a European Blue Flag for its beaches. The Old Town has fine examples of 12th-century architecture, including the Château St-Bernard and the Tour St-Blaise, built by the Knights Templar. Toulon's naval legacy remains a draw for visitors, and the National Maritime Museum celebrates its seafaring past. The bustling market is one of the largest in the region.

Toulon is not regarded as the most desirable area by foreign property buyers, and its rapid turnover of property is driven by the local French population. Prices are reasonable when compared with those on the French Riviera. An average three-bedroom property in the area costs just under €512,000.

The average rent for a one-bedroom apartment is €376 per week, while a similar two-bedroom house rises to €678 per week. Expect to pay at least €1,883 for five or more bedrooms.

Key facts
■ **POPULATION** 166,442
■ **TAXES** Taxe d'habitation 5.29%, taxe foncière 6.40%
■ **AIRPORT** Toulon/Hyères Aéroport, boulevard de la Marine, 83400 Hyères, Tel: +33 (0) 4 94 00 83 83
■ **SCHOOLS** See Aix-en-Provence and Marseilles
■ **MEDICAL** Hôpital Font-Pré, 1208 avenue Colonel Picot, Toulon, Tel: +33 (0) 4 94 61 61 61 ■ Hôpital Chalucet, rue Chalucet, Toulon, Tel: +33 (0) 4 94 22 77 77 ■ Hôpital Georges Clemenceau, 421 avenue Infanterie de Marine du Pacifique, La Garde, Tel: +33 (0) 4 94 08 86 86
■ **PROS** Ouerse and Pierre-Sieu are excellent locations to buy a vineyard, which can be purchased for less than the price of a flat in London ■ Toulon has a fine Mediterranean climate
■ **CONS** Destroyed in the Second World War, Toulon has been rebuilt and is no longer an authentic Provençal town.

CANNES

5 Glitzy Cannes combines history, beautiful architecture, ornate palace-style hotels, well-heeled holiday-makers and its world-renowned film festival. The price of property in Cannes has been rising fast, but that hasn't deterred British buyers, who are prepared to shell out for a place in the sun with sophistication. In terms of the European summer rental market, the French Riviera is the most popular area for holiday-makers – even more than Spain, Greece and Italy – so buying to rent on the Riviera is an excellent investment.

Summer rental prices on the Riviera are very high due to the limited length of the season, with prices varying from €633 per week for a one-bedroom apartment to around €2,774 per week for a five-bedroom house. Undoubtedly, Cannes is phenomenally expensive and you won't be able to pick up much for under €570,000 bar the odd small apartment. Four-bedroom homes cost around €1,262000

while a decent-sized villa with terracing and a swimming pool will set you back more than double that.

Five kilometres inland from Cannes lies the hilltop village of Mougins, where Picasso made his home. It's famous for its picturesque narrow lanes, restaurants, and while it isn't cheap, prices can be half of what they are in Cannes.

Rentals, both short and long term, are highly lucrative here, and during the Film Festival, those who own property can name their price.

Key facts
■ **POPULATION** 67,304
■ **TAXES** Taxe d'habitation 5.29%, taxe foncière 6.40%
■ **AIRPORT** Cannes Airport, Aéroport Cannes-Mandelieu, 06150 Cannes la Bocca, +33 (0) 4 89 88 98 28
■ **SCHOOLS** Mougins School, 615 avenue Dr Maurice Donat, Font de l'Orme, BP 401, 06251 Mougins Cedex, Tel: +33 (0) 4 93 90 1547. ■ CIV International School of Sophia Antipolis, BP 097, 06902 Sophia Antipolis, Tel: +33 (0) 4 92 96 52 24
■ **MEDICAL** Centre Hospitalier de Cannes, 13 avenue des Broussailles, Cannes, Tel: +33 (0) 4 93 69 70 00, www.hopital-cannes.fr
■ **PROS** Nice's posh relation, so there are many more amenities on offer
■ **CONS** There are not many native first-time buyers because of tight planning regulations ■ Villas can range from €700,000 plus; there is no ceiling.

ANTIBES

6 Antibes has proved an attractive location to buyers mesmerised by its setting, stunning views and sunny disposition. It is famous for its jazz festival, the military citadel Fort Carré and the lovely Old Town, where artists and writers including Picasso and Graham Greene chose to live. Residents and visitors have the pick of 48 beaches, from small coves to sheltered, family-friendly bays.

Foreign buyers don't seem to be drawn to any particular style of property, although traditional Provençal villas still sell strongly and are easy to find a rental market for. The secluded area of Cap d'Antibes, just outside the centre of town, has retained some woodland despite increasing development and is extremely expensive. A luxuriously appointed villa here, with private swimming pool and six or more bedrooms, can cost upwards of €4,000,000.

Property prices are rising faster in Cap than anywhere else on the Côte d'Azur. The best value is to be found inland towards Mougins, Valbonne and Biot. Due to its proximity to Nice and the A8, the town of Villeneuve-Loubet has proved particularly attractive to overseas buyers; expect to pay €501,000 for a two-bedroom studio. Most rentals here are short term. The average weekly rent during peak season for a one-bedroom apartment is €571, while a two-bedroom apartment can command €998, and a five-bedroom house an average of €1,400.

Key facts
■ **POPULATION** 72,412
■ **TAXES** Taxe d'habitation 5.29%, taxe foncière 6.40%
■ **AIRPORT** Nice/Côte d'Azur Airport, Chambre de Commerce et d'Industrie, 06281 Nice, Cedex 3, Tel: +33 (0) 4 93 21 30 30
■ **SCHOOLS** See Cannes and Nice
■ **MEDICAL** Hospitalier Centre d'Antibes Juan-les-Pins, 7 route Nationale, 06600 Antibes, Tel: +33 (0) 4 92 91 77 77, www.ch-antibes.fr
■ **PROS** A real town with a strong community, there is always activity here ■ The property market is a safe investment ■ Popular with yachting enthusiasts ■ Antibes has a good infrastructure, with the N98, A8 and D5 roads running directly into town
■ **CONS** Villas and houses are only ever on the market for a short period.

NICE

7 In Nice, location is paramount, with Nice West being a popular choice due to its proximity to the airport and the availability of more land to build on. Other hotspots include the green and tranquil Mont Boron, one of the most exclusive areas on the Côte d'Azur, tucked away to the east of the Old Town with spectacular views and a wealth of belle époque buildings. The area to the north of the main station, a kilometre from the seafront, is home to Nice's cheapest properties, and thus most of the bargains, while old Nice is favoured because the flower markets, restaurants and pedestrian zones create an attractive environment within the centre of town.

Nice is an expensive area but the boroughs can yield cheaper properties. Potential buyers are mostly interested in second homes, choosing properties with a swimming pool and sea views. Brand new homes are in demand, with the opportunity they bring to customise interiors before the work is completed. Almost half of the new developments are bought as weekend or second homes. Two-bedroom homes cost an average of €448,000, although it's possible to pick up apartments a little cheaper. However, you will more often than not have to pay more than €908,000 for four bedrooms.

This is an ever-popular summer destination and rentals are big business for the native population, with excellent prospects for long- and short-term lets. The average rent per week for a one-bedroom apartment is €484; a three-bedroom apartment will generate €798 a week, and a similar five-bedroom house around €1,351.

Key facts
■ **POPULATION** 345,892
■ **TAXES** Taxe d'habitation 5.29%, taxe foncière 6.40%.
■ **AIRPORT** Nice/Côte d'Azur Airport, Chambre de Commerce et d'Industrie, 06281 Nice, Cedex 3, Tel: +33 (0) 4 93 21 30 30
■ **SCHOOLS** The International School of Nice, 15 avenue Claude Debussy, 06200 Nice, Tel: +33 (0) 4 93 21 04 00. See also Cannes
■ **MEDICAL** Centre Hospitalier Universitaire de Nice, Hôpital de Cimiez, 4 avenue Reine Victoria, BP 1179, 06003 Nice, Cedex 1, Tel: +33 (0) 4 92 03 77 77
■ **PROS** Nice has excellent transport networks ■ As an international hotspot, Nice has undeniable glamour ■ Mild, sunny winters and very temperate summers.
■ **CONS** Area is packed during summer and very busy.

MARSEILLE

8 A melting pot of nationalities with a rich cultural heritage, Marseille is associated with the golden age of maritime prosperity in the late 19th century. The city is now being revitalised thanks to regeneration and investment projects in many of its districts, with the aim of creating a gateway to Europe. The second largest city in France, Marseille offers fine architecture, museums and excellent theatres. Along the Vieux Port at place Thiars are trendy bars and restaurants, while early risers can visit the fish market to source ingredients for the local speciality, bouillabaisse. Ferries run between the Vieux Port and Château d'If.

Marseille's regeneration has helped the foreign property market prosper. There are more than 100 quartiers, many with their own village life, while the upmarket 8th district offers two-bedroom studios in a modern apartment block from €305,000. If you're looking for a coastal village, try Ensuès-la-Redonne,

20 kilometres west of Marseille. Looking out over the sea, this location has beautiful bays and deep rocky inlets extending all along the coast with the city as a backdrop. A modern, three-bedroom villa here has a starting price of around €455,000.

There is a healthy year-round student rentals market, and holiday-makers in July and August. The average weekly rent for a one-bedroom apartment is €366 a week, rising to €556 for two bedrooms and arouond €732 for three.

Key facts
■ **POPULATION** 807,071
■ **TAXES** Taxe d'habitation 8.70%, taxe foncière 7.15%
■ **AIRPORT** Marseille/Provence Airport, BP7 Aéroport, 13727 Marignane, Tel: +33 (0) 4 42 14 14 14
■ **SCHOOLS** EPIM – Marseille International School, 156-178 Bd Perier, 13008 Marseille, Tel: +33 (0) 4 91 53 00 00. See also Aix-en-Provence
■ **MEDICAL** Centre Hospitalier Universitaire La Timone, 264 rue St-Pierre, 13005 Marseille, Tel: +33 (0) 4 91 38 60 00
■ **PROS** City improvements have attracted foreign buyers ■ Toulon is within easy reach
■ **CONS** The city has managed to shake off its rather seedy image within France; this lingers with some foreign buyers.

AIX-EN-PROVENCE & ST-RÉMY-DE-PROVENCE

9 Dating back to Roman times and much loved by the painter Cézanne, Aix-en-Provence is well-known for its impressive monuments and cultural heritage. The old town is ringed by boulevards and squares while the main street, Cours Mirabeau, is lined with trees, cafés, bookshops and spectacular fountains. Aix has a deserved reputation as the most beautiful city in southern France.

The market town of St-Rémy-de-Provence lies 75 kilometres from Aix, surrounded by lush green perfumed valleys. Its ancient streets are lined with beautifully restored houses.

This area is very expensive and development land is restricted. Quality properties and beautiful scenery have attracted buyers to homes in the village of Venelles, perched six kilometres from Aix. A typical four-bedroom property costs over €634,000. St-Victoire offers a more rural environment in which a renovated property is substantially cheaper.

St-Rémy is much sought after for its properties, particularly by those who appreciate its unhurried pace of life. It's very expensive, so you'll probably have to be very busy to afford such unhurriedness. In St-Rémy prices start at €900,000 for a maison de maître, while if you want a luxury four-bedroom, 19th-century stone farmhouse don't expect any change from €1,700,000.

The region offers excellent rental potential as there are no shortage of people – french and from abroad – wanting to spend time here. Rent for a one-bedroom apartment averages €465 per week. In Le Thalonet, a house costing €400,000 can be let for about €3,000 a month. The average rent for a pretty standard two-bedroom apartment is around €565 per week.

Key facts
■ **POPULATION** Aix-en-Provence 134,222, St-Rémy-de-Provence 9,429
■ **TAXES** Taxe d'habitation 8.70%, taxe foncière 7.15%
■ **AIRPORT** Marseille/Provence Airport, BP7 Aéroport, 13727 Marignane, Tel: +33 (0) 4 42 14 14 14
■ **SCHOOLS** École Val St-André, 19 avenue Malacrida, 13100 Aix-en-Provence, Tel: +33 (0) 4 42 27 14 47. ■ International School of Provence, Domaine des Pins, 55 Route Bouc Bel Air, Luynes, 13080, Aix-en-Provence, Tel: +33 (0) 4 42 24 03 40
■ **MEDICAL** Centre Hospitalier du Pays d'Aix, avenue des Tamaris, 13616 Aix-en-Provence, Cedex 1, Tel: +33 (0) 4 42 33 56 50, www.ch-aix.fr
■ **PROS** The large student population fuels the rentals market ■ Aix-en-Provence is more desirable than the Var, as all amenities are found in the town ■ **CONS** Studio apartments are in very short supply ■ The St-Rémy triangle is a very expensive area to buy in.

PORTO-VECCHIO (CORSICA)

10 Blessed with breathtaking mountain scenery, lakes and more than 600 kilometres of dramatic coastline, Corsica is frequently described as the 'Scented Isle' as the heady aroma of the huge forests and the fragrant low-lying scrub vegetation fills the air. Its principal towns are Ajaccio (where none other than Napoléon was born in 1769), Bastia, Sartène and Bonifacio. French is the official language, though many native locals speak Corsican (Corsu).

The port of Porto-Vecchio, with its marina and ferry links to mainland France and Italy, is one of the most popular areas of Corsica, simply because it is so accessible. Its maze of narrow streets is lined with exclusive shops and stylish boutiques, fashionable restaurants and lively bars. The resort is best known for its beaches, such as the Palombaggia and Cala Rossa, which are some of the most popular in the whole of Corsica, perhaps France as a whole.

While short-term holiday rentals dominate the island's property market, many locals cash in on the busy summer months by investing in rental properties. Though the winter months are nowhere near as profitable, property is still expensive and this reflects the island's exclusive nature and unique atmosphere. Traditional properties vary from white stone villas with red-roof tiling to the Provençal terracotta-based villa. Expect to pay around €352,000 for a two-bedroom house, and around €545,000 for a three-bedroom villa with pool.

Rental income for an average two-bedroom property is €847 a week, rising to €1,463 for a similar five-bedroom house. A property with a pool can expect a season lasting from May until the end of October.

Key facts
■ **POPULATION** 10,326
■ **TAXES** Taxe d'habitation 9.74%, taxe foncière 6.32%
■ **AIRPORT** Ajaccio Airport, 20090 Ajaccio Cedex, Tel: +33 (0) 4 95 23 56 56, www.ajaccio.aeroport.fr
■ **SCHOOLS** See Nice
■ **MEDICAL** Centre Hospitalier Général, route Impériale, 20200 Bastia, Tel: +33 (0) 4 95 59 11 11
■ **PROS** The Porto-Vecchio area has beautiful beaches and is close to Bonifacio and Bastia
■ **CONS** The difficulty and expense in reaching the island have an impact on rental potential ■ To preserve the island's beautiful lush greenery, direct flights are limited to connections from Paris, Nice and Marseille.

BRIANÇON & SURROUNDING ALPINE RESORTS

11 Briançon, Europe's highest town, is the largest settlement in the Serre Chevalier area, a grouping of Hautes-Alpes ski resorts in the Guisane valley linked by 77 lifts and 250 kilometres of runs. The area offers 300 days of sunshine per year in addition to excellent skiing throughout winter. The popular villages of Chantemerle and Villeneuve are both located near the ski lifts. Chantemerle, the largest, has an attractive town popular with tourists and locals centre, while Villeneuve, also picturesque, is a further 10-minute ride away.

Le Monêtier-les-Bains (at 1,200 metres) is a typical Savoyard village, with rustic charm and little development. It has been a hot spa for hundreds of years and you can still take the waters there. The villages are not very far apart and are well served by a regular and reliable local bus service.

Briançon is a pleasant old town in a beautiful setting, with hilltop fortifications. Its steep streets, shops and restaurants create a lively ambience. However, the town is not fully served by ski buses, which can result in long walks for skiers to and from the ski lifts. Two-bedroom homes in Briançon average just over €258,000, although small apartments are cheaper. If you're looking to buy a four-bedroom home in the region, you'll need a budget of around €437,000.

The rental potential is excellent, with the opportunity for four months' ski rental and three months' summer rental. A two-bedroom apartment can be rented for an average of €500 per week, while a similar four-bedroom home can generate €800 per week.

Key facts
■ **POPULATION** 17,023
■ **TAXES** Taxe d'habitation 4.65%, taxe foncière 12.56%%
■ **AIRPORT** Turin International Airport, Strada San Maurizio 12, 10072 Caselle Torinese, Tel: +39 (0) 11 567 6361/2
■ **SCHOOLS** See Nice
■ **PROS** Aspres and Serres village houses range massively in price ■ Property is excellent value and many French are choosing to buy in this area, instead of purchasing a ski lodge and summer home ■ The south coast is a two-hour drive away
■ **CONS** The cold climate can be discouraging to some. ●

Property guide

Properties in Provence are far pricier than in many other rural areas of France and as demand continues to soar there are few bargains to be had

Traditional village houses, with their brightly painted shutters, are much sought after and bargains are rare

The Côte d'Azur, with its golden beaches, Mediterranean climate and exclusive resorts, is one of France's prime property hotspots, geared primarily at the high end of the market. Sales to relocators and holiday-home hunters are booming. Here the average five-bedroom property in Nice with sea views will set you back €1,490,000. Further back from the seafront, it's possible to find more reasonably priced accommodation, but local first-time buyers have been priced out of the market. Cheaper properties exist in Nice's Riquier borough, a favourite with locals, with a good rental market.

Though property in St-Tropez does still hold its value, prices do not have the potential to rise at the rate witnessed in Cannes. Mougins, Menton and Juan-les-Pins offer less space for more money. The new-build market is booming on the Côte d'Azur with superb apartment complexes offering swimming, tennis and beautiful gardens. Starting prices for apartments range from €215,000 for a two-bedroom property, up to €723,000, while high-spec villas start at €568,000. If you are lucky enough to track down a cottage for under €40,000, it will require a complete overhaul to make it habitable. Village houses in Var and Alpes-Maritime cost around €330,000 for a two-bedroom property.

Corsica, with its idyllic location and beaches, has a booming tourist industry. The market is for short-term lets, but properties are pricy, and two-bedroom apartments cost upwards of €352,000.

Provençal holiday homes have high income potential during May to October. With its year-round rental market, and celebrity tenants during the Film Festival, Cannes is a fantastic buy-to-let prospect. High changeover fees for the upkeep of holiday properties in St-Rémy can make buy-to-let homes here unprofitable. Maussane, Pont Royal and Les Baux form an expensive tourist triangle, whose busy rental market can justify a costly investment. ●

TYPICAL PROPERTIES

■ Rural homes of Provence are Mediterranean in style, built from limestone, with deep, narrow doors and windows framed with brightly painted, slatted shutters

Mas
■ The term mas describes any Provençal two-storey farmhouse, with barn and stables
■ The buildings are long and narrow, and some have a tower-shaped dovecote
■ Walls are made from local stone, giving mas a beige and ochre appearance
■ Roofs are often clad in pink-red roman canal tiles
■ The original floors were made of clay slabs

Magnanerie
■ Unique to southern France, these stone buildings were constructed for the cultivation of silk worms, or magnans
■ Cultivating silk worms during the 18th and 19th century was an important source of wealth for many villages. Very few unconverted magnaneries exist today
■ Magnaneries are very narrow, have several floors, and sometimes large arcades
■ Many of these buildings are still surrounded by the mulberry trees on which the silk worms were once reared

WHAT CAN YOU GET FOR YOUR EUROS?

MODERN VILLA

This three-bedroom villa is set in a large 2,000 square metre garden in the quiet coastal resort of Ensuès-La-Redonne. It has a self-contained studio apartment on the ground floor, making it a great rental investment. The airport is only 20 minutes away, as are Aix-en-Provence and Marseille. Other features include a pool, tower, conservatory, terrace, automatic garden watering system and fireplace.

€1,089,000 CODE FRA

COASTAL VILLA

This five-bedroom, three-bathroom home offers beautiful sea views of both sides of the Bay of Cavalaire, including the Cap Cavalaire and Bon Porteau. The property has a guest studio and a swimming pool, set in over a quarter of an acre of grounds in a quiet location in the Cavalaire hills. It's within easy reach of the beach, shops and restaurants, and is about an hour away from the airports in Nice and Toulon.

€875,000 CODE SIF

PROVENÇAL MAS

This fantastic, well-restored Provençal mas, dating from the 19th century, incorporates four separate gîtes, meaning it has the potential to be a great business, or an incredibly private residence. The main house has three bedrooms and two bathrooms, while there's a pool in the grounds. It's set on the edge of Rasteau, a village known for its wines, and it's only 75 mintues from Marseilles airport.

€980,000 CODE SIF

PROPERTY IN ROQUEFORT-LES-PINS

Located in a residential domaine, this is a charming Provençal property composed of two villas. Both properties enjoy open views over the surrounding hills and they're set in grounds of 3,300 square metres. This includes a spacious swimming pool and pool house. One house boasts four bedrooms and a living room with fireplace, while the other is split into two one-bedroom apartments.

€1,590,000 CODE SIF

WELL-LOCATED HOUSE

This five-bedroom villa is in a great location: it overlooks a golf course and is only ten minutes' drive from the beach. It's in Valescure, a prestigious residential quarter of St Raphael, and this fantastic property also boasts a jacuzzi, sauna, wine cellar, bar room and games/music room. There's a pool in the 1,600 square metres of land, as well as a pretty terraced area with built-in barbeque.

€894,785 CODE VEF

COASTAL VILLA

This lovely villa is in a residential area just outside the Roman town of Frejus, five minutes from the golf course and 10 minutes from the beach. The living and dining rooms boast open fires, with patio doors onto a balcony and terrace, overlooking the swimming pool. There are four bedrooms, cellars, a built-in barbeque and a separate holiday apartment, with fantastic letting potential.

€689,165 CODE VEF

AVERAGE HOUSE PRICES CÔTE D'AZUR, PROVENCE & CORSICA

	2-bed		3-bed		4-bed		5-bed	
Vaucluse	€215,498	(145,607)	€320,483	(£216,543)	€402,705	(£272,098)	€568,663	(£384,232)
Inland Var	€330,959	(£223,621)	€337,583	(£228,097)	€407,785	(£275,531)	€623,211	(£421,089)
St-Tropez	€729,752	(£493,076)	€1,486,827	(£1,004,613)	€2,217,355	(£1,498,213)	€3,912,967	(£2,643,897)
Toulon	€288,281	(£194,785)	€512,393	(£346,212)	€714,743	(£482,935)	€758,260	(£512,338)
Cannes	€572,989	(£387,155)	€724,196	(£489,322)	€1,261,543	(£852,394)	€1,744,436	(£1,178,673)
Antibes	€501,138	(£338,607)	€579,343	(£391,448)	€1,025,635	(£692,997)	€1,491,324	(£1,007,652)
Nice	€448,212	(£302,846)	€791,535	(£534,821)	€908,267	(£613,694)	€1,158,049	(£782,466)
Marseille	€304,697	(£205,877)	€455,034	(£307,456)	€609,205	(£411,625)	€1,019,905	(£689,125)
Aix-en-Provence & St-Rémy	€289,273	(£195,455)	€465,109	(£314,263)	€633,909	(£428,317)	€855,946	(£578,342)

PROPERTY GUIDE

Buyer's reference

All the resources a house hunter could need, from price matrices to essential contacts and a useful glossary

House price matrix

	2-bed	3-bed	4-bed	5-bed
BRITTANY				
Dinard, Dinan, St-Malo	€220,243 (£148,813)	€288,119 (£194,675)	€377,238 (£254,891)	€425,465 (£287,477)
Rennes	€194,253 (£131,252)	€272,262 (£183,961)	€292,200 (£197,433)	€413,383 (£279,313)
Lorient	€191,551 (£129,427)	€242,426 (£163,802)	€295,117 (£199,404)	€313,443 (£211,786)
Brest	€204,780 (£138,365)	€260,599 (£176,081)	€292,165 (£197,409)	€307,511 (£207,778)
Quimper	€141,140 (£95,365)	€229,801 (£155,271)	€264,837 (£178,944)	€306,901 (£207,366)
Guingamp	€129,369 (£87,412)	€168,626 (£113,937)	€239,526 (£161,842)	€264,918 (£178,999)
Golfe Du Morbidan	€288,789 (£195,128)	€355,490 (£240,196)	€446,640 (£301,784)	€511,812 (£345,819)
NORMANDY				
Deauville	€283,919 (£191,837)	€368,432 (£248,941)	€422,566 (£285,518)	€1,032,761 (£697,812)
Trouville	€183,200 (£123,784)	€254,564 (£172,003)	€448,169 (£302,817)	€615,671 (£415,994)
HonFleur	€210,865 (£142,477)	€242,483 (£163,840)	€353,715 (£238,997)	€382,449 (£258,412)
Rouen	€199,684 (£134,922)	€236,856 (£160,038)	€277,369 (£187,412)	€406,974 (£274,983)
Caen	€209,899 (£141,824)	€ 235,436 (£159,079)	€318,089 (£214,925)	€441,666 (£298,423)
Avranches	€216,972 (£146,603)	€294,996 (£199,322)	€361,919 (£244,540)	€550,296 (£371,822)
Dieppe	€196,672 (£132,887)	€238,604 (£161,219)	€292,563 (£197,678)	€406,048 (£274,357)
NORD-PAS-DE-CALAIS & PICARDY				
Le-Touquet-Paris-Plage	€302,214 (£204,199)	€573,708 (£387,641)	€674,618 (£455,823)	€710,121 (£479,812)
Amiens	€190,080 (£128,433)	€229,516 (£155,079)	€279,653 (£188,955)	€279,653 (£197,804)
Lille	€188,834 (£127,591)	€231,519 (£156,432)	€316,530 (£213,872)	€480,712 (£324,806)
Somme Valley	€138,690 (£93,710)	€190,486 (£128,707)	€200,419 (£135,417)	€ 238,105 (£160,882)
Montreuil & Hesdin	€132,536 (£89,552)	€217,983 (£147,286)	€281,189 (£189,993)	€304,921 (£206,028)
ILE-DE-FRANCE				
Arrondissement 1	€650,905 (£439,801)	€706,910 (£477,642)		
Arrondissement 2		€1,050,108 (£709,533)		
Arrondissement 3	€569,668 (£384,911)	€856,390 (£578,642)	€3,160,553 (£2,135,509)	
Arrondissement 4		€1,639,683 (£1,107,894)	€1,680,720 (£1,135,622)	€2,341,552 (£1,582,130)
Arrondissement 6	€852,232 (£575,833)	€1,722,286 (£1,163,707)	€1,953,385 (£1,319,855)	
Arrondissement 7	€586,741 (£396,447)	€1,441,552 (£974,022)	€1,628,105 (£1,100,071)	€5,901,383 (£3,987,421)
Arrondissement 8	€1,025,603 (£692,975)	€898,210 (£606,899)	€1,122,316 (£758,322)	€2,429,107 (£1,641,289)
Arrondissement 16	€677,693 (£457,901)	€1,335,282 (£902,218)	€1,446,731 (£977,521)	€3,770,874 (£2,547,888)
Arrondissement 17	€1,032,169 (£697,412)	€1,174,382 (£793,502)	€1,360,525 (£919,274)	€2,919,748 (£1,972,803)
Versailles	€595,577 (£402,417)	€773,794 (£522,834)	€970,764 (£655,922)	€1,292,563 (£873,354)
CHAMPAGNE-ARDENNE				
Charleville-Méziéres	€132,418 (£89,472)	€206,908 (£139,803)	€215,612 (£145,684)	€307,003 (£207,435)
Reims & ...pernay	€165,539 (£111,851)	€240,224 (£162,314)	€289,083 (£195,327)	€353,308 (£238,722)
Chalons-en-Champagne	€160,183 (£108,232)	€198,987 (£134,451)	€261,085 (£176,409)	€293,936 (£198,606)
ALSACE, LORRAINE & FRANCHE-COMTE				
Strasbourg	€309,772 (£209,306)	€407,596 (£275,403)	€445,158 (£300,783)	€603,665 (£407,882)
Metz & Nancy	€232,315 (£156,970)	€280,378 (£189,445)	€299,794 (£202,564)	€412,835 (£278,943)
The Vodges	€196,623 (£132,854	€206,764 (£139,706)	€249,665 (£168,693)	€262,608 (£177,438)
Besancon	190,113 (£128,455)	€251,497 (£169,931)	€273,094 (£185,432)	€328,340 (£221,852)
THE LOIRE (CENTER & PAYS-DÈ-LA-LOIRE)				
Vendèe coast	€149,961 (101,325)	€257,937 (£174,282)	€295,308 (£199,533)	€410,028 (£277,046)
Saumur & Angers	€193,453 (£130,712)	€278,555 (£188,213)	€296,467 (£200,316)	€369,521 (£249,677)
Nantes	€247,752 (£167,400)	€286,304 (£193,449)	€ 371,588 (£251,073)	€568,574 (£384,172)
Le Mans	€183,135 (£123,740)	€207,001 (£139,866)	€279,768 (£189,033)	€289,273 (£294,607)
Tours & The Touraine	€180,759 (£122,135)	€254,373 (£171,874)	€338,214 (£228,523)	€446,140 (£301,446)
BURGUNDY				
Cote d'Or	€192,392 (£129,995)	€188,217 (£127,174)	€243,070 (£164,237)	€408,993 (£276,347)
Saone-et-Loire (Cluny & Macon)	€203,366 (£137,410)	€263,811 (£178,251)	€268,449 (£181,385)	€299,580 (£202,419)
Morvan Regional Park	€115,311 (£77,913)	€187,103 (£126,421)	€199,532 (£134,819)	€328,342 (£221,853)
Auxerre	€125,390 (£84,723)	€190,486 (£128,707)	€234,167 (£158,221)	€248,200 (£167,703)
Chatillon-sur-Seine	€139,596 (£94,322)	€172,301 (£116,420)	€189,959 (£128,351)	€441,654 (£298,415)

House price matrix

	2-bed	3-bed	4-bed	5-bed
POITOU-CHARENTES				
Ile de RÈ & La Rochelle	€293,797 (£198,512)	€421,413 (£284,739)	€423,894 (£286,415	€486,484 (£328,706)
Charente	€164,746 (£111,315)	€199,222 (£134,610)	€252,283 (£170,462)	€354,480 (£239,514)
Poiters	€ 161,960 (£109,433)	€244,901 (£165,474)	€353,148 (£238,614)	€389,161 (£262,947)
Chatellerault	€152,204 (£102,841)	€183,485 (£123,977)	€205,278 (£138,702)	€351,412 (£237,441)
LIMOSINE & VUVERGNE				
Limonges	€181,461 (£122,609)	€257,657 (£174,093)	€277,251 (£187,332)	€423,877 (£286,404)
Clemont-Ferrand	€139,580 (£94,311)	€190,356 (£128,619)	€197,516 (£133,457)	€299,926 (£202,653)
Volcanic Mountains & Lakes of Auvergne	€116,820 (£78,933)	€187,089 (£126,412)	€188,408 (£127,303)	€211,123 (£142,651)
Correze	€94,609 (£63,925)	€173,299 (£117,094)	€255,508 (£172,641)	€299,509 (£202,371)
Vichy	€120,583 (£81,475)	€190,193 (£128,509)	€201,891 (£136,413)	€293,424 (£198,260)
RHONE-ALPS				
Lake Annecy	€351,667 (£237,613)	€516,665 (£349,098)	€529,561 (£357,812	€606,643 (£409,894X
Lake Geneva	€408,633 (£276,104	€428,317 (£289,404	€497,322 (£336,029.00)	€556,009 (£375,682)
Mgeve	€559,700 (£378,176)	€860,365 (£581,328)	€1,146,261(£774,501)	€1,324,104(£894,665)
Chamonix	€842,441 (£569,217)	€965,837 (£652,593)	€1,258,196(£850,133	€1,276328 (£862,384)
Meribel	€802,297 (£542,093)	€1,477,928(£998,600)	€2,049,360(£1,384,703)	---
Courchevel	€802,297 (£542,093)	€1,477,92 (£998,600)	€2,049,360(£1,384,703)	---
Les Menuires	€315,916 (£213,457)	€338,379 (£228,635)	€590,084 (£398,706)	€930,592 (£628,779)
Val d'Isere	€876,608 (£592,303)	€1,480,904(£1,000,611)	€2,187,738(£1,478,202)	€2,645,230(£1,787,318)
Grenole	€270,353 (£182,67)	€354,331 (£239,413)	€445,585 (£301,071)	€537,136 (£362,930)
Les Portes Du Solleil (les Gets & Morzine)	€388,260 (£262,338)	€487,877 (£329,647)	€583,676 (£394,376)	€841,014 (£568,253)
Lyon	€366,464 (£247,611)	€419,069 (£283,155)	€502,905 (£339,801)	€772,598 (£522,026)
Beaujolais	€218,522 (£147,650)	€288,315 (£194,808)	€378,985 (£256,071))	€551,183 (£372,421)
AQUITANE				
Cap Ferret & Bay of Arcachon	€321,543 (£217,259)	€406,449 (£274,628)	€543,948 (£367,533)	€684,701 (£462,636)
Dordogne	€180,275 (£121,808)	€211,814 (£143,118)	€359,515 (£242,916)	€392,632 (£265,292)
Agen	€160,849 (£108,682)	€172,306 (£116,423)	€312,956 (£211,457)	€471,628 (£318,668)
Bordeaux	€283,433 (£191,509)	€368,041 (£248,677)	€475,948 (£321,587)	€632,716 (£427,511)
Biarritz	€338,356 (£228,619)	€454,866 (£307,342)	€563,954 (£381,050)	€704,818 (£476,229)
MIDI-PYRANEES				
Cahors & Rocamador	€184,504 (£124,665)	€312,703 (£211,286)	€368,759 (£249,162)	€423,735 (£286,308)
Gascony/Gers	€170,063 (£114,908)	€230,851 (£164,089)	€331,200 (£223,784)	€430,358 (£290,783)
Toulouse	€211,466 (£142,883)	€292,043 (£197,327)	€430,444 (£290,841)	€527,186 (£356,207)
Bagneres-de-Bigorre	€175,776 (£118,768)	€210,294 (£142,091)	€271,545 (£183,477)	€457,179 (£308,905)
LANGUEDOC-ROUSSILLON				
Perpignan	€203,354 (£137,402)	€240,964 (£162,814)	€301,138 (£203,472)	€444,893 (£300,604)
Southern Roussillon	€242,588 (£163,911)	€381,952 (£258,076)	€461,506 (£311,829)	€656,770 (£443,764)
Montpelier	€224,477 (£151,674)	€346,240 (£233,946)	€412,409 (£278,655)	€632,904 (£427,638)
Carcassone	€166,320 (£112,379)	€216,513 (£146,293)	€284,694 (£192,361)	€351,420 (£237,446)
Nimes	€202,595 (£136,889)	€347,779 (£234,986)	€435,228 (£294,073)	€446,785 (£301,882)
Beziers & Narbonne	€200,424 (£135,422)	€ 218,846 (£147,869)	€257,330 (£173,872)	€339,590 (£229,453)
COTE D'AZUR, PROVENCE & CORSICA				
Vaucluse (Luberon)	€215,498 (£145,607)	€320,483 (£216,543)	€402,705 (£272,098)	€568,663 (£384,232)
Inland Var (Draguignan, Ste-Maxime)	€330,959 (£223,621)	€337,583 (£228,097)	€407,785 (£275,531)	€623,211 (£421,089)
St-Tropez	€729,752 (£493,076)	€1,486,827(£1,004,613)	€2,217,355(£1,498,213)	€3,912,967(£2,643,897)
Toulon	€288,281 (£194,785)	€512,393 (£346,212)	€714,743 (£482,935)	€758,260 (£512,338)
Cannes	€572,989 (£387,155)	€724,196 (£489,322)	€1,261,543(£852,394)	€ 1,744,436(£1,178,673)
Antibes	€501,138 (£338,607)	€579,343 (£391,448)	€1,025,635(£692,997)	€1,491,324(£1,007,652)
Nice	€448,212 (£302,846)	€791,535 (£534,821)	€908,267 (£613,694)	€1,158,049(£782,466)
Marseille	€304,697 (£205,877)	€455,034 (£307,456)	€609,205 (£411,625)	€1,019,905(£689,125)
Aix-en-Provence & St Remy-de-Provence	€289,273 (£195,455)	€465,109 (£314,263)	€633,909 (£428,317)	€855,946 (£578,346)
Porto-Vecchio (Corsica)	€351,619 (£237,581)	€544,943 (£368,205)	€704,626 (£476,099)	€774,973 (£523,631)
Briancon & Surrounding Alpine Resorts	€257,844 (£174,219)	€350,566 (£236,869)	€437,233 (£295,428)	€470,058 (£317,607)

Apartment price matrix

	1-bed	2-bed	3-bed	4-bed
BRITTANY				
Dinard, Dinan, St-Malo	€173,710 (£117,372)	€250,244 (£169,084)	€316,367 (£213,762)	€338,169 (£228,493)
Lorient	€101,976 (£68,903)	€139,518 (£94,269)	€180,315 (£121,835)	€215,499 (£145,608)
Golfe du Morbihan	€132,351 (£89,427)	€205,191 (£138,643)	€245,264 (£165,719)	€270,002 (£182,434)
Brest	€80,081 (£54,109)	€127,993 (£86,482)	€183,197 (£123,782)	€218,529 (£147,655)
Quimper	€86,175 (£58,227)	€95,837 (£64,755)	€167,833 (£113,401)	€274,787 (£185,667)
Guingamp	€132,393 (£89,455)	€138,658 (£93,688)	€181,783 (£122,827)	€244,800 (£165,406)
Rennes	€137,899 (£93,175)	€161,685 (£109,247)	€219,192 (£148,103)	€255,744 (£172,800)
NORMANDY				
Deauville	€175,680 (£118,703)	€270,361 (£182,677)	€431,926 (£291,842)	€458,623 (£309,881)
Trouville	€124,781 (£84,312)	€376,010 (£254,061)	€352,497 (£238,174)	-
HonFleur	€122,951 (£83,075)	€187,178 (£126,472)	€302,742 (£204,556)	€417,277 (£281,944)
Rouen	€131,204 (£88,652)	€199,336 (£134,687)	€251,571 (£169,981)	€278,869 (£188,425)
Caen	€109,333 (£73,874)	€187,185 (£126,477)	€235,265 (£158,963)	€240,335 (£162,389)
Avranche	€120,929 (£81,709)	€130,880 (£88,433)	€137,061 (£92,609)	€205,058 (£138,553)
Dieppe	€100,557 (£67,944)	€154,406 (£104,329)	€221,680 (£149,784)	€280,714 (£189,672)
NORD-PAS-DE-CALAIS				
Le Touquet-Paris-Plage	€174,555 (£117,943)	€294,293 (£198,847)	€456,513 (£308,455)	€559,774 (£378,225)
Amiens	€132,359 (£89,432)	€161,990 (£109,453)	€248,964 (£168,219)	€285,959 (£193,216)
Lille	€136,843 (£92,461)	€224,400 (£151,622)	€280,057 (£189,224)	€335,046 (£226,383X)
Somme Valley	€115,764 (£78,219)	€155,947 (£105,370)	€170,820 (£115,419)	€257,403 (£173,921)
Montreeuil-Hesdin	€143,194 (£96,753)	€190,542 (£128,745)	€271,306 (£183,315)	€322,114 (£217,645)
ILE DE FRANCE				
1st Arrondissement	€456,545 (£308,477)	€694,447 (£469,221)	€1,277,670 (£863,291)	€2,352,610 (£1,589,602)
2nd Arrondissement	€440,498 (£297,634)	€713,605 (£482,166)	€729,938 (£493,202)	€1,434,849 (£969,493)
3rd Arrondissement	€382,155 (£258,213)	€600,623 (£405,827)	€864,463 (£584,097)	€1,484,568 (£1,003,087)
4th Arrondissement	€364,605 (£246,355)	€717,797 (£484,998)	€825,342 (£557,664)	€1,346,637 (£909,989)
6th Arrondissement	€451,095 (£304,794)	€886,641 (£599,082)	€2,491,464 (£1,683,422)	€2,641,760 (£1,784,973)
7th Arrondissement	€440,865 (£297,882)	€855,953 (£578,347)	€1,298,498 (£877,364)	€2,652,682 (£1,792,353)
8th Arrondissement	€317,642 (£214,623)	€1,072,416 (£724,606)	€1,612,761 (£1,089,704)	€1,523,376 (£1,029,306)
16th Arrondissement	€313,003 (£211,489)	€863,449 (£583,412)	€1,131,890 (£764,791)	€1,483,529 (£1,002,385)
17th Arrondissement	€289,527 (£195,627)	€424,535 (£286,848)	€695,459 (£469,905)	€1,464,070 (£989,237)
Versailles	€292,208 (£197,438)	€344,322 (£232,650)	€576,079 (£389,243)	€734,552 (£496,319)
CHAMPAGNE-ARDENE				
Chareville-Mezieres	€92,409 (£62,439)	€121,277 (£81,944)	€159,296 (£107,633)	€190,829 (£128,939)
Reims & Epernay	€191,546 (£129,423)	€276,348 (£186,722)	€294,466 (£198,964)	€339,840 (£229,622)
Chalons-en-Champagne	€103,329 (£69,817)	€144,076 (£97,349)	€160,776 (£108,633)	€255,233 (£172,455)
ALSACE, LORRAINE & FRENCH-COMTE				
Strasbourg	€116,000 (£78,379)	€161,946 (£109,423)	€310,271 (£209,643)	€564,776 (£381,606)
Metz & Nancy	€120,551 (£81,454)	€202,598 (£136,891)	€239,871 (£162,075)	€434,260 (£293,419)
The Vosges	€109,981 (£74,312)	€131,280 (£88,703)	€199,200 (£134,595)	€234,525 (£158,463)
Besaccon	€83,538 (£56,445)	€121,852 (£82,333)	€219,352 (£148,211)	€280,717 (£189,674)
Lons-Le-saunier, Haut Jura & Vallee des Lacs	€116,066 (£78,423)	€140,021 (£94,609)	€160,464 (£108,422)	€196,604 (£132,841)
THE LOIRE				
Vendee coast	€100,496 (£67,903)	€125,700 (£84,933)	€160,790 (£108,642)	€258,072 (£174,373)
Saumur & Angers	€135,137 (£91,309)	€148,674 (£100,456)	€165,492 (£111,819)	€241,158 (£162,945)
Nantes	€146,435 (£98,943)	€161,953 (£109,428)	€231,964 (£156,733)	€318,929 (£215,493)
Le Mans	€136,685 (£92,355)	€157,608 (£106,492)	€189,775 (£128,227)	€215,471 (£145,589)
Oreleans	€107,143 (£72,394)	€141,208 (£95,411))	€211,156 (£142,673)	€277,211 (£187,305)
Tours & the Touraine	€145,738 (£98,472)	€157,652 (£106,522)	€181,955 (£122,943)	€234,850 (£158,683)
BURGUNDY				
Cote D'Or	€126,412 (£85,414)	€211,169 (£142,682)	€234,776 (£158,633)	€287,546 (£194,288)
Saone-et-Loire (Cluny & Macon)	€107,957 (£72,944)	€145,740 (£98,473)	€188,899 (£127,635)	€280,329 (£189,412)
Morvan Regional Park	-	-	-	-
Auxerre	€129,266 (£87,342)	€190,792 (£128,914)	€211,167 (£142,681)	€256,859 (£173,554)
Chatillon-Sur-Sein	-	-	-	-

Apartment price matrix

	1-bed	2-bed	3-bed	4-bed
POITOU-CHARENTES				
Ile de Re & La Rochelle	€126,649 (£85,574)	€181,128 (£122,384)	€425,655 (£287,605)	€450,544 (£304,422)
Charente	€96,849 (£65,439)	€132,403 (£89,462)	€153,545 (£103,747)	€188,609 (£127,439)
Poitiers	€68,288 (£47,802)	€116,354 (£81,448)	€144,166 (£101,266)	€215,888 (£150,422)
Challerault				
LIMOUSIN & AUVERGNE				
Limoges	€95,192 (£64,319)	€116,098 (£78,445)	€162,250 (£109,629)	€351,430 (£237,453)
Clemont-Ferrand	€92,525 (£62,517)	€132,344 (£89,422)	€205,093 (£138,577)	€331,000 (£223,649
Volcanic Mountains & Lakes	€86,174 (£58,226)	€95,310 (£64,399)	€149,046 (£100,707)	€264,168 (£178,492)
Correze	€78,355 (£52,943)	€130,007 (£87,843X)	€156,323 (£105,624)	€172,396 (£116,484)
Vichy	€91,003 (£61,489)	€115,892 (£78,306)	€122,206 (£82,572)	€191,856 (£129,633)
RHONES-ALPES				
Lake Annecy	€220,827 (£149,208)	€265,488 (£179,384)	€335,248 (£226,519)	€422,470 (£285,453)
Lake Geneva	€203,560 (£137,541)	€187,686 (£126,815)	€287,228 (£194,073)	€420,876 (£284,376)
Megeve	€218,452 (£147,603)	€346,577 (£234,174)	€521,580 (£352,419)	€569,208 (384,600)
Chamonix	€236,539 (£159,824)	€570,505 (£385,477)	€576,643 (£389,624)	€627,971 (£424,305)
Meribel	€360,662 (£243,691)	€899,610 (£607,845)	€923,417 (£623,931)	€1,525,009(£1,030,412)
Courchevel	€250,759 (£169,432)	€736,154 (£497,402)	€734,525 (£496,301)	€744,875 (£503,294)
Les Menuires	€159,755 (£107,943)	€264,074 (£178,429)	€428,616 (£289,606)	€611,346 (£413,072)
Val d-Isere	€307,314 (£207,645)	€472,833 (£319,482)	€850,453 (£574,631)	€1,394,620(£942,311)
Grenoble	€161,963 (£109,435)	€242,548 (£163,884)	€274,409 (£185,412)	€436,410 (£294,872)
Les Porter du Soliel	€171,200 (£115,676)	€269,943 (£182,394)	€310,623 (£209,878)	€527,553 (£356,455)
Lyon	€189,993 (£128,374)	€264,328 (£178,600)	€304,037 (£205,431)	€537,216 (£362,984)
Beaujolais	€150,453 (£101,658)	€203,177 (£137,282)	€160,645 (£108,544)	€236,344 (£159,692)
AQUITAINE				
Cap Ferret & Bay of Arcachon	€228,392 (£154,319)	€248,973 (£168,225)	€352,851 (£238,413)	€569,240 (£384,622)
Dordogne	€102,577 (£69,309)	€187,104 (£126,422)	€236,708 (£159,938)	€379,580 (£256,473)
Agen	€79,060 (£53,419)	€107,526 (£72,653)	€161,993 (£109,455)	€362,804 (£245,138)
Bordeaux	€131,117 (£88,593)	€164,639 (£111,243)	€272,780 (£184,311)	€394,926 (£266,842)
Biarritz & Bayonne	€179,134 (£121,037)	€276,674 (£186,942)	€425,415 (£287,443)	€521,961 (£352,677)
MIDI-PYRANEES				
Cahors & Rocamadour	€120,238 (£81,242)	€142,596 (£96,349)	€185,689 (£125,466)	€280,349 (£189,425)
Gascony / Gers	€88,255 (£59,632)	€111,655 (£75,443)	€188,415 (£127,308)	€249,313 (£168,455X)
Toulouse	€132,378 (£89,445)	€181,147 (£122,397)	€231,921 (£156,704)	€575,606 (£388,923)
Bagneres-de-Bigorree	€85,604 (£57,841)	€110,945 (£84,963)	€160,464 (£108,422)	€250,080 (£168,973)
LANGUEDOC-ROUSSILLON				
Perpignan	€141,046 (£95,302)	€161,943 (£109,421)	€202,603 (£136,894)	€230,396 (£155,673)
Southern Roussillon	€144,042 (£97,326)	€156,215 (£105,551)	€188,498 (£127,364)	€228,386 (£154,315)
Montpelier	€230,313 (£155,617)	€264,049 (£178,412)	€290,575 (£196,335)	€422,520 (£285,487)
Carcassonne	€93,117 (£62,917)	€116,114 (£78,456)	€189,929 (£128,331)	€287,968 (£194,573)
Mines	€143,875 (£97,213)	€156,353 (£105,644)	€203,979 (£137,824)	€280,658 (£189,634)
Beziers & Narbonne	€102,743 (£69,421)	€203,368 (£137,411)	€231,500 (£156,419)	€264,095 (£178,443
COTE D'AZUR, PROVENCE & CORSICA				
Vacluse (Luberon)	€172,135 (£116,308)	€218,479 (£147,621)	€250,035 (£168,943)	€310,566 (£209,842)
Inland Var (Draguignan, Ste-Maxime)	€144,804 (£97,841)	€196,678 (£132,891)	€261,217 (£176,498)	€440,804 (£297,841)
St-Tropez	€280,346 (£189,423)	€573,710 (£387,642)	€613,609 (£414,60)	€737,547 (£498,343)
Toulon	€181,177 (£122,417)	€249,378 (£168,499)	€258,891 (£174,927)	€290,750 (£196,453)
Cannes	€277,667 (£187,613)	€507,524 (£342,922)	€571,681 (£386,271)	€713,849 (£482,331)
Antibes	€280,610 (£189,602)	€308,893 (£208,712)	€478,994 (£323,645)	€700,658 (£473,418)
Nice & area	€220,833 (£149,212)	€277,711 (£187,643)	€383,845 (£259,355)	€573,707 (£387,640)
Marseille	€141,240 (£95,433)	€181,886 (£122,896)	€258,706 (£174,802)	€421,224 (£284,611)
Aix-en-Provence & St-Rémy-de-Provence	€215,643 (£145,705)	€309,231 (£208,940)	€428,272 (£289,373)	€543,888 (£367,492)
Porto-Vecchio (Corsica)	€182,938 (£123,607)	€258,971 (£174,981)	€378,894 (£256,010)	€487,640 (£329,487
Briancon	€139,120 (£94,000)	€165,958 (£112,134)	€220,403 (£148,921)	€354,590 (£239,588

Lettings price matrix

	1-bed	2-bed	3-bed	4-bed	5+-bed
BRITTANY					
Dinard, Diana, St-Malo	£273 €404	£295.00 €436	£405 €599	£520 €769	£845 €1,250
Lorient	£255 €377	£362 €535	£455 €673	£530 €784	£725 €1,073
Golfe du Morbihan	£322 €477	£415 €614	£495 €733	£1,205 €1,783	£1,554 €2,300
Brest	£295 €437	£342 €506	£460 €681	-	-
Quimper	£325 €481	£355 €525	£538 €796	£695 €1,029	£900 €1,332
Guingamp	£343 €508	£391 €579	£454 €672	£582 €861	£845 €1,251
Rennes	£232 €343	£409 €605	£525 €777	£583 €863	£1,124 €1,66
NORMANDY					
Deauville	£374 €554	£425 €629	£656 €971	£733 €1,085	£1,154 €1,708
Trouville	£342 €506	£566 €838	£672 €995	£695 €1,029	£853 €1,260
Honfleur	£315 €466	£364 €539	£469 €694	£682 €1,009	£731 €1,082
Rouen	-	-	-	£894 €1,323	£1,109 €1,641
Caen	£321 €475	£366 €542	£523 €774	£926 €1,370	£1,382 €2,045
Avranches	£319 €472	£398 €589	£438 €648	£476 €704	£621 €919
Dieppe	£337 €499	£384 €568	£416 €616	£482 €713	-
NORD-PAS-DE-CALAIS & PICARDY					
Le-Touquet-Paris-Plage	£305 €451	£382 €565	£566 €838	£894 €1,323	£1,275 €1,88
Amiens	£220 €326	£374 €554	-	-	-
Lille	£362 €536	£439 €650	£512 €758	£608 €900	£935 €1,384
Somme Valley	£266 €394	£300 €444	£355 €525	£537 €795	£742 €1,098
Maontreuil & hesdin	£206 €305	£354 €524	£379 €561	-	-
IL-DE-FRANCE					
Arrondissement 1	£335 €496	£431 €638	£742 €1,098	£896 €1,326	£1,078 €1,595
Arrondissement 2	£349 €517	£488 €722	£568 €841	£822 €1,217	£973 €1,440
Arrondissement 3	£389 €576	£475 €703	£662 €980	£849 €1,257	£1,076 €1,592
Arrondissement 4	£429 €635	£574 €850	£685 €1,014	£834 €1,234	£1,107 €1,638
Arrondissement 6	£478 €707	£755 €1,117	£899 €1,331	£1,330 €1,968	£1,764 €2,611
Arrondissement 7	£421 €623	£489 €724	£633 €937	£722 €1,069	£893 €1,322
Arrondissement 8	£479 €709	£601 €889	£654 €968	£921 €1,363	£995 €1,473
Arrondissement 16	£385 €570	£473 €700	£712 €1,054	£866 €1,282	£1,372 €2,031
Arrondissement17	£410 €607	£541 €801	£622 €921	£723 €1,070	-
Versailles	-	-	-	-	-
CAMPAGNE ARDENNE					
Charleville-Mexieres	£282 €417	£304 €450	£369 €546	£545 €807	£672 €99 5
Reims & Epernay	£254 €376	£355 €525	£505 €747	£489 €724	£564 €835
Chalons-en-Champagne	£289 €428	£324 €480	£405 €599	-	-
ALSACE, LORRAINE, & FRANCE-COMTE					
Strasbourg	£220 €326	£289 €428	£395 €585	£527 €780	-
Metz & Nancy	£275 €407	£386 €571	£449 €665	£455 €673	£564 €835
The Vosges	£242 €358	£276 €408	£304 €450	£602 €891	£627 €928
Besancon	£233 €345	£272 €403	£451 €667	£542 €802	£841 €1,245
Lons-le-Sn, Ht-Jura & Vallee des Lacs	£389 €576	£397 €588	-	-	£703 €1,040
THE LOIRE					
Vendee coast	£409 €605	£415 €614	£462 €684	£1,011 €1,496	£1,346 €1,992
Saumur & Angers	£247 €366	£361 €534	£522 €773	£686 €1,015	£911 €1,348
Nantes	£331 €490	£374 €554	-	-	-
Le Mans	-	-	-	-	-
Orleans	£389 €576	£476 €704	£582 €861	-	-
Tours & the Touraine	£255 €377	£417 €617	£455 €673	£972 €1,439	£1,102 €1,631
BURGUNDY					
Cote D'or	-	£458 €678	£623 €922	£705 €1,043	£894 €1,323
Saone-et-Loire (Cluny & Macon)	£422 €625	£478 €707	£504 €746	£633 €937	£1,208 €1,788
Morvan Regional Park	-	-	-	-	-
Auxerre	-	-	-	-	-
Chatillon-sur-seine	-	-	-	-	-

Lettings price matrix

	1-bed	2-bed	3-bed	4-bed	5+-bed
POITOU-CHARENTES					
ile de Re & la Rochelle	£238 €352	£359 €531	£427 €632	£574 €850	£932 €1,379
Charente	£227 €336	£313 €463	£413 €611	£562 €832	£694 €1,027
Poitiers	£325 €481	£568 €841	£829 €1,227	£1,493 €2,210	-
Chatellerault	£334 €494	£356 €527	£428 €633 -	-	
LIMOSINE & AUVERGNE					
Limonges	£255 €377	£349 €517	£405 €599	£536 €793	-
Clement-Ferrand	-	-	-	£564 €835	-
Volcanic Mountains & Lakes	£257 €380	£276 €408	£425 €629 £	647 €958	£1,345 €1,991
Correze	£205 €303	£227 €336	£351 €519	£425 €629	£719 €1,064
Vichy	£195 €289	£245 €363	£394 €583	-	
RHONE-ALPES					
Lake Annecy	£295 €437	£387 €573	£469 €694	£1,210 €1,791	-
Lake Geneva	£355 €525	£456 €675	£512 €758	£1,235 €1,828	£2,148 €3,179
Megeve	£405 €599	£438 €648	£695 €1,029	£1,080 €1,598	£2,185 €3,234
Chamonix	£350 €518	£425 €629	£517 €765	£609 €901	£855 €1,265
Meribel	£327 €484	£458 €678	£780 €1,154	£1,050 €1,554	£1,935 €2,864
Courchevel	£365 €540	£495 €733	£646 €956	£1,208 €1,788	£2,139 €3,166
Les Menuires	£355 €525	£490 €725	£622 €921	-	-
Val D'Isere	£705 €1,043	£1,184 €1,752	£2,033 €3,009	-	-
Grenoble	£252 €373	£349 €517	£495 €733	£672 €995	-
Les Portes du Soleil	£416 €616	£468 €693	£544 €805	£623 €922	£954 €1,412
Lyon	£237 €351	£495 €733	£728 €1,077	£946 €1,400	-
Beaujolais	-	-	-	-	-
AQUITAINE					
Cap Ferret & Bay of Arcachon	£387€573	£395 €585	£527 €780	£519 €768	£894 €1,323
Dordogne	£255 €377	£384 €568	£492 €728	£658 €974	£837 €1,239
Agen	£294 €435	£568 €841	£574 €850	£633 €937	£921 €1,363
Bordeaux	£325 €481	£613 €907	£684 €1,012	£1,237 €1,831	£1,542 €2,282
Biarritz & Bayonne	£309 €457	£382 €565	£505 €747	£672 €995	£853 €1,262
MIDI-PYRANEES					
Cahors & Rocamadour	£372 €551	£389 €576	£562 €832	£790 €1,169	£1,235 €1,828
Gascomy/Gers	£255 €377	£430 €636	£597 €884	£728 €1,077	£794 €1,175
Toulouse	£255 €377	£429 €635	£656 €971	-	-
Bagneres-de-Bigorre	-	£394 €583	£585 €866	-	-
LANGUEDOC-ROUSSILLON					
Perpignan	£287 €425	£339 €502	£572 €847	£1,185 €1,754	-
Southern Roussillon	£321 €475	£455 €673	£734 €1,086	£1,006 €1,489	£1,742 €2,578
Montpelier	£195 €289	£336 €497	£451 €667	£611 €904	£924 €1,368
Carcassonne	£347 €514	£389 €576	£575 €851	£694 €1,027	£785 €1,167
Nimes	£228 €337	£397 €588	£684 €1,012	£905 €1,339	£1,129 €1,671
Beziers & Narbonne	£246 €364	£455 €673	£632 €935	£781 €1,156	£1,236 €1,829
COTE D'AZUR, PROVENCE & CORSICA					
Vaucluse (Luberon)	£256 €379	£359 €531	£461 €682	£722 €1,069	£877 €1,298
Inland Var (Draguignan, Ste-Maxime)	£391 €579	£482 €713	£649 €961	£1,037 €1,535	£1,235 €1,828
St-Tropez)	£327 €484	£505 €747	£738 €1,092	£1,350 €1,998	£1,625 €2,405
Toulon	£254 €376	£458 €678	-	-	£1,239 €1,834
Cannes	£428 €633	£599 €887	£783 €1,159	£1,295 €1,917	£1,874 €2,774
Antibes	£386 €571	£674 €998	£821 €1,215	£937 €1,387	£1,406 €2,081
Nice * Area	£327 €484	£468 €693	£539 €798	£682 €1,009	£1,351 €1,999
Marseille	£247 €366	£376 €556	£495 €733	£608 €900	£942 €1,394
Aix-en-Provence & St-Remy-de-Prov	£314 €465	£382 €565	£577 €854	£794 €1,175	£1,231 €1,822
Porto-Vecchio (Corsica)	£493 €730	£572 €847	£615 €910	£822 €1,217	£989 €1,464
Briancon	-	-	-	-	

Glossary

nm = masculine noun
nf = feminine noun

A

acompte (nm)
deposit
acte (nm)
deed
agent immobilier (nm)
estate agent
artisan (nm)
builder, skilled craftsman
assurance multirisques habitation (nf)
comprehensive household insurance

B

bail (nm)
lease
    bail à long terme
    long term lease
bastide (nf)
    (maison) Provençal country house
    (ville) walled town
bâtiment (nm)
building

C

caisse (nf)
office, fund
    caisse primaire d'assurance maladie (CPAM)
    state health insurance centre
carte (nf)
card, permit
cave (nf)
cellar
caveau (nm)
small cellar
centre des impôts (nm)
local tax office
certificat (nm)
certificate
chambre (nf)
bedroom, chamber
chauffage (nm)
heating
clause (nf)
clause
colombage (nm)
half-timbering
compromis de vente (nm)
sales contract
conservation des hypothèques (nf)
land registry
contrat (nm)
contract
    contrat de réservation
    reservation contract for a property

that has yet to be constructed
contribution sociale (nf)
social charge
copie authentique (nf)
certified copy
copropriété (nf)
co-ownership
    charges de copropriété
    maintenance/service charges
    immeuble en copropriété
    block of flats
cotisation (nf)
contributions
cuisine (nf)
kitchen

D

demande de prêt (nf)
loan application
département (nm)
administrative area
dépendance (nf)
outbuilding
dépôt de garantie (nm)
deposit
domicile (nm)
place of residence, home
droit (nm)
right, duty, law
duplex (nm)
maisonette

E

eau de la ville (nf)
mains water
en propriété libre
freehold
expert immobilier (nm)
valuer
expertise (nf)
valuation, survey

F

ferme (nf)
farm, farmhouse
fermette (nf)
small farmhouse
fosse septique (nf)
septic tank

G

gendarmerie (nf)
police station
géomètre (nm)
land surveyor
grange (nf)
barn
grenier (nm)
attic

H

hypothèque (nf)
mortgage, remortgage

I

immobilier (nm)
property
impôt (nm)
tax
indivision (nf)
joint ownership

L

location (nf)
letting, rented accommodation
longère (nf)
longhouse or long barn

M

mairie (nf)
town hall
maison (nf)
house
mandat (nm)
power of attorney
manoir (nm)
country manor
mas (nm)
stone farmhouse (particularly in
Provence)

N

notaire (nm)
notary (the clerk at the town hall (mairie)
who oversees the conveyancing)

O

occupant(e) (nm/f)
occupier
offre (nf)
offer, bid

P

parcelle de terre (nf)
plot of land
pavillon (nm)
typical modern house
permis de construire (nm)
planning permission
pierre (nf)
stone
  en pierre
  built of stone
  pierre de taille
  sandstone, limestone
pigeonnier (nm)
dovecote
plan (nm)
plan, outline
préfecture (nf)
administrative offices of the local
state representative
prélèvement automatique (nm)
direct debit
prêt (nm)
loan
promesse de vente (nf)

sales agreement

R

rectorat (nm)
local education authority

S

salle (nf)
room
salon (nm)
sitting room
séjour (nm)
living room
société civile immobilière (SCI)
(nf)
property-holding company
sous-seing privé (nm)
private agreement
surface au sol
floor space
surface habitable (nf)
living space
**système d'écoulement des
eaux** (nm)
drainage

T

taxe (nf)
tax
titre (nm)
title deed

toit (nm)
roof
toiture (nf)
roofing
tout-à-l'égout (nm)
mains drainage
type (T) (nm)
(followed by a number) property with a
set number of main rooms
  T4
  four-room flat

U

usufruit (nm)
lifetime interest

V

vendre (verb)
to sell
  à vendre
  for sale
vendeur (nm)
seller
vente (nf)
sale
versement (nm)
payment
villa (nf)
detached modern house
volet (nm)
shutter

Index to agents

FIR 1ST-FOR-FRENCH-PROPERTY
0870 7202966
www.1st-for-french-property.co.uk

FPS FRENCH PROPERTY SHOP
01233 666902
Elwick Club, Church Road, Ashford, Kent
TN23 1RD, United Kingdom
sales@frenchpropertyshop.com

FRA FRANCOPHILES
01622 688165
www.francophiles.co.uk

SIF SIFEX
+44 (0) 207 384 120
Fax: +44 (0) 207 384 2001
info@sifex.co.uk
www.sifex.co.uk

VEF VEF
020 7515 8660
www.vefuk.com

LAT LATITUDES
020 8951 5155
www.latitudes.co.uk
sales@latitudes.co.uk

Index to advertisers

MAISON DE LA FRANCE

ACKNOWLEDGEMENTS

Contributors
Leaonne Hall
Kelly-Marie Dudley
Sarah Nichol
Joanna Styles

Legal
Laurence Boone **Barclays Bank**
Miles Dobson **Affordable French Homes**
Stefano Lucatello **International Property Law Centre**
Debbie Stacey **Kingfisher Leisure Marketing Ltd**

Regional info
Karine Beauvallet **Demeures de France**
Karine Chaumont and Liz Oliver **Francophiles Ltd**
Sarah Francis **Sifex**
Benjamin Haas **Burgundy4u**
Jenny Kearton **VEF**
Nicholas Stallwood **French Property Shop**